T0288040

PREDICTION REVISITED

PREDICTION REVISITED

THE IMPORTANCE OF OBSERVATION

MEGAN CZASONIS
MARK KRITZMAN
DAVID TURKINGTON

WILEY

Published by John Wiley & Sons, Inc., Hoboken, New Jersey.
Published simultaneously in Canada.

For general information on our other products and services or for technical support, please contact our Customer Care Department within the United States at (800) 762-2974, outside the United States at (317) 572-3993 or fax (317) 572-4002.

Wiley also publishes its books in a variety of electronic formats. Some content that appears in print may not be available in electronic formats. For more information about Wiley products, visit our web site at www.wiley.com.

Library of Congress Cataloging-in-Publication Data is Available:

ISBN 9781119895589 (hardback)
ISBN 9781119895602 (ePDF)
ISBN 9781119895596 (epub)

Cover Design: Wiley
Cover Image: © akinbostanci/Getty Images

SKY10034029_041822

Contents

Timeline of Innovations

Relevance is the centerpiece of our approach to prediction. The key concepts that give rise to relevance were introduced over the past three centuries, as illustrated in this timeline. In Chapter 8, we offer more detail about the people who made these groundbreaking discoveries.

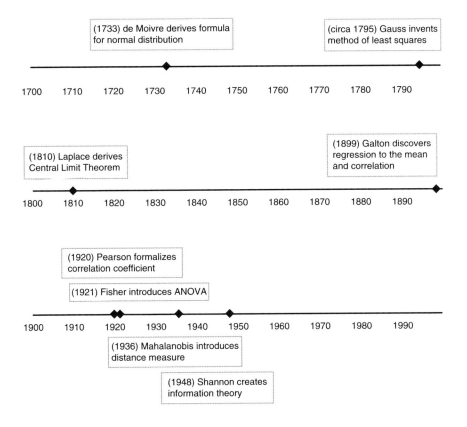

Essential Concepts

This book introduces a new approach to prediction, which requires a new vocabulary—not new words, but new interpretations of words that are commonly understood to have other meanings. Therefore, to facilitate a quicker understanding of what awaits you, we define some essential concepts as they are used throughout this book. And rather than follow the convention of presenting them alphabetically, we present them in a sequence that matches the progression of ideas as they unfold in the following pages.

Observation: One element among many that are described by a common set of attributes, distributed across time or space, and which collectively provide guidance about an outcome that has yet to be revealed. Classical statistics often refers to an observation as a multivariate data point.

Attribute: A recorded value that is used individually or alongside other attributes to describe an observation. In classical statistics, attributes are called independent variables.

Outcome: A measurement of interest that is usually observed alongside other attributes, and which one wishes to predict. In classical statistics, outcomes are called dependent variables.

Arithmetic average: A weighted summation of the values of attributes or outcomes that efficiently aggregates the information contained in a sample of observations. Depending on the context and the weights that are used, the result may be interpreted as a typical value or as a prediction of an unknown outcome.

Spread: The pairwise distance between observations of an attribute, measured in units of surprise. We compute this distance as the average of half the squared difference in values across every pair of observations. In classical statistics, the same quantity is usually computed as the average of squared deviations of observations from their mean and is referred to as variance. However, the equivalent evaluation of pairwise spreads reveals why we must divide by $N - 1$ rather than N to obtain an unbiased estimate of a sample's variance; it is because the zero distance of an observation with itself (the diagonal in a matrix of pairs) conveys no information.

Information theory: A unified mathematical theory of communication, created by Claude Shannon, which expresses messages as sequences of 0s and 1s and, based on the inverse relationship of information and probability, prescribes the optimal redundancy of symbols to manage the speed and accuracy of transmission.

Circumstance: A set of attribute values that collectively describes an observation.

Informativeness: A measure of the information conveyed by the circumstances of an observation, based on the inverse relationship of information and probability. For an observation of a single attribute, it is equal to the observed distance from the average, squared. For an observation of two or more uncorrelated attributes, it is equal to the sum of each individual attribute's informativeness. For an observation of two or more correlated attributes—the most general case—it is given by the Mahalanobis distance of the observation from the average of the observations. Informativeness is a component of relevance. It does not depend on the units of measurement.

Co-occurrence: The degree of alignment between two attributes for a single observation. It ranges between −1 and +1 and does not depend on the units of measurement.

Correlation: The average co-occurrence of a pair of attributes across all observations, weighted by the informativeness of each observation. In classical statistics, it is known as the Pearson correlation coefficient.

Covariance matrix: A symmetric square matrix of numbers that concisely summarizes the spreads of a set of attributes along with the signs and strengths of their correlation. Each element pertains to a pair of attributes and is equal to their correlation times their respective standard deviations (the square root of variance or spread).

Mahalanobis distance: A standardized measure of distance or surprise for a single observation across many attributes, which incorporates all the information from the covariance matrix. The Mahalanobis distance of a set of attribute values (a circumstance) from the average of the attribute values measures the informativeness of that observation.

Half of the negative of the Mahalanobis distance of one circumstance from another measures the similarity between them.

Similarity: A measure of the closeness between one circumstance and another, based on their attributes. It is equal to the opposite (negative) of half the Mahalanobis distance between the two circumstances. Similarity is a component of relevance.

Relevance: A measure of the importance of an observation to forming a prediction. Its components are the informativeness of past circumstances, the informativeness of current circumstances, and the similarity of past circumstances to current circumstances.

Partial sample regression: A two-step prediction process in which one first identifies a subset of observations that are relevant to the prediction task and, second, forms the prediction as a relevance-weighted average of the historical outcomes in the subset. When the subset from the first step equals the full-sample, this procedure converges to classical linear regression.

Asymmetry: A measure of the extent to which predictions differ when they are formed from a partial sample regression that includes the most relevant observations compared to one that includes the least relevant observations. It is computed as the average dissimilarity of the predictions from these two methods. Equivalently, it may be computed by comparing the respective fits of the most and least relevant subsets of observations to the cross-fit between them. The presence of asymmetry causes partial sample regression predictions to differ from those of classical linear regression. The minimum amount of asymmetry is zero, in which case the predictions from full-sample and partial-sample regression match.

Fit: The average alignment between relevance and outcomes across all observation pairs for a single prediction. It is normalized by the spreads of relevance and outcomes, and while the alignment for one pair of observations may be positive or negative, their average always falls between zero and one. A large value indicates that observations that are similarly relevant have similar outcomes, in which case one should have more confidence in the prediction. A small value indicates that relevance does not line up with the outcomes, in which case one should view the prediction more cautiously.

Bias: The artificial inflation of fit resulting from the inclusion of the alignment of each observation with itself. This bias is addressed by partitioning fit into two components—outlier influence, which is the fit of observations with themselves, and agreement, which is the fit of observations with their peers—and using agreement to give an unbiased measure of fit.

Outlier influence: The fit of observations with themselves. It is always greater than zero, owing to the inherent bias of comparing observations with themselves, and it is larger to the extent that unusual circumstances coincide with unusual outcomes.

Agreement: The fit of observations with their peers. It may be positive, negative, or zero, and is not systematically biased.

Precision: The inverse of the extent to which the randomness of historical observations (often referred to as noise) introduces uncertainty to a prediction.

Focus: The choice to form a prediction from a subset of relevant observations even though the smaller subset may be more sensitive to noise than the full sample of observations, because the consistency of the relevant subset improves confidence in the prediction more than noise undermines confidence.

Reliability: The average fit across a set of prediction tasks, weighted by the informativeness of each prediction circumstance. For a full sample of observations, it may be computed as the average alignment of pairwise relevance and outcomes and is equivalent to the classical R-squared statistic.

Complexity: The presence of nonlinearities or other conditional features that undermine the efficacy of linear prediction models. The conventional approach for addressing complexity is to apply machine learning algorithms, but one must counter the tendency of these algorithms to overfit the data. In addition, it can be difficult to interpret the inner workings of machine learning models. A simpler and more transparent approach to complexity is to filter observations by relevance. The two approaches can also be combined.

Preface

The path that led us to write this book began in 1999. We wanted to build an investment portfolio that would perform well across a wide range of market environments. We quickly came to the view that we needed more reliable estimates of volatilities and correlations—the inputs that determine portfolio risk—than the estimates given by the conventional method of extrapolating historical values. Our thought back then was to measure these statistics from a subset of the most unusual periods in history. We reasoned that unusual observations were likely to be associated with material events and would therefore be more informative than common observations, which probably reflected useless noise. We had not yet heard of the Mahalanobis distance, nor were we aware of Claude Shannon's information theory. Nonetheless, as we worked on our task, we derived the same formula Mahalanobis originated to analyze human skulls in India more than 60 years earlier.

As we extended our research to a broader set of problems, we developed a deep appreciation of the versatility of the Mahalanobis distance. In a single number, his distance measure tells us how dissimilar two items are from each other, accounting not only for the size and alignment of their many features, but also the typical variation and covariation of those features across a broader sample. We applied the method first to compare periods in time, each characterized by its economic circumstances or the returns of financial assets, and this led to other uses. We were impressed by the method's potential to tackle familiar problems in new ways, often leading to new paths of understanding. This eventually led to our own discovery that the prediction from a linear regression equation can be equivalently expressed as a weighted average of the values of past outcomes, in which the weights are the sum of two Mahalanobis distances: one that measures unusualness and the other similarity. Although

xv

we understood intuitively why unusual observations are more informative than common ones, it was not until we connected our research to information theory that we fully appreciated the nuances of the inverse relationship of information and probability.

Our focus on observations led us to the insight that we can just as well analyze data samples as collections of pairs rather than distributions of observations around their average. This insight enabled us to view variance, correlation, and R-squared through a new lens, which shed light on statistical notions that are commonly accepted but not so well understood. It clarified, for example, why we must divide by $N-1$ instead of N to compute a sample variance. It gave us more insight into the bias of R-squared and suggested a new way to address this bias. And it showed why we square distances in so many statistical calculations. (It is not merely because unsquared deviations from the mean sum to zero.)

But our purpose goes beyond illuminating vague notions of statistics, although we hope that we do this to some extent. Our larger mission is to enable researchers to deploy data more effectively in their prediction models. It is this quest that led us down a different path from the one selected by the founders of classical statistics. Their purpose was to understand the movement of heavenly bodies or games of chance, which obey relatively simple laws of nature. Today's most pressing challenges deal with esoteric social phenomena, which obey a different and more complex set of rules.

The emergent approach for dealing with this complexity is the field of machine learning, but more powerful algorithms introduce complexities of their own. By reorienting data-driven prediction to focus on observation, we offer a more transparent and intuitive approach to complexity. We propose a simple framework for identifying asymmetries in data and weighting the data accordingly. In some cases, traditional linear regression analysis gives sufficient guidance about the future. In other cases, only sophisticated machine learning algorithms offer any hope of dealing with a system's complexity. However, in many instances the methods described in this book offer the ideal blend of transparency and sophistication for deploying data to guide us into the future.

We should acknowledge upfront that our approach to statistics and prediction is unconventional. Though we are versed, to some degree, in classical statistics and have a deep appreciation for the insights gifted to us by a long line of scholars, we have found it instructive and pragmatic to reconsider the principles of statistics from a fresh perspective—one that is motivated by the challenge we face as financial researchers and by our quest for intuition. But mostly we are motivated by a stubborn refusal to stop asking the question: Why?

Practitioners have difficult problems to solve and often too little time. Those on the front lines may struggle to absorb everything that technical training has to offer. And there are bound to be many useful ideas, often published in academic articles and books, that are widely available yet seldom used, perhaps because they are new, complex, or just hard to find.

Most of the ideas we present in this book are new to us, meaning that we have never encountered them in school courses or publications. Nor are we aware of their application in practice, even though investors clearly thrive on the quality of their predictions. But we are not so much concerned with precedence as we are with gaining and sharing a better understanding of the process of data-driven prediction. We would, therefore, be pleased to learn of others who have already come to the insights we present in this book, especially if they have advanced them further than we do in this book.

1

Introduction

We rely on experience to shape our view of the unknown, with the notable exception of religion. But for most practical purposes we lean on experience to guide us through an uncertain world. We process experiences both naturally and statistically; however, the way we naturally process experiences often diverges from the methods that classical statistics prescribes. Our purpose in writing this book is to reorient common statistical thinking to accord with our natural instincts.

Let us first consider how we naturally process experience. We record experiences as narratives, and we store these narratives in our memory or in written form. Then when we are called upon to decide under uncertainty, we recall past experiences that resemble present circumstances, and we predict that what will happen now will be like what happened following similar past experiences. Moreover, we instinctively focus more on past experiences that were exceptional rather than ordinary because they reside more prominently in our memory.

Now, consider how classical statistics advises us to process experience. It tells us to record experiences not as narratives, but as data. It suggests that we form decisions from as many observations as we can assemble or from a subset of recent observations, rather than focus on

1

observations that are like current circumstances. And it advises us to view unusual observations with skepticism. To summarize:

Natural Process
- Records experiences as narratives.
- Focuses on experiences that are like current circumstances.
- Focuses on experiences that are unusual.

Classical Statistics
- Record experiences as data.
- Include observations irrespective of their similarity to current circumstances.
- Treat unusual observations with skepticism.

The advantage of the natural process is that it is intuitive and sensible. The advantage of classical statistics is that by recording experiences as data we can analyze experiences more rigorously and efficiently than would be allowed by narratives. Our purpose is to reconcile classical statistics with our natural process in a way that secures the advantages of both approaches.

We accomplish this reconciliation by shifting the focus of prediction away from the selection of variables to the selection of observations. As part of this shift in focus from variables to observations, we discard the term *variable*. Instead, we use the word *attribute* to refer to an independent variable (something we use to predict) and the word *outcome* to refer to a dependent variable (something we want to predict). Our purpose is to induce you to think foremost of experiences, which we refer to as observations, and less so of the attributes and outcomes we use to measure those experiences. This shift in focus from variables to observations does not mean we undervalue the importance of choosing the right variables. We accept its importance. We contend, however, that the choice of variables has commanded disproportionately more attention than the choice of observations. We hope to show that by choosing observations as carefully as we choose variables, we can use data to greater effect.

Relevance

The underlying premise of this book is that some observations are relevant, and some are not—a distinction that we argue receives far less attention than it deserves. Moreover, of those that are relevant, some observations are more relevant than others. By separating relevant observations from those that are not, and by measuring the comparative relevance of observations, we can use data more effectively to guide our decisions. As suggested by our discussion thus far, relevance has two components: similarity and unusualness. We formally refer to the latter as informativeness. This component of relevance is less intuitive than similarity but is perhaps more foundational to our notion of relevance; therefore, we tackle it first.

Informativeness

Informativeness is related to information theory, the creation of Claude Shannon, arguably the greatest genius of the twentieth century.[1] As we discuss in Chapter 2, information theory posits that information is inversely related to probability. In other words, observations that are unusual contain more information than those that are common. We could stop here and rest on Shannon's formidable reputation to validate our inclusion of informativeness as one of the two components of relevance. But it never hurts to appeal to intuition. Therefore, let us consider the following example.

Suppose we would like to measure the relationship between the performance of the stock market and a collection of economic attributes (think variables) such as inflation, interest rates, energy prices, and economic growth. Our initial thought might be to examine how stock returns covary with changes in these attributes. If these economic attributes behaved in an ordinary way, it would be difficult to tell which of the attributes were driving stock returns or even if the performance of the stock market was instead responding to hidden forces. However, if one of the attributes behaved in an unusual way, and the stock market return we observed was also notable, we might suspect that these two occurrences are linked by more than mere coincidence. It could be evidence of a fundamental relationship. We provide a more formal explanation of informativeness in Chapter 2, but for now let us move on to similarity.

---

[1] Some might prefer to assign this accolade to Albert Einstein, but why quibble? Both were pretty smart.

Similarity

Imagine you are a health care professional charged with treating a patient who has contracted a life-threatening disease. It is your job to decide which treatment to apply among a variety of available treatments. You might consider examining the outcomes of alternative treatments from as large a sample of patients with the same disease as you can find, reasoning that a large sample should produce more reliable guidance than a small sample. Alternatively, you might focus on a subset of the large sample comprising only patients of a similar age, with similar health conditions, and with similar behavior regarding exercise and smoking. The first approach of using as large a sample as possible to evaluate treatments would undoubtedly yield the more robust treatment; that is, the treatment that would help, at least to some extent, the largest number of patients irrespective of each person's specific features. But the second approach of focusing on a targeted subset of similar patients is more likely to identify the most effective treatment for the specific patient under your care.

We contrived these examples to lend intuition to the notions of informativeness and similarity. In most cases, though, informativeness and similarity depend on nuances that we would fail to detect by casual inspection. Moreover, it is important that we combine an observation's informativeness and similarity in proper proportion to determine its relevance. This would be difficult, if not impossible, to do informally.

Fortunately, we have discovered how to measure informativeness, similarity, and therefore relevance, in a mathematically precise way. The recipe for doing so is one of the key insights of this book. However, before we reveal it, we need to establish a new conceptual and mathematical foundation for observing data. By viewing common statistical measures through a new lens, we hope to bring clarity to certain statistical concepts that, although they are commonly accepted, are not always commonly understood. But our purpose is not to present these new statistical concepts merely to enlighten you; rather, we hope to equip you with tools that will enable you to make better predictions.

Roadmap

Here is what awaits you. In Chapter 2, we lay out the foundations of our approach to observing information from data. In Chapter 3, we characterize patterns between multiple attributes. In Chapter 4, we introduce relevance and show how to use it to form predictions. In Chapter 5, we discuss how to measure confidence in predictions by considering the tradeoff between relevance and noise. In Chapter 6, we apply this new perspective to evaluate the efficacy of prediction models. In Chapter 7, we compare our relevance-based approach to prediction to machine learning algorithms. And lastly, in Chapter 8, we provide biographical sketches of some of the key scientists throughout history who established the theoretical foundation that underpins our notion of relevance.

In each chapter, we first present the material conceptually, leaning heavily on intuition. And we highlight the key takeaways from our conceptual exposition. Then, we present the material again, but this time mathematically. We conclude each chapter with an empirical application of the concepts, which builds upon itself as we progress through the chapters.

If you are strongly disinclined toward mathematics, you can pass by the math and concentrate only on the prose, which is sufficient to convey the key concepts of this book. In fact, you can think of this book as two books: one written in the language of poets and one written in the language of mathematics, although you may conclude we are not very good at poetry.

We expect some readers will view our key insight about relevance skeptically, because it calls into question notions about statistical analysis that are deeply entrenched in beliefs from earlier training. To get the most out of this book, we ask you to suspend these beliefs and give us a chance to convince you of the validity of our counterclassical interpretation of data by appealing to intuition, mathematics, and empirical illustration. We thank you in advance for your forbearance.

2

Observing Information

Our journey into data-driven prediction begins with some basic ideas. In this chapter, we set forth principles which may at first seem obvious, but which, upon deeper inspection, have profound implications. These ideas lay the foundation for everything that follows.

Observing Information Conceptually

Whenever we approach a new dataset the first order of business is to get our bearings. We have before us a series of observations, each of which is described by a set of attributes. The observations could be of people, described by attributes like age, health, education, salary, and place of residence. They could be times at-bat for a major league baseball player, with attributes of runs-batted-in, home runs, walks, strikeouts, weather conditions, and where the game took place. Or the observations could be periods of economic performance measured by attributes such as growth in output, inflation, interest rates, unemployment, stock market returns, and perhaps the political parties in power at the time. What matters is that we have a set of observations characterized by a consistent collection of attributes. A conventional statistics approach would have us focus on these attributes and refer to them as variables, but as we stated earlier, we ask that you indulge us as we focus mainly on how we observe these attributes.

We begin by summarizing the observations as averages. Through-out this book we will compute many averages. We use the average as a device to let the data speak. Sometimes this process will act demo-cratically, assigning equal weight to each observation. Other times, we will overweight more relevant observations at the expense of others. In either case, our goal is to separate information from noise. The humble arithmetic average does this job well.

Central Tendency

After attending the West of England Fat Stock and Poultry Exhibition in 1906, the British polymath Francis Galton was struck by the surprising power of a simple average. As he documented in an article soon after the exhibition, 787 people guessed the weight of an ox that had been slaugh-tered for market, with the hope of winning a prize. Galton found that the average of their guesses came remarkably close to the true weight, delivering more accuracy than any individual guess, including those of the proclaimed experts in attendance. James Suroweicki pays homage to this effect in his 2004 book *The Wisdom of Crowds*. Among the myriad examples he includes is a more practical equivalent of Galton's exper-iment, whereby people guess the number of jelly beans in a jar. The punchline of these experiments is that when conditions are right, an average guess is eerily precise.

Suppose we choose a single attribute for whatever data we have in mind and compute its average across observations. The result provides a measure of central tendency, as it surely lies within the range of values we observe. There are, of course, other ways to gauge the characteristic value of an attribute. The median splits observed values in half and points to the dividing line, while the mode represents the most common occurrence. The median and mode are sometimes considered better measures of cen-tral tendency because they are less sensitive to outliers than the average, and therefore generally more stable. But as we have already mentioned and will soon show, unusual observations are the most informative of all.

Assume we compute the average for every attribute in our dataset. Now, in addition to having counted the number of observations, we know what types of values to expect for each attribute. Observing a value of 0.00001, 1, 1,000,000, or −1,000,000 should not necessarily surprise us so long as that value is near the average, because this means it is within the range of recorded experience.

Spread

Consider a set of observations for an attribute, which we plot along a line as shown in Exhibit 2.1. Are these observations tightly clustered or broadly dispersed? A natural way to address this question—though interestingly not the typical way—is to consider the distance between two observations of a pair. In other words, if we present you with two random observations from the set, how far apart should you expect them to be? The answer to this question involves taking another average. This time, however, we do not average over every observation, but over every pair of observations.

In an analysis of basketball greats, this calculation might involve comparing points per game for Michael Jordan to LeBron James, Wilt Chamberlain to Jordan, and Chamberlain to James. For three players there are three distinct pairs, for 10 players there would be 45 pairs, and for N players there would be $(N - 1)/2$ pairs. Imagine lining up each player's name in a row and a column to form a grid. Of all the N^2 matchups, we remove the N diagonal entries that compare a player to himself and divide the remainder by 2 to remove redundancies. We want to average across all these pairs.

Let us assert, boldly and without any justification for now, that the quantity we are most interested in measuring is half the squared distance between any two observations. This choice leads us to an important equivalence. It turns out that the average across pairs yields precisely the same result as the textbook formula for variance. The equivalence holds even though the conventional formula for variance measures deviations from average, rather than deviations across every pair. It helps explain a feature of the well-known sample variance formula that may at first seem puzzling: the requirement to divide by $N - 1$ instead of N to obtain an unbiased result. This pairwise perspective makes clear why we must use one fewer than the number of observations in the classical formula. It arises directly from the fact that we exclude the trivial comparisons of

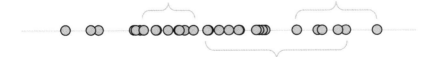

Exhibit 2.1 Spreads

values to themselves, which would otherwise impart an overconfidence bias (see the math section for more detail).

Yet a puzzle remains. Why should we focus on half the squared distance between values? It would seem much simpler to record the distance and leave it at that. This choice is worth considering carefully. There is something special about half the squared distance, and we will encounter this theme repeatedly. Why should we square the distance? And why should we divide it in half?

Information Theory

The first part of the answer rests on insights from Claude Shannon, the father of information theory. Shannon was a creative genius who laid the foundation for our modern information age. In 1937, while a graduate student at MIT, he introduced new rigor to circuit design, proving that mere electrical switches can implement logical reasoning to solve problems. After earning his PhD at MIT, Shannon went to work at Bell Laboratories, a storied innovation hub where dozens of brilliant minds crossed paths in the twentieth century. Nine alumni have received Nobel prizes, mostly in physics, with credit to work they did at Bell Labs. Shannon himself is notably absent from this list; it is not for lack of profundity or practical impact of his work, but because the Nobel Prize has no clear category for his contributions to humanity (he received many other awards). He introduced the field of cryptography after working on practical problems of message encryption during World War II. He defined the universal language of computing in terms of the binary digits of 0 and 1, recognizing that all information boils down to this form. And, in a breakthrough 1948 paper, he unveiled the contribution for which he is best known, a unified mathematical theory of communication that spawned several fields of study and decades of further innovation.

But by his own admission, Shannon did not set out with grand plans to change the world. He was at heart an eccentric tinkerer with a healthy sense of humor. It is safe to assume these personality traits fueled his creative spirit. He was known for riding a unicycle down the hallways of Bell Labs while juggling. And it is entertaining to note that a man who made so many practical contributions was also at times captivated by so-called useless machines—contraptions whose only purpose when switched on is to turn themselves back off with a mechanical arm. Shannon built many such machines and displayed one in his office. Together with his colleague Edward Thorpe he devised a computer that they concealed and wore to casinos to gain a statistical advantage at the roulette table. As William Poundstone recounts in *Fortune's Formula*, the pair of inventors figured they could exploit tiny probability advantages that arose from the tilt of roulette wheels. Though imperceptible to the naked eye, off-kilter wheels land on some numbers more than they should, and the wearable device allowed inputs by foot pedal to inform which numbers to bet on. Alas, he did not become rich from gambling. Later in life, Shannon spent a great deal of time contemplating artificial intelligence and experimenting with it. To this end he built a robotic mouse to navigate a maze, and much more.

Shannon's theory of information relates to our present discussion. He formalized the essential notion that information must be a sort of inverse of probability. To emphasize this point, let us start by acknowledging that it is not newsworthy when a likely outcome occurs. Rare events, on the other hand, are notable. Shannon showed, with mathematical precision, that rare events convey more information than common ones.

We can illustrate this fact using everyday examples and basic intuition. Suppose a friend tells you that she went to the grocery store, bought some apples, and came home: it was uneventful. We can easily understand and visualize this story by drawing on common experience. Now suppose another friend tells you that she went to the store and something truly crazy happened. From our perspective as a listener this could be anything; we need more information to understand. Moreover, the story might take a while, because when things are unusual there is more to explain.

Here is another example. Is it more informative to learn that on a given day it was 80° F in Singapore or that it was 80° F in Boston? Those who know Singapore might recognize this temperature as typical for every day of the year. Learning that a day's temperature was 80° tells us next to nothing. In fact, people often joke that there are two climates in Singapore: indoors and outdoors. In Boston, however, we recognize immediately that an 80° day is almost surely in the summer and definitely not in the winter (even after we consider global warming—at least, so far). Whether a fact is informative depends on the range of outcomes we expect. It is a fundamental truth that information comes from surprise.

Surprise is related to probability. And probability, in turn, is essentially a fancy way of counting. Precision is important. The probability of an event represents the number of ways it can happen divided by the total number of possibilities. These possibilities explode into a huge number of permutations. And yet a single piece of information can rule out large swaths of them. With each piece of information we lose, possibilities grow exponentially. With each piece of information we gain, possibilities rapidly contract. This inverse relationship, and the power of information to proscribe probabilities, sits at the core of Shannon's information theory.

The relationship of information to probability is profound and important, so it is worth investing some more time on this topic. Consider the following experiment. Ask 10 friends, independently, to choose a number between 1 and 10. Once you have collected their responses, add them up. What do you expect the result to be? We can build intuition by focusing on the extremes. It is quite hard to get 100; this only happens when everyone selects the number 10. The probability of this outcome is 1 divided by 10^{10} or 1 in 10 billion. To put this in perspective, you are about 20,000 times more likely to be struck by lightning this year. Now consider that if you know the result is 100, you also know that each person must have picked 10, which means you know precisely what happened. There is no more information to be gained. By contrast, if the sum is 50, there are millions of possible configurations, and you have a cloud of uncertainty over which numbers each of your friends chose.

The more extreme the value, the more you know for sure. But by how much? What is the informational difference between a sum of 100 versus 99? To arrive at 99, you need one out of 10 people to pick 9 instead of 10. There are 10 ways that could happen. So, in terms of probability, a value of 99 is 10 times more likely than 100. It represents one unit less of information because you know someone chose 9, but you do not know who. To get 98, you need one friend to pick 8 or two friends to pick 9. There are 10 ways for one person to pick 9, and for each of those we have nine ways for another person to pick 9. Half of these 90 combinations are redundant, however, so we are left with 45 possibilities. Add to this 10 ways for one person to pick 8. In total, there are 55 ways to arrive at a sum of 98. Compared to the sum of 99, you now have one less piece of information because you know that two of the numbers (or one of the numbers, twice) must be incrementally lower than 10, but you do not know which friends chose the incrementally lower numbers. The bottom line is that probabilities multiply and information adds. They are intimately connected. The lower the probability of an event, the more information it conveys, and vice versa.

Let us return to the task of measuring dispersion. When we observe a pair of observations, what we really want to know is not merely the distance between the two observations, but rather how notable is their spread. Here again, we gain considerable insight by thinking about spread in terms of pairs. The key insight is that larger spreads become rare at an accelerating pace. A spread twice as large conveys not twice as much information but four times as much. This occurs because spreads depend jointly on two observations, and though a large spread is a single number, it tells us something about two occurrences at once. The only assumption we need to ground this truth is that there are boundaries of possibility in the attributes we measure. So long as possibilities are not infinite, we will always struggle to find huge distances, because they require observations to fall at opposite extremes. Two observations that lie close together might be located anywhere in the range of values. Two observations with a moderate distance require that at least one of them not be near the center of the distribution. And two observations with a very large distance require that both be at opposite extremes. Therefore, because information is inversely related to probability, and because distance depends on a compound probability of two outcomes, we must square distances to gauge their informativeness. The average squared distance across all pairs tells us the information we should expect, on average, from a randomly chosen pair.

A gambling example will make this point more concrete. Indeed, games of chance have motivated philosophers of probability as far back as the seventeenth century. There are many examples, but take the case of rolling two dice and obtaining the sum, as a player does in the popular casino game of craps. The total of a roll ranges from 2 to 12, with 7 being the most common outcome. Let us now arrange every possibility in a row and in a column, creating a triangle of unique pairs, as shown in Exhibit 2.2. Each element in this triangle is a distance between the outcomes of two throws. Notice that there are many ways to get a distance of 2 but only one way to get a distance of 10. Like a giant funnel, the possibilities collapse within this triangle as we push to the extremes. The farther we push into large pairwise differences, the faster the numbers become compressed in the narrower section of the funnel. Ultimately, the information contained in a distance is very close to

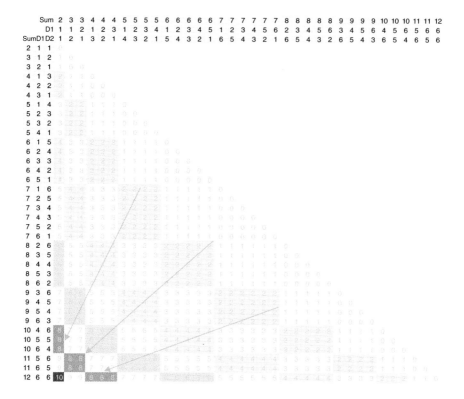

Exhibit 2.2 Triangle of Pairs

half of that distance squared. This fact is enshrined in the Central Limit Theorem, a result that is widely acknowledged as the most important in all of statistics. It makes precise what we mean by very close and explains why sums of independent observations invariably give rise to the familiar bell-shaped curve we call the normal distribution. Far from being arbitrary, this law of nature can be found almost everywhere around us, and it justifies our use of half the squared distance as a measure of the informativeness of a spread.

The Strong Pull of Normality

The discovery of the normal distribution did not come easily in the course of history. Nor did recognition of its profound importance. This might seem surprising, because once we know of the normal distribution it is quite easy to find examples of it all around us. Francis Galton was so taken by the normal distribution that he commissioned the construction of what he called a quincunx.[1] It generates a histogram of the normal probability curve by allowing pellets to cascade down a lattice of pins, falling randomly to the left or right of each pin. Few fall to the far left or to the far right; most cluster near the middle. Galton famously used this contraption to show, right before one's eyes, that the normal curve arises time and again from nothing more than the aggregation of the simplest random outcomes. With a bit more patience and even less technology, you can observe the same thing by tallying the number of heads you get from a sequence of coin flips. It is plausible that this is what the French mathematician Abraham de Moivre had in mind as he worked on his book *The Doctrine of Chances* in London, after having fled religious persecution and imprisonment in France. In 1733 de Moivre published his finding that for the sum of many binomial outcomes, such as coin flips, the occurrence of large deviations from average decays exponentially as a function of the distance squared. Though this discovery was a triumph, it was not well-known nor widely applied until much later.

In the 1770s, Pierre-Simon Laplace confronted similar ideas but in a more general context than just the coin flip equivalent. Though aware of de Moivre's work, Laplace appears to have been somewhat tormented for decades by the question of what curve best reflects the rarity of extreme events. After multiple false starts, he presented the essence of the Central Limit Theorem in 1810. It was a profound breakthrough.

Meanwhile, in 1805, another French mathematician named Adrien-Marie Legendre was actively promoting his method of least squares for solving the day's most pressing problems in astronomy. Departing from tradition, he blended noise-prone measurements together in what would later be seen as a form of linear regression analysis. The widespread attention he gained led to a conflict with Carl Friedrich Gauss, who argued he had invented the same method a decade earlier, although he did not publish his result at the time. Nonetheless, Gauss eventually outdid Legendre by connecting the method of least squares to the normal distribution in his 1809 book about the orbits of heavenly bodies around the sun.

Gauss's reference to the normal distribution was a minor side note at the end of his book. He was fond of using the arithmetic average of observations to mitigate measurement errors, and he asked himself:

---

[1] This curious term derives originally from the Roman word for five-twelfths, often depicted on currency as five dots. The term came to mean an arrangement of five dots in a lattice, such as on the side of a die, and eventually to describe such a lattice pattern in general.

Under what circumstances is the average the best choice? After all, one might use the median or some other more intricate blend. Gauss found that the average is optimal so long as errors conform to the curve of a normal distribution, and from this follows the theory of least squares. In his book *The History of Statistics*, Stephen M. Stigler argues that these advances were crystallized with a final stroke of genius from Laplace, who seized upon Gauss's result and realized that if errors themselves arose from the average of random effects, then they would forever gravitate toward the normal curve. Whenever independent random effects combine to form the attributes we observe—whether through genetic recombinations, market price adjustments toward equilibrium, or repeated experiments—we should expect departures from average to approach the normal curve. Thus, if we merely assume that possibilities have bounds and observations arise from the aggregation of smaller independent events, it is wise to focus on half the squared distance between observations.[2]

In summary, we wish to stress once more the intuitive benefit that comes from pairwise comparisons. To our knowledge, none of the historical development, from de Moivre to Gauss to Laplace and others, proceeded in this direction. They focused instead on errors from the average, which is mathematically equivalent. We do not intend to minimize in any way the deep understanding and precision that come from the early expositions of these ideas, nor do we suspect we are the first to stress the points we make. But it remains that those who seek an intuitive understanding have much to gain from considering a pairwise view of these ideas.

- First, it becomes clear that when considering every pairwise comparison among N observations, we should ignore trivial comparisons of each observation to itself because they convey no information. The smaller set of remaining observations explains why we divide by $N - 1$ to arrive at an unbiased measure of a data sample's variance.

- Second, the distance between pairwise observations reveals why the rarity of large distances grows with the square of the distance. This fact, anchored by the constant pull toward normality of the Central Limit Theorem explains why, by default, the spread should be

---

[2] While Laplace is widely credited with originating the Central Limit Theorem, its formalization and subsequent generalization progressed for many years after and included substantial contributions from others. See Chapter 8 to learn more about Laplace.

measured as squared deviations rather than absolute value deviations or anything else.

- And third, pairwise comparisons relate the notion of pairwise similarity between observations to that of a single observation's distance from average, which we will soon show is a measure of informativeness.

The resulting measure of spread is called the variance. It represents the squared distance from average that equates to one unit of information. We will continue to anchor to units of information, but at times it is convenient to take the square root of the variance, converting it to units of physical distance from average. This measure is called the standard deviation.

A Constant of Convenience

Let us turn to the question of why we multiply the squared spread by one half. One might assume this choice of multiple comes from some deep principle of information, but to the contrary, it is arbitrary and inconsequential. The choice defines a unit of squared distance, and we have argued that decisions should be made from squared units. But information equates to surprise, which means that each measurement is divided by the average of what we expect for that measurement across a broader sample. Any constant multiple will be the same in the numerator and denominator of such a ratio, and it will always cancel out. For this reason, the information that we observe is independent of the units of measurement, including any units we might introduce after squaring distances.

The choice of multiple has no more consequence for any method we present than does the use of Fahrenheit versus Celsius, meters versus feet, or the definition of a year as one lap of the Earth around the Sun. One might argue for the aesthetic appeal of one half, which has the consequence that one unit of variance locates the inflection point on the normal distribution (see the appendix to this chapter for details). However, we could as easily define that location as a thousand milli-standard-deviations, or something else entirely. A more pragmatic justification for one half is that it replicates the conventional definition of variance, which we demonstrate in the mathematics section that follows. We will stick to this convention so that it is easier to appreciate the connection of our approach to common statistical formulas.

Throughout this book we will sometimes focus on pairwise squared distances and other times on squared distances from the average. They are linked by the fact that their respective averages are equal. But this equivalence requires distances from average to be, on average, twice as large. When we choose to scale pairwise distances by one half, it means that we do not have to scale distances to average because their required scaling factor equals 1. This allows us to preserve the conventional formulas for distance to average.

Our key point is that squaring pairwise distances is essential but multiplying that result by a further constant is not. All that matters is that we scale distances to average by twice as much.

Key Takeaways

- A dataset can be thought of as a series of observations, each of which is described by a set of attributes.
- Classical statistics refers to attributes as variables.
- Our purpose is to provide a balanced view of data by shifting our focus from attributes (variables) to observations.
- The arithmetic average is a remarkably effective way of separating information from noise.
- Information is directly related to surprise and inversely related to probability.
- Probability depends on the spread between observations.
- The conventional approach to summarizing the spread of a set of observations is to compute the average squared deviation of the observations from their arithmetic average, which is called variance.
- However, it may be more insightful to view variance equivalently as half the average squared distance across every pair of observations.
- Measuring variance as a function of pairwise distance reveals why we must divide by $N - 1$ rather than N to obtain an unbiased estimate of a sample's variance in the traditional formula; it is because the zero distance of an observation with itself (the diagonal in a matrix of pairs) conveys no information.
- Because distances between pairs depend on two observations jointly, large distances are rare.

- A distance twice as large as another conveys four times as much information.

- We square distances to reflect the heightened importance of large spreads, which arises from their rarity and thus their informativeness.

- We multiply squared pairwise distances by one half to match the common definition of variance. But this scaling is optional and arbitrary. Information is related to surprise, and it is measured as a ratio of one observation (or pair) to the average of many observations (or pairs). Therefore, it does not depend on the units of measurement, and scaling the squared distance has no effect.

- To preserve an important equivalence, however, we must scale distances from average by twice as much as we scale pairwise distances.

Observing Information Mathematically

Let us begin with some basic definitions. Our starting point is a rect-angular dataset in two dimensions. There are N rows, each of which represents an observation. Each observation contains the same set of M measurements arranged in columns. Depending on the application, we may refer to a subset comprising K of these measurements as attributes that describe the circumstances of that observation, and we may refer to some of the measurements as outcomes. We assume that every one of the $N \times M$ cells in the data matrix contains a real number. This setup is quite general and accommodates many different types of data.

For now, we will consider just one attribute, which could be any column of the full dataset. We will call this attribute x_A. The capital subscript A refers to the attribute, or column, in the data. We denote a particular observation of x_A as $x_{i,A}$, where the subscript i indicates an observation, or row, in the data.

Throughout this book, the act of learning or predicting from data often involves taking an arithmetic average over observations. As a gen-eral construct, these averages consist of an object of interest, denoted obj_i for a given observation, and some form of weight that accompanies each observation. We use the term *weight* loosely, as the values that scale each observation may be positive, negative, or zero, and they need not sum to a specific number (although they often do).

Average

Our first task is to determine a typical value for x_A. Even though we do not yet know anything about the nature of the data in our sample, it is still helpful to introduce the concept of informativeness as the weight—or scale factor—that we apply to each observation. In this context, we denote an observation's informativeness as $info_i$. The average value of x_A is then given by:

$$\bar{x}_A = \frac{1}{N} \sum_i info_i obj_i \tag{1}$$

Where:

$$info_i = 1 \tag{2}$$

$$obj_i = x_{i,A} \tag{3}$$

Therefore:

$$\bar{x}_A = \frac{1}{N} \sum_i x_{i,A} \tag{4}$$

In these expressions, we notate summation using shorthand of just i under the summation symbol. This shorthand should be taken to mean the sum over all $i = 1, 2, \ldots, N$. Here, informativeness equals 1 for all observations because we do not yet have any basis to distinguish among them.

Spread

We would like to measure the typical spread between observations of x_A to gauge how tightly or loosely clustered the observations are as a group. An intuitive, though nontraditional, approach to answering this question is to consider the average spread between every pair of observations. If the average distance between pairs is small, then they are tightly clustered; if it is large, then they are broadly dispersed. Note that this concept is defined without reference to the average value. We write this sum across pairs as a double sum across indexes for i and j.

$$\sigma_{x_A}^2 = \frac{1}{N(N-1)} \sum_i \sum_j info_{ij} obj_{ij} \tag{5}$$

Where:

$$info_{ij} = 1 \tag{6}$$

$$obj_{ij} = \frac{1}{2}(x_{i,A} - x_{j,A})^2 \tag{7}$$

Therefore:

$$\sigma_{x_A}^2 = \frac{1}{N(N-1)} \sum_i \sum_j \frac{1}{2}(x_{i,A} - x_{j,A})^2 \tag{8}$$

These choices demand some justification. As before, the informativeness of every item—in this case a pair—is equal to 1 because we do not yet have any information by which to distinguish the various pairs. The object of interest reflects the difference between the two observations in a pair, but crucially it is not a simple difference: it is half the squared difference. We are interested in a squared distance because the information contained in a pair's spread is inversely related to its probability, and the probability of successively larger spreads drops at an accelerating pace. This occurs because larger distances require that both observations be extreme in the opposite direction, a joint occurrence that becomes increasingly rare as low probabilities are multiplied together. We apply a scalar multiple of one half to the squared distance, although this choice has no consequence on any of the analysis that follows in this book. It does not matter because, as we will show, the entire purpose of computing the average squared distance is to normalize individual squared distances as a ratio. The ratio of a squared distance to the average squared distance is a measure of information that does not depend on the units of measurement. Any multiplicative constant will be canceled out in this ratio.

It is important to recognize that the distance of an observation from itself contains no information whatsoever, because we know, trivially and in advance, that the squared difference will equal zero. There is no potential for surprise. Therefore, we should exclude self-comparisons from the pairwise sum. If we visualize pairwise differences arranged in a grid of rows and columns, we must disregard the values of zero on the diagonal. This means that there are $N^2 - N$, or $N(N-1)$, informative pairs to consider. This value appears as the denominator for the normalization of our average. Because our measure of distance between observations is symmetric, the sum counts each pair twice—once as i, j and again as j, i. However, this is not a problem. We rewrite the sum equivalently in terms of distinct pairs (the lower triangle of a pairwise comparison grid). In this formulation, we avoid double-counting and divide the sum by half of the number from before:

$$\sigma_{x_A}^2 = \frac{1}{\frac{N(N-1)}{2}} \sum_{\substack{\text{distinct} \\ \text{pairs } i, j}} \frac{1}{2}(x_{i,A} - x_{j,A})^2 \tag{9}$$

We have suggestively labeled this result as $\sigma_{x_A}^2$, which is typically used to represent the variance of a series of observations. Traditionally, the variance is defined as the average squared difference of every observation from average. As we show in the following equations, these two definitions are equivalent. For notational simplicity, we suppress the subscript of A.

$$\sigma_x^2 = \frac{1}{N(N-1)} \sum_i \sum_j \frac{1}{2}(x_i^2 + x_j^2 - 2x_ix_j) \tag{10}$$

$$\sigma_x^2 = \frac{1}{N(N-1)} \sum_i \sum_j \frac{1}{2}(x_i^2 + x_j^2) - \frac{1}{N(N-1)} \sum_i \sum_j x_ix_j \tag{11}$$

$$\sigma_x^2 = \frac{1}{(N-1)} \sum_i \frac{1}{N} \sum_j x_i^2 + \frac{1}{N(N-1)} \sum_i \sum_j x_ix_j - \frac{2}{N(N-1)} \sum_i \sum_j x_ix_j \tag{12}$$

We now reindex i to k in the middle term, and add a sum over i divided by N:

$$\sigma_x^2 = \frac{1}{(N-1)} \sum_i \frac{1}{N} \sum_j x_i^2 + \frac{1}{N^2(N-1)} \sum_i \sum_j \sum_k x_jx_k - \frac{1}{N(N-1)} \sum_i \sum_j 2x_ix_j \tag{13}$$

$$\sigma_x^2 = \frac{1}{(N-1)} \sum_i \left(x_i^2 + \frac{1}{N^2} \sum_j \sum_k x_jx_k - \frac{1}{N} \sum_j 2x_ix_j \right) \tag{14}$$

We rewrite the terms in the parentheses as the result of a difference, squared:

$$\sigma_x^2 = \frac{1}{(N-1)} \sum_i \left(x_i - \frac{1}{N} \sum_j x_j \right)^2 \tag{15}$$

$$\sigma_x^2 = \frac{1}{(N-1)} \sum_i (x_i - \bar{x})^2 \tag{16}$$

Notice that in Equation 16 we divide by $N-1$, even though N observations are included in the sum. This statistic is commonly known as the sample variance, and it corrects for the bias that would occur if we were to divide the sum by N. If we were to use N, we would underestimate the amount of variation in the data. Viewing this calculation from the perspective of observation pairs, it is highly intuitive why we must choose $N-1$. It is a consequence of ignoring each observation's distance from itself, which clearly contains no information. These values equal zero, so there is no need to excise them from the sum. It suffices, in this case, to exclude them from the count of informative observations.

The relationship between pairwise distance and distance from average reveals another important connection. It shows that there is a deep linkage between the pairwise distances that occur in a dataset and the measurement of one unit of information (or surprise), which is based on the squared distance of the observations from their center (the average). In Chapter 4, we extend these ideas to define multivariate similarity and informativeness, which together provide a precise definition of relevance.

In Chapters 5 and 6, we apply pairwise averages to assess the quality of fit that supports a prediction. In that case, considering the information content and bias of each pairwise comparison leads to insights about the bias of the traditional R-squared statistic and how to deal with it.

Lastly, we note that it is sometimes convenient to express the typical spread in units of what we might call physical distance—the sort that can be measured with a ruler—instead of squared distance. The square root of the variance, called the standard deviation and denoted as σ_x, expresses the spread in units of physical distance:

$$\sigma_x = \sqrt{\sigma_x^2} \tag{17}$$

Information Distance

Now that we know the typical distance between observations in terms of surprise, which equals an attribute's variance, we can express the distance between observations in units of information. We define the information distance between two observations $x_{i,A}$ and $x_{j,A}$ for an attribute A as half the squared distance between them divided by the average of the same quantity across all pairs of observations:

$$d(x_{i,A}, x_{j,A}) = \frac{\frac{1}{2}(x_{i,A} - x_{j,A})^2}{\frac{1}{N(N-1)} \sum_k \sum_l \frac{1}{2}(x_{k,A} - x_{l,A})^2} \tag{18}$$

$$d(x_{i,A}, x_{j,A}) = \frac{\frac{1}{2}(x_{i,A} - x_{j,A})^2}{\sigma_{x_A}^2} \tag{19}$$

It is clear from Equations 18 and 19 that $d(x_i, x_j)$ is invariant to the units in which x is measured, and it is invariant to the constant multiple of $\frac{1}{2}$ that appears in both the numerator and the denominator.

When we define an information distance between one observation $x_{i,A}$ and the average value of the attribute $\bar{x}_A$, the multiple of $\frac{1}{2}$ doubles to become 1, maintaining the consistency that is illustrated in Equations 8 through 16. Therefore, we define information distance from average as the squared distance from average divided by the average of the same quantity across all observations:

$$d(x_{i,A}, \overline{x}_A) = \frac{(x_{i,A} - \overline{x}_A)^2}{\frac{1}{N-1} \sum_k (x_{k,A} - \overline{x}_A)^2} \tag{20}$$

$$d(x_{i,A}, \overline{x}_A) = \frac{(x_{i,A} - \overline{x}_A)^2}{\sigma^2_{x_A}} \tag{21}$$

The following important equivalence links these two definitions:

$$\frac{1}{N(N-1)} \sum_i \sum_j d(x_{i,A}, x_{j,A}) = \frac{1}{N-1} \sum_i d(x_{i,A}, \overline{x}_A) \tag{22}$$

This relationship allows us to translate between information that is measured between two observations and information that is measured between one observation and the broader average. A factor of $\frac{1}{2}$ (or 2, depending on how you prefer to view it) is an integral part of this translation.

Information distance is a foundational concept that will recur throughout the book.

Observing Information Applied

In this section we apply the concepts and equations we have thus far presented. The practical goal we set forth in our empirical example is to predict the strength of the U.S. economy in the forthcoming year. Keep in mind, however, that the purpose of this example is to illuminate the value of an observation-centric approach and not to prescribe the best prediction model. We intentionally keep it simple. We will use this same economic dataset as we extend our example to the more advanced notions we discuss in subsequent chapters.

Our dataset contains $M = 5$ economic measurements[3] for $N = 294$ observations,[4] each indexed to the end of a calendar quarter: March 31 (Q1), June 30 (Q2), September 30 (Q3), and December 31 (Q4) from 1947 through the middle of 2020. One of the five measurements we consider an outcome; it is the percentage change in gross domestic product (GDP) that occurred during the following year (four quarters). Note that these measurements overlap sequentially, because we record

---

[3] Subsequent GDP growth is the percentage change in nominal GDP (seasonally-adjusted) over the next four quarters. Nominal GDP is available quarterly from the Federal Reserve Economic Data (FRED) repository maintained by the Federal Reserve Bank of Saint Louis starting in Q1 1947 (code: GDP). Industrial production is the trailing 12-month percentage change in the monthly Industrial Production Index, which is available from FRED starting in January 1919 (code: INDPRO). Nonfarm payrolls is the trailing 12-month percentage change in monthly Nonfarm Payrolls, which is available from FRED beginning in January 1939 (code: PAYEMS). The return of the stock market is the trailing 12-month price return of the S&P 500 Composite Index. Beginning in December 1964, we calculate the returns from monthly data from Datastream. Prior to December 1964, we calculate the returns from monthly data from Robert Shiller's website. The slope of the yield curve is measured as the average difference between the 10-year U.S. Treasury yield and the U.S. Federal Funds Rate over the preceding 12 months. Both series are available monthly from FRED (codes: GS10 and FEDFUNDS, available April 1953 and July 1954, respectively). Prior to July 1957, we source the 10-year U.S. Treasury yield from Robert Shiller's website and proxy the Federal Funds Rate with the annual U.S. 1-month T-bill rate from Ibbotson.

[4] Observations correspond to quarter-end. For example, Q1 1947 refers to values as of March 31, 1947. In the case of industrial production and nonfarm payrolls, which are published with roughly two- and one-week delays, respectively, we lag the data by one month so that it corresponds to what would be observable as of the end of each quarter. For example, at the end of Q1 1947 (March 31, 1947), the latest Industrial Production Index would correspond to February 1947. Therefore, we calculate its one-year percentage change based on the period February 1946 through February 1947. We do the same for nonfarm payrolls. All other attributes are available without delay and therefore correspond to values at the end of each quarter.

a new value every quarter but with a year-ahead window. This overlap does not cause any problems. In fact, it is helpful because it allows us to observe yearly values without needing to choose an arbitrary time of year to make the measurements. And yearly changes are helpful because, unlike quarter-to-quarter changes, they are more stable, and they are not distorted by seasonality.

Exhibit 2.3 illustrates how we measure subsequent GDP growth each quarter and the way in which observations overlap.

We observe four other attributes every quarter in a similar fashion; however, these look back to what happened in the four quarters prior to each date. The first two attributes relate to recent economic activity. Industrial production reflects the year-over-year growth in output for a core segment of the economy. Nonfarm payrolls capture the year-over-year growth in labor force participation, without the seasonal volatility of farming. The next two attributes come from financial markets. The one-year return of the stock market, in aggregate, often serves as a bellwether. Stock prices reflect expectations for the future, and though markets may at times behave irrationally, they are at least somewhat linked to the profitability of companies and the sentiment of investors. The final attribute is the slope of the yield curve, defined as the excess rate of return on offer for U.S. 10-year bonds, above and beyond the short-term policy rate set by the Federal Reserve (the federal funds rate). A positive or large value means the yield curve slopes

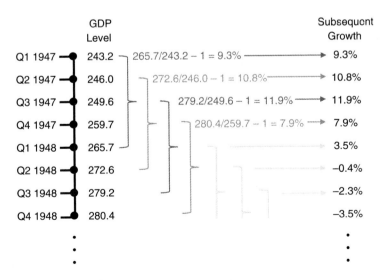

Exhibit 2.3 Subsequent GDP Growth

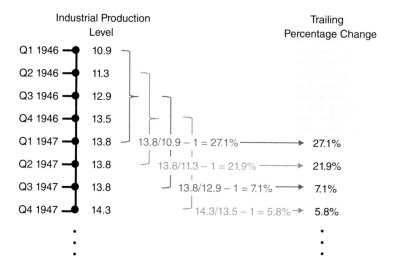

Exhibit 2.4 Trailing Percentage Changes in Industrial Production

up, which is common during robust markets. A negative value has often presaged economic downturns in the past.

Exhibit 2.4 illustrates how we calculate the trailing percentage change in industrial production each quarter.

Exhibit 2.5 shows a sample of our dataset arranged in rows and columns. Though there are 294 observations, we display only the first four and last four in this exhibit.

Our first order of business is to figure out what types of values to expect. We apply Equation 4 to measure the arithmetic averages of outcomes and attributes across the full sample of observations. Exhibit 2.6 reports these values.

Next, we want to summarize the spread of each set of observations. For example, if we plot all observed values of industrial production on a line, as shown in Exhibit 2.7, and randomly select any two observations, how far apart should we expect them to be?

Notice that in Exhibit 2.7, many observations congregate toward the middle of the range. However, it is difficult to discern just how many fall toward the center of the distribution when the circles sit on top of one another. Alternatively, Exhibit 2.8 shows the number of observations that fall within narrow ranges of values for industrial production. This representation is called a histogram. Notice that the shape of the distribution resembles a bell-shaped curve.

Exhibit 2.5 Dataset[5]

	Outcomes	Attributes			
	Subsequent GDP Growth	Industrial Production	Nonfarm Payrolls	Stock Market Return	Slope of the Yield Curve
Q1 1947	9.3%	27.1%	11.0%	−13.5%	1.9%
Q2 1947	10.8%	21.9%	5.5%	−20.1%	1.9%
Q3 1947	11.9%	7.1%	3.1%	−0.2%	1.9%
Q4 1947	7.9%	5.8%	2.5%	−0.7%	1.8%
•	•	•	•	•	•
•	•	•	•	•	•
•	•	•	•	•	•
Q3 2019	−1.7%	−1.4%	1.2%	2.2%	0.2%
Q4 2019	−1.0%	−1.9%	1.4%	28.9%	0.0%
Q1 2020	2.6%	−1.4%	1.6%	−8.8%	0.0%
Q2 2020	16.7%	−16.2%	−11.7%	5.4%	0.1%

Exhibit 2.6 Arithmetic Averages

	Outcomes	Attributes			
	Subsequent GDP Growth	Industrial Production	Nonfarm Payrolls	Stock Market Return	Slope of the Yield Curve
Average	6.3%	3.1%	1.8%	8.6%	1.1%

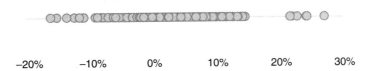

−20%   −10%   0%   10%   20%   30%

Exhibit 2.7 Industrial Production

[5] As described in a previous footnote, observations correspond to quarter-end. For example, Q1 1947 refers to values as of March 31, 1947. In the case of industrial production and nonfarm payrolls, which are published with roughly two- and one-week delays, respectively, we lag the data by one month so that it corresponds to what would be observable as of the end of each quarter.

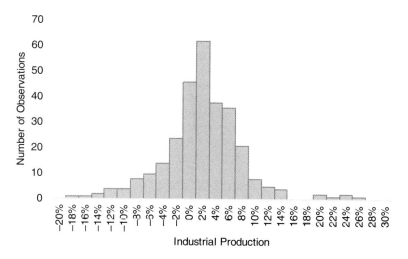

Exhibit 2.8 Histogram of Industrial Production

The conventional approach to summarizing the spread across observations is to compute the average squared deviation of observations from their arithmetic average, which is called variance. As we discussed previously, an alternative but equivalent approach is to estimate variance as a function of the pairwise distances between observations. Exhibit 2.9 illustrates this approach for industrial production. Here, we create a 294-by-294 table for all pairs of observations of industrial production. This corresponds to 86,436 pairs (294 × 294 = 86,436). Again, for ease of visualization, we only show pairs formed from the first four and last four observations, but we can imagine a giant table containing every number. Each cell in this table reports, for the case of industrial production, one half of the squared distance (Equation 7) between the observation that corresponds to its row and the observation that corresponds to its column. The average of these distances equals industrial production's variance. However, recall that the 294 diagonal entries merely compare observations to themselves. They are precisely zero and contain no information, so we exclude them from our count when we calculate the average spread across pairs. As described by Equation 8 and shown at the bottom of Exhibit 2.9, we sum the pairwise distances across the full table and divide by the number of off-diagonal pairs, which equals 86,142 (86,436 total pairs − 294 diagonal pairs = 86,142).

For comparison, Exhibit 2.10 illustrates the conventional approach (Equation 16) to calculating variance and how it is equivalent to the pairwise approach.

Exhibit 2.9 Pairwise Spreads and Variance Calculation—Industrial Production

		1	2	3	4	• • •	291	292	293	294
1	Q1 1947	0.0%	0.1%	2.0%	2.3%		4.1%	4.2%	4.1%	9.4%
2	Q2 1947	0.1%	0.0%	1.1%	1.3%		2.7%	2.8%	2.7%	7.3%
3	Q3 1947	2.0%	1.1%	0.0%	0.0%		0.4%	0.4%	0.4%	2.7%
4	Q4 1947	2.3%	1.3%	0.0%	0.0%		0.3%	0.3%	0.3%	2.4%
	•									
	•									
	•									
291	Q3 2019	4.1%	2.7%	0.4%	0.3%		0.0%	0.0%	0.0%	1.1%
292	Q4 2019	4.2%	2.8%	0.4%	0.3%		0.0%	0.0%	0.0%	1.0%
293	Q1 2020	4.1%	2.7%	0.4%	0.3%		0.0%	0.0%	0.0%	1.1%
294	Q2 2020	9.4%	7.3%	2.7%	2.4%		1.1%	1.0%	1.1%	0.0%

Sum of pairwise spreads	312.0
Number of pairs excluding pairs of observations with themselves	86,142
Variance	0.4%

Exhibit 2.10 Conventional Variance Calculation— Industrial Production

		Observed Value	Squared Deviation from Average
1	Q1 1947	27.1%	5.8%
2	Q2 1947	21.9%	3.6%
3	Q3 1947	7.1%	0.2%
4	Q4 1947	5.8%	0.1%
	•	•	•
	•	•	•
	•	•	•
291	Q3 2019	−1.4%	0.2%
292	Q4 2019	−1.9%	0.2%
293	Q1 2020	−1.4%	0.2%
294	Q2 2020	−16.2%	3.7%

Average	3.1%

Sum of squared deviations	1.1
Number of observations − 1	293
Variance	0.4%

Exhibit 2.11 Arithmetic Averages, Variances, and Standard Deviations

	Outcomes	Attributes			
	Subsequent GDP Growth	Industrial Production	Nonfarm Payrolls	Stock Market Return	Slope of the Yield Curve
Average	6.3%	3.1%	1.8%	8.6%	1.1%
Variance	0.1%	0.4%	0.1%	2.6%	0.0%
Standard deviation	3.7%	6.0%	2.4%	16.2%	1.3%

Exhibit 2.11 shows the arithmetic averages, variances, and standard deviations for outcomes and attributes across the full-sample of observations.

Appendix 2.1: On the Inflection Point of the Normal Distribution

The normal distribution arises because of mathematical law, as Pierre-Simon Laplace elegantly demonstrated with his famous Central Limit Theorem. But it also describes the variation of many natural occurrences. For example, the time intervals between eruptions of the geyser Old Faithful in Yellowstone National Park are normally distributed.

Our purpose in this brief digression is to explain an intriguing feature of the normal distribution, which is the inflection point on either side of its peak, giving rise to its characteristic bell shape. The height of the normal curve measures occurrences defined along the horizontal axis. Its tails measure unusual occurrences, and its peak measures the average occurrence, as well as the most likely occurrence, and the middle occurrence. The question we seek to address is why the rate of change first accelerates and then decelerates as we move from the extreme left tail toward the peak. Why don't the occurrences increase at a constant pace, accelerate all the way to the peak, or increase at a decreasing rate as they approach the peak? The same questions, of course, apply as we move left from the extreme right tail to the peak. Given this symmetry, we will focus mainly on the left half of the distribution.

The normal distribution is a continuous distribution, which means it assumes there are an infinite number of observations covering all possible values along a continuous scale. For example, we can think of time as being distributed along a continuous scale. The challenge of continuous distributions is lack of transparency. Because we cannot directly observe continuous units, we would need to use calculus to understand the forces that give rise to the normal distribution's unique shape. Thankfully, those of us who prefer a noncalculus explanation can instead explore a close cousin of the normal distribution, the binomial distribution, which is an easily observable discrete distribution that converges to the normal distribution as the number of trials increases. Abraham de Moivre proved this fact in 1733 when he derived the formula for the normal distribution.

The binomial distribution captures the sum of many yes/no outcomes, like the total number of heads in a sequence of coin flips. Though the probability could be skewed, let us stick with the notion of a fair coin, which gives a 50% chance of flipping either a head or a tail. Each occurrence has simple odds, and it follows that every unique sequence of heads and tails is equally likely. Thus, the probability of obtaining a particular sum—like getting three heads out of 10 flips—is just a matter of counting how many of the possible sequences lead to this result.

The key to understanding the inflection points of the normal distribution has to do with the relationship between permutations and combinations. To understand this relationship, it is more convenient to think of flipping several different coins rather than flipping the same coin several times. Therefore, let us consider flipping 10 different dollar coins: the American dollar, Australian dollar, Bahamian dollar, Bermudan dollar, Canadian dollar, Hong Kong dollar, Jamaican dollar, New Zealand dollar, Singapore dollar, and Taiwanese dollar. In case you are interested, there are 21 countries that have dollar currencies, not including those that use the American dollar as their currency.

Before we proceed, it might be helpful to review the difference between a permutation and a combination. A permutation refers to one of the many ways you could arrange the coins in a sequence, whereas a combination refers to a unique group of coins, irrespective of their order. This means that each combination may be arranged into many different permutations.

Let us start at the left tail of the binomial distribution, which would be to flip no heads. There is only one way for this outcome to occur: to flip a tail with all 10 coins. Thus, this outcome has only one permutation and one combination. Now let us move slightly to the right of the binomial distribution and consider the ways in which we can flip precisely one head in total. It would be to flip a head with any of the dollars and a tail for all the others; thus, there are 10 ways this can happen, leading to

10 permutations and 10 combinations. Now let us consider an outcome of two heads. For each dollar that could come up heads, there are nine other dollars that could also come up heads. So, there are 90 permutations of two heads. However, half of these permutations are redundant. If, for example, we first flip the Singapore dollar and get a head and then subsequently flip the New Zealand dollar and get a second head, that counts as one permutation, assuming the other coins produced tails. But if we first flip the New Zealand dollar and get a head and then later flip the Singapore dollar and get another head, that counts as a second permutation of two heads, but it is still the same combination of two heads. The binomial distribution gives the probabilities of distinct outcomes, which is to say, combinations, not permutations.

The key insight here is that as we consider larger and larger numbers of heads, two things happen. First, the permutations expand because there are more ways to sequence five heads, for example, than there are to sequence two heads. But second, a greater fraction of five permutations is redundant than would be the case with two heads. By the time we get to 10 heads, there are more than 3.6 million sequences in which we could arrive at 10 heads. To name just two: we could flip the coins in the alphabetical order of their country and end up with 10 heads, or we could flip them in reverse alphabetical order and end up with the same outcome. Only the first permutation we count is a unique combination, and the other 3,628,799 attempts eventually converge to it. The number of ways to arrive at a redundant outcome grows rapidly as we consider an increasing number of heads.

Another way to think about it is from the perspective of combinations. If we flip a head with the Bahamian dollar, there are nine other coins with which to produce a combination of two heads. However, if we flip heads with both the Bahamian dollar and Canadian dollar, there are only eight other coins with which to produce a distinct combination of three heads. As we increase the number of heads, we have more ways to arrange their sequence but fewer unused coins to produce new combinations. This tradeoff determines how fast the combinations expand as we consider larger numbers of heads.

Exhibits 2.12 and 2.13 help to explain this tradeoff. Exhibit 2.12 presents detailed information about the permutations and combinations of heads as we consider larger numbers of heads, while Exhibit 2.13 shows the distribution of distinct combinations of different numbers of heads. If we divide the number of combinations by their sum it would

Exhibit 2.12 Flipping 10 Coins

A	B	C	D	E	F	G	H	I
Heads	Permu-tations	Combi-nations	Redundant Permuta-tions	Incremental Expan-sion	Redundancy Ratio	Permu-tation Multiple	Redun-dancy Multiple	Net Multiple
0	1	1	0		1			
1	10	10	0	9	1	10	1	10.0
2	90	45	45	35	2	9	2	4.5
3	720	120	600	75	6	8	3	2.7
4	5,040	210	4,830	90	24	7	4	1.8
5	30,240	252	29,988	42	120	6	5	1.2
6	51,200	210	15,990	−42	720	5	6	0.8
7	604,800	120	604,680	−90	5,040	4	7	0.6
8	1,814,400	45	1,814,355	−75	40,320	3	8	0.4
9	3,628,800	10	3,628,790	−35	362,880	2	9	0.2
10	3,628,800	1	3,628,799	−9	3,628,800	1	10	0.1

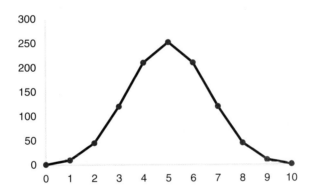

Exhibit 2.13 Distribution of Combinations

give us a probability distribution, which would have the exact same shape.

Column A in Exhibit 2.12 shows the possible number of heads from flipping 10 different coins. Column B shows the possible permutations for each number of possible heads. As we increase the number of heads, most of these permutations include the same coin more than once; it just appears in a different position within the sequence. Column C shows how many of these permutations result in distinct combinations of heads; that is, permutations that have at least one different coin from all the other permutations. It is important to note that the number of permutations grows with the number of heads until it levels off at the end, while the number of combinations first grows and then decreases. Column D shows the number of redundant permutations. It equals the number of permutations less the number of combinations. Column E shows the incremental expansion of combinations. It equals the difference in combinations as we consider greater numbers of heads. Column F shows the ratio of redundant permutations, which equals the number of permutations divided by the number of combinations. For example, for five heads the number of permutations is 120 times the number of combinations. Column G shows the multiple by which the number of permutations grows. As we move from no heads to one head, the number of permutations grows at a multiple of 10 (10/1). Then when we move to two heads, it grows at a multiple of 9 (90/10), and so on. Column H shows the multiple by which the redundancy ratio grows. And Column I shows the net multiple, which equals the permutation multiple divided by the redundancy multiple. Column I also gives the multiple by which combinations grow. Therefore, we can compute it by dividing the numbers in Column C by their preceding numbers.

Columns E and I explain why the binomial distribution (and therefore the normal distribution) is shaped the way it is. These columns capture the tradeoff between growth in permutations and growth in redundancy. Column I addresses the change in the absolute number of heads. It reveals that expanding permutations dominate increasing redundancy up to five heads, thereby increasing the number of combinations. But as we consider more than five heads, redundancy overtakes growth in permutations, as evidenced by the net multiple shifting from a value greater than 1.0 to a value less than 1.0. Column E addresses the incremental expansion of combinations. It reveals that incremental expansion increases up to four heads and then begins to decrease and turn negative after five heads. The point at which it begins to decrease marks the inflection point of the distribution, and the point at which it shifts from positive to negative marks the peak of the distribution.

Based on Exhibit 2.12, these points occur at four and five heads, respectively, but in theory the inflection point occurs between three and four heads. Because we consider only 10 tosses, the results in Exhibit 2.12 are too coarse to reveal the precise location of the inflection point. Exhibit 2.13, however, shows that the curve is convex from zero heads to three heads and then concave from three heads to five heads, suggesting that the inflection point is located between three and four heads. And it reveals the peak to be located at five heads.

Mathematically, we know that the inflection point occurs one standard deviation below the average. We compute the standard deviation of a binomial distribution as:

$$\sigma = \sqrt{np(1-p)} \tag{23}$$

Here σ equals standard deviation, n and p equals the number of trials, and p equals the probability of a head. Therefore, given 10 trials and a probability of 0.5, the standard deviation equals 1.58, and the inflection point should occur at 3.42 heads (the average of 5 minus the standard deviation of 1.58). If there were such a thing as a fractional head, this indication of the inflection point would be consistent with both the table in Exhibit 2.12 and the graph in Exhibit 2.13.

But rather than contemplate fractional heads, we repeat the same experiment with 30 trials instead of 10. Exhibit 2.14 shows the distinct combinations (in millions) and their incremental expansion at each step. By incremental expansion, we mean the change in the number of combinations as we consider larger numbers of heads, which we plot as the light gray line. The inflection points occur at the peak and trough of the light gray line. The more trials we include, the smoother these curves will become. In the limit, they converge precisely to the normal distribution, and the inflection points coincide exactly with one standard deviation above and below the average.

The same result holds for binary probabilities other than 50%. In fact, it holds for the sum of any independent outcomes even if they are not binary. In every case, the possible ways of obtaining an extreme value

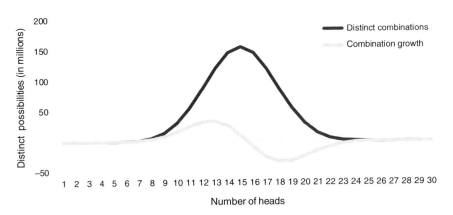

Exhibit 2.14 Counting Distinct Combinations for 30 Trials

are few, and they expand quickly at first. But by the time we get to one standard deviation below average, the number of combinations continues to expand but by smaller and smaller increments until the incremental change reaches zero at the average number of combinations. Then the number of combinations begins to fall steeply as we consider numbers up to one standard deviation above the average, at which point the incremental decrease in the number of combinations begins to slow down.

Now let's consider the inflection point mathematically rather than visually. Mathematically, the binomial distribution is given by:

$$P(X = k) = \frac{n!}{(n-k)!k!}p^k(1-p)^{n-k} \tag{24}$$

Here, n is the total number of trials, k is the number of heads we wish to consider, p is the probability of heads on each trial, and ! denotes the factorial function which is the product of every integer from 1 to the number specified. We can compute the growth multiplier in possibilities from k to $k+1$ as:

$$\frac{P(X = k+1)}{P(X = k)} = \left(\frac{p}{1-p}\right)\left(\frac{n-k}{k+1}\right) \tag{25}$$

We can ignore the constant term involving p, and note that the ratio is determined by the numerator, $n - k$, which represents permutations, and the denominator, $k + 1$, which represents redundancy. This fraction is approximately equal to $\frac{n}{k} - 1$, the percentage by which n is larger than k. When k is small, the multiple will be large. It will decrease to the point where at the center of the distribution, n is twice as large as k and the resulting multiple will be 1.

To map this to the standard normal distribution, we use the probability density function:

$$\varphi(z) = \kappa e^{\left(\frac{1}{2}z^2\right)} \tag{26}$$

Here, z is assumed to be a z-score that is normalized by subtracting the average and dividing by the standard deviation, and κ is a normalization constant (the details of which do not matter for the point we wish to make). The first and second derivatives of this function are:

$$\varphi'(z) = -z\varphi(z) \tag{27}$$

$$\varphi''(z) = (z^2 - 1)\varphi(z) \tag{28}$$

The first derivative implies that the rate of increase when z is very negative is a positive number (z) times the current probability. As z moves toward its center value of zero, this rate of increase correspondingly falls to zero. The inflection point occurs when the first derivative is flat, which means the second derivative is zero. This clearly happens when z equals 1 or −1, which is one standard deviation above or below the average.

You may now lay to rest any nagging anxieties you may have had about this topic.

References

Bellhouse, D., and C. Genest. 2007. "Maty's Biography of Abraham De Moivre. Translated, Annotated and Augmented." *Statistical Science* 22 (1): 109–136.

Bernstein, P. 1996. *Against the Gods*, New York: John Wiley & Sons, 125–129.

Fischer, Hans. 2011. *A History of the Central Limit Theorem: From Classical to Modern Probability Theory.* New York: Springer.

Rosenfeld, R. 2019. *"Origin of the Normal Curve—Abraham De Moivre (1667–1754)."* Vermont Mathematics Initiative.

Shannon, C. 1948. "A Mathematical Theory of Communication." *The Bell System Technical Journal* 27 (July, October): 379–423, 623–656.

Stigler, Stephen M. 1986. *The History of Statistics: The Measurement of Uncertainty before 1900.* Cambridge, MA and London: The Belknap Press of Harvard University Press.

Surowiecki, James. 2004. *The Wisdom of Crowds: Why the Many Are Smarter Than the Few and How Collective Wisdom Shapes Business, Economies, Societies and Nations.* New York: Anchor Books.

3

Co-occurrence

So far, we have only considered attributes separately. When we observe more than one attribute, how do we know if their joint occurrence is typical? The answer lies in learning how they tend to co-occur. Whereas previously we looked at pairs of observations, we now investigate pairs of attributes.

Co-occurrence Conceptually

Imagine you are a sales analyst for an online retailer, and you want to forecast how much a customer will spend based on a collection of attributes about this person. For example, suppose you know this person's age, annual income, time spent on your website, and education level. Before you take the leap of predicting, which we will come to later, you must first understand the typical relationship between these attributes. Only then can you gauge whether this customer is an archetype or an anomaly.

First, consider the relationship between age and income. Here, your observation is a single customer; age and income form a pair of attributes. You select at random a person who is 25 years old and earns $75,000 per year. What does the alignment of these attributes say about this shopper? Is this shopper:

- Younger with lower income, implying a positive relationship?
- Younger with higher income, implying a negative relationship?
- Older with higher income, implying a positive relationship?
- Older with lower income, implying a negative relationship?

Start with what you know. By applying the techniques in Chapter 2, you know that:

- The average age of your customer base is 35 years, with a standard deviation of plus or minus 20 years around this average.
- The average annual income is $100,000, with a standard deviation of $50,000.

You can now conclude that the individual you are studying is relatively young (10 years below average), with an annual income $25,000 under that of your typical customer. Because both attributes are below average, the nature of their relationship is positive.

The question now becomes: How strong is this association? First, we need to put each attribute's distance from average into context. To do this, we divide the distance from average by the standard deviation of the attribute. The result tells us how extreme this single observation is, given the distribution of all customers. For age, we get a value of -0.5 (-10 years/20 years $= -0.5$), half a standard deviation below average. For income, we find the same result ($-\$25,000/\$50,000 = -0.5$). These ratios are called z-scores. They provide a measure of surprise: the unusualness of a single observation for a single attribute. Importantly, z-scores do not depend on the units of measurement. Notice that when we cite the z-scores above, we drop the label of years in the case of age and $ for salary. The z-scores are standardized, which allows us to compare attributes that may otherwise be quoted in different units.

In Exhibit 3.1, we plot our target individual's age and income as z-scores in two dimensions. The upward slope of a line that connects this observation with the center of the chart reveals the positive dynamic at play. The 45-degree slope means that, in this example, the attributes moved in perfect unison. In fact, any observation that falls on this line has the same one-to-one relationship between age and income. It does not matter whether both attributes are above or below their averages, or whether their magnitude is $+4$, -0.5, or 0.01. If they are on this line, they co-occur in lockstep.

It is no accident that every point on a line through the center has the same co-occurrence. This is essential to ensure that information about co-occurrence is distinct, and therefore additive to the information we already have. Recall from Chapter 2 that information is additive so long as it reveals something we did not already know. Everything we know so far comes from viewing the attributes in isolation. We know the degree of surprise, or information, each one carries: its squared z-score. By

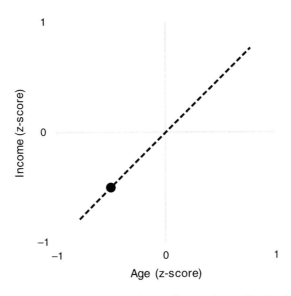

Exhibit 3.1 Two Positively Related Attributes for a Single Observation

extension, the combined surprise of observing two attribute values is nothing more than the average of their individual surprises. So, the first thing we learn about the joint observation of two attributes is the level of surprise they collectively bring.

But knowing only the total surprise paints an incomplete picture. When viewed on a graph, the remaining possibilities trace a circle, such as the one shown in Exhibit 3.2. We know the radius of this circle, but we are ignorant of our location along its boundary. Every position is viable, so we need more information to locate an observation. Put differently, we can describe an observation—a point with two values—in terms of radial coordinates. The distance from center reveals the collective information, or surprise, that the attributes bring on their own. The direction we must travel to reach our observation from the center reveals the pattern of co-occurrence. These two measures are distinct.

Creating the perfect measure of co-occurrence resembles an engineering problem. How should we capture this information in a concise numeric form? Let us explore this question using basic principles as our guide. To start, we acknowledge that co-occurrence is bounded. The most concordant experience happens when two attributes deviate in the same direction and by the same extent. These outcomes are, in fact, redundant, because they carry the same information. In this instance we set co-occurrence equal to 1, representing the unity of both results.

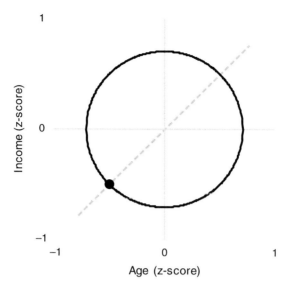

Exhibit 3.2 Possible Co-occurrence Patterns for Attributes with a Given Average Information

There is also a limit to how divergent two outcomes can be. The largest divergence occurs when two attributes move by the same extent, but in opposite directions. (Remember that we are holding constant the amount of total surprise and just looking at the pattern.) In this case, we set co-occurrence equal to −1. This choice serves two purposes. First, it preserves an important symmetry. If we were to redefine one attribute arbitrarily as its mirror opposite by multiplying every value by −1, the most divergent event should now register as the most concordant one, and it should have a co-occurrence of 1. Second, we want to distinguish between perfect unison and perfect opposition. The negative sign keeps track of this distinction.

As we traverse any circle on our graph paper where the sum of surprise is constant, we should expect co-occurrence to vary smoothly between its two extremes, from +1 to −1, and back again. We need to define a measure with these properties.

Unfortunately, the difference between observations—which we used effectively in Chapter 2—will not suffice here. Differences do not indicate location. For example, a positive z-score paired with a negative z-score can produce the same difference as two positives or two negatives. Instead of a difference, we need a product. When the signs are the same, we record positive alignment, and when the signs do not match, we record negative alignment. By virtue of the sign of the alignment, the product records the sameness or differentness of two z–scores. And when one of the z–scores is zero, which means it does not deviate from the norm at all, the co–occurrence is zero, as it should be.

The product of two z–scores still embeds information about total surprise, which we prefer to keep separate. Dividing by total surprise gives the measure we want. To confirm: if we double both z–scores, the product will increase by a factor of 4. The collective surprise, which equals the average squared z–score, will also increase by a factor of 4, leaving the co–occurrence unchanged. The divisor also scales the measure as needed. When the two z–scores match, co–occurrence correctly delivers a value of 1. If we then double just one of these z–scores, we break its perfect alignment. The product of z–scores increases by a factor of 2, yet the divisor increases by more $(0.5 \times (2^2 + 1^2) = 2.5)$. As a result, the imbalance in z–scores causes the co–occurrence to fall as expected. Dividing by total surprise ensures that all observations on the same line through the center of the chart have the same degree of co–occurrence, regardless of their distance from the center.

Exhibit 3.3 illustrates a variety of patterns and their co–occurrence.

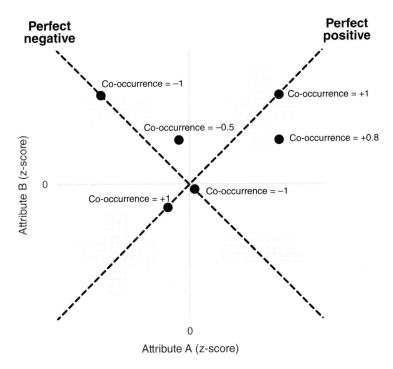

Exhibit 3.3 Co-occurrence for Single Observations

Returning to our online retail example, you now know that the co-occurrence between your individual customer's age and income is exactly 1 $((0.5 + 0.5)/((0.5^2 + 0.5^2)/2))$. The calculation faithfully captures the correspondence between this pair of attributes for this person. But is this finding representative of the broader customer base? To answer this question, we need a summary.

Correlation as an Information-Weighted Average of Co-occurrence

Fast-forward to the point where you have calculated the co-occurrence between age and annual income for 100 customers. How do you determine the typical co-occurrence across all of them? Once again, we turn to the arithmetic average to summarize the tendency of a series. It makes sense to view the typical co-occurrence between a pair of attributes as an average across observations. However, we must recognize that some observations are more informative than others, and we should over-weight them. Therefore, we must determine the informativeness of each observation.

We previously established that informativeness is related to unusualness. Moreover, unusualness is defined within the context of what we know about the data. In our example, we know the age and annual income of 100 people, along with their averages and standard deviations. What makes a person unusual within this context? It would be someone whose age and income are collectively different than the norm. Perhaps this person is extremely young or old, with a slightly atypical income level. Or perhaps this person's income deviates dramatically from average. Perhaps both are extreme. Whatever the case, it makes intuitive sense that these observations contain the most information about the co-occurrence of age and income. As a counterexample, someone who is precisely average in both respects tells us nothing about this person's joint tendencies; co-occurrence relies on the attributes' deviations from average. It is not until you consider people with more intriguing characteristics that you can start to draw reliable conclusions.

In fact, any data that is interesting to analyze likely comes from noisy processes and is measured imperfectly. It is prudent to be skeptical by picturing a cloud of uncertainty around every observation we see. Our measure of informativeness fights against this cloud. When informativeness is large and we estimate a particular value of co-occurrence, we can be confident that the other observations in the cloud exhibit similar co-occurrence. Hence, the measurement is robust to the noise. When informativeness is small, other observations in the cloud may have contradictory co-occurrence scores, so we are wise to discount what we observe. Noise easily overwhelms estimates close to the center, and if we are not careful, these estimates can mislead or distract us. Co-occurrence of informative observations is more reliable.

Mathematically, for our present purposes, an observation's informativeness is the attribute pair's collective surprise as we described earlier: the average squared z-score of the attribute values. In the next chapter, we refine this definition to also consider the average co-occurrence between attributes. However, we defer that discussion because for now we want to focus on their pairwise relationship.

There are two other features worth noting about this definition of informativeness. First, it is equal to the denominator in our measure of the co-occurrence of a single observation. This is important for reasons we will describe soon. Second, it is the average of two squared distances: the standardized distance of the first attribute from its average and the standardized distance of the second attribute from its average. This definition is consistent with the notion set forth in Chapter 2, that the expected information for a pair of observations—or, in this case, a pair of attributes—is the average of their squared distances. This concept recurs throughout the book.

We summarize the typical co-occurrence between a pair of attributes as the information-weighted average co-occurrence across observations. The resulting estimate turns out to equal the well-known Pearson correlation coefficient, an essential concept of classical statistics.

The Pearson correlation owes its name and final form to Karl Pearson, a seminal figure in modern statistics. However, as Pearson acknowledged in his 1920 paper "Notes on the History of Correlation," the concept of correlation can be traced to earlier work by Carl Friedrich Gauss and Francis Galton, among others. In fact, Galton may be considered the inventor of correlation, the discovery of which he recounted in his 1890 paper "Kinship and Correlation."

Galton was fascinated by the quantitative study of heredity. Over the course of the 1870s and 1880s, he produced a body of research based on studying parent–offspring relationships in peas and later humans. It was through this research, which Galton summarized in his 1889 book *Natural Inheritance*, that regression analysis was born.

Interestingly, Galton conceived of regression analysis, a relatively complex concept that we discuss in the following chapter, before he introduced the notion of correlation. A key tool in his analyses were frequency tables that tabulated people according to a given trait and the same trait of their parents. For example, if height was the characteristic of interest, the columns would represent a range of heights across adult children and the rows would represent a range of heights across their parents. Each cell would report the number of adult children with a given combination of their own height and the average of their parents' heights. Though these tables may sound simple, they were revolutionary in that they were some of the first descriptions of a bivariate normal distribution (a normal distribution of observations characterized by two attributes). They also formed the basis for regression analysis, as Galton would draw lines through the tables to describe the relationship between parent and offspring traits. As Pearson remarks in his paper on the history of correlation, "That Galton should have evolved all this from his observations is to my mind one of the most noteworthy scientific discoveries arising from pure analysis of observations" (Pearson, 1920).

Though these tables also formed the basis for correlation, Galton had not fully conceived of the concept when he wrote *Natural Inheritance*. As he recalls in "Kinship and Correlation," it was not until the book was set for print that Galton recognized the significance of correlation. At the time, Galton was involved in two seemingly unrelated projects. One was an anthropological endeavor, investigating the relationship between an individual's thigh bone length and this individual's height. The other was a forensic project for criminal identification, investigating the relationship between various dimensions of a person's body. In conducting this research, it dawned on Galton that, in principle, the two pursuits were identical to his studies on heredity. And with that, Galton conceived of correlation as a generalized concept. Realizing the significance of his discovery and worried that he had not included it in his book, Galton quickly wrote a seminal article on correlation, "Co-relations and their Measurements, Chiefly from Anthropometric Data," which was published in 1889, just days before the release of his book.

Though this paper introduced the concept of correlation, the math still needed some refinement. Moreover, Galton had only imagined correlation as a positive relationship. By the mid-1890s, these remaining pieces were in place, thanks to work by W. F. R. Weldon, who studied anatomical correlations in shellfish, and Karl Pearson, a close friend of Weldon who finalized the mathematical formula for his product–moment correlation in 1895. It is this definition of correlation, also known as the Pearson correlation, that has become a critical tool of statistical analysis.

Let us now return to our observation-centric view of correlation. Just as a single observation for a given attribute is likely to deviate from its average, so too may the co-occurrence of a single observation deviate from its average. The Pearson correlation provides a useful guide for the expected relationship between two attributes. Nonetheless, it remains valuable to measure their alignment, or co-occurrence, from one observation to the next.

Let us summarize how we measure the pattern of co-occurrence between a pair of attributes:

- Co-occurrence describes the sign and strength of alignment between two attributes. It is invariant to the sum of their magnitudes in isolation.

- For a single observation, the co-occurrence of a pair of attributes is equal to the product of their z-scores divided by the average of their squared z-scores. Co-occurrence varies between −1 and +1, which imply perfect, negative alignment and perfect, positive alignment, respectively.

- For purposes of measuring co-occurrence, an observation's informativeness is defined as the combined surprise of the attributes: the average of their squared z-scores.

- An information-weighted average of co-occurrences across multiple observations is equivalent to the Pearson correlation of the attributes' observed values over the same set of observations.

Pairs of Pairs

In our discussion of co-occurrence so far, we have referred to deviations from average. It is just as natural, or perhaps even more so, to think about deviations between pairs of observations, as we did for spreads in Chapter 2. Recall that to compute variance, we took half the squared difference for each pair of observations and averaged across all $N(N-1)$ pairs. Because we excluded the trivial zero difference between an observation's value with itself, we ended up with the common formula for variance in which observations are compared to the average. But we gained a clearer understanding of why we must divide by $N-1$ instead of N when these estimates come from a sample of observations.

The same principle applies to co-occurrence. We do not need to compare two attributes' values to the average; we can compare them to other observations—their peers. Unfortunately, this becomes cumbersome to describe in words because we need to deal with two kinds of pairs: pairs of attributes and pairs of observations. Nevertheless, here is a description of how it works. Imagine that for any two observations you choose, whichever one has higher values for attribute A also has higher values for attribute B. This means that they are clearly aligned. It means that the differences between observation 1 and 2 co-occur for A and B. To measure the extent of the co-occurrence, we normalize by standard deviation and construct the same metric as before. The only difference is that now we must multiply by 1 over the square root of 2 because we are dealing with pairs (this carries over from the multiple of one-half that is contained in the formula for pairwise variance). Taking the normalized spreads for each of the two attributes, we compute our measure of alignment and average it across every pair of observations. Working through the math, we see once again why the conventional formula for correlation divides by $N-1$. Pairs that compare observations to themselves will always have an alignment of zero. These pairs contain no information, and they should be excluded from the average.

We decided to present the conceptual portion of this chapter using comparisons to the average so that we do not have to describe pairs of pairs repeatedly. It is, however, easier to articulate pairs of pairs mathematically and by example, so that is how we proceed in the mathematical and empirical sections of this chapter.

Across Many Attributes

It is often the case that we want to analyze more than two attributes. Returning to our example, we know the typical relationship between a customer's age and income, but there are two more attributes to consider: time spent on your website and education level. With a total of four attributes ($K = 4$), we have six ($K(K - 1)/2$) unique pairwise relationships to estimate. When we summarize these relationships in a K by K table, as illustrated in Exhibit 3.4, we produce a correlation matrix. Each cell contains the correlation of the row attribute with the column attribute. For example, the correlation between age and income is 0.57, while the correlation between age and time spent browsing the website is −0.23. Note that the diagonal cells are all equal to 1 because they

Exhibit 3.4 Correlation Matrix

	Age	Income	Time on website	Education level
Age	1.00	0.57	−0.23	0.78
Income	0.57	1.00	−0.12	0.62
Time on website	−0.23	−0.12	1.00	−0.05
Education level	0.78	0.62	−0.05	1.00

represent each attribute's correlation with itself. Moreover, the top right triangle of correlations is the mirror image of the bottom left triangle. That is because the correlation for each pair is reported twice in this matrix. If we strip out these redundancies and remove the trivial values along the diagonal, there are $K(K-1)/2$ pieces of information.

An important and perhaps less obvious feature of correlation matrices is that the pairwise correlations between two attributes, A and B, and between attributes B and C, imply an expected relationship between attributes A and C. For example, if A and B have a strong, positive correlation and B and C have a strong, positive correlation, A and C must also relate positively to one another. As a real-world example, imagine you and your friend Joe watch most of the same TV shows, and the same is true of you and your friend Amy. It's likely the case that Joe and Amy also watch similar TV shows.

It is important for the correlation matrix to be internally consistent. Mathematically, it allows us to perform certain calculations, which we describe in the next chapter. The need for consistency underscores the complexity in analyzing many attributes. The example of Joe and Amy is relatively easy to imagine, as we describe the implied relationship between three attributes with only three unique pairs. But this quickly becomes difficult for 10 attributes with 45 unique pairs, or 20 attributes with 190 unique pairs. In all cases, each pairwise correlation must be consistent with the others. If our observations correctly characterize our attributes, and if we have at least as many observations as we have attributes in our matrix, this consistency will occur naturally.

The final step, before moving on to prediction, is to integrate all we have learned so far into a covariance matrix. So far, we have described how to estimate an attribute's central tendency (average), dispersion (standard deviation), and pairwise co-occurrence (correlation). We combine this information by multiplying each correlation in the matrix by the standard deviations of the respective attributes. The result is the covariance, which we summarize across all pairs in a K by K table called the covariance matrix. Whereas correlations describe the direction and strength of a relationship, covariances add information about the size of the deviations from average. Covariances can be negative or positive, retaining the sign of the correlation. Moreover, covariances are measured in squared units because they include the product of two standard deviations. As we have come to appreciate by now, squared distances provide essential information about a dataset.

Covariance matrices play a prominent role in the remainder of this book. They allow us to quantify the unusualness of observations that are characterized by a collection of many attributes. And unusualness underlies the concept of relevance, which is at the heart of this book.

Key Takeaways

- For a single attribute, an observation's squared distance from average divided by the average squared distance from average gives a measure of surprise or unusualness.

- The square root of this quantity is called a z-score.

- A z-score does not depend on the unit of measurement; it is standardized.

- Given a two-dimensional plot of z-scores whose center is located at the coordinate of zero for both values, the distance from the center tells us the magnitude of surprise, and the direction from the center tells us the pattern of co-occurrence.

- We measure co-occurrence for a pair of observations as the product of their z-scores divided by the average of their squared z-scores. This measure has desirable properties.

- The information-weighted average co-occurrence for a pair of attributes across all observations is equal to the well-known Pearson correlation.

- A matrix of such correlations yields $K(K-1)/2$ pieces of information. We subtract 1 because the diagonal shows the correlation of each attribute with itself, and we divide by 2 because the upper right triangle of the matrix repeats the correlations in the lower left triangle.

- The correlation of attribute A with attribute B, together with the correlation of attribute B with attribute C, imposes upper and lower bounds on the correlation of A with C.

- The correlation matrix gives information about the strength and direction of the relationships among attributes, but it reveals nothing about the size of their co-movement.

- We multiply correlations by the standard deviations of their respective attributes to compute covariances.

- Covariances, which are measured in squared units, add information about the average size of the deviations from average.

Co-occurrence Mathematically

In Chapter 2, we introduced measures of the typical value and spread in values for individual attributes. These measures summarize the way an attribute tends to occur in isolation based on observed experience. Our next task is to observe how two attributes co-occur. From earlier, we know that the information contained in a given pair of observations for attribute A is its information distance. Again, recall that the $\frac{1}{2}$ in the numerator merely cancels a $\frac{1}{2}$ that is implicitly contained in the denominator, because variance is an average of half the squared distances of all pairwise observations.

$$d(x_{i,A}, x_{j,A}) = \frac{\frac{1}{2}(x_{i,A} - x_{j,A})^2}{\sigma_{x_A}^2} \tag{29}$$

Likewise, the information contained in the same observation pair for another attribute B is $d(x_{i,B}, x_{j,B})$. The collective information for both attributes is the average, $\frac{1}{2}(d(x_{i,A}, x_{j,A}) + d(x_{i,B}, x_{j,B}))$. But note that this value tells us nothing about the relationship between the underlying attribute values for this pair. We would like to devise a metric that adds distinct information about attribute co-occurrence. From first principles, we can specify that our desired metric of co-occurrence should satisfy the following properties:

1. It should be distinct from the sum of individual attribute information, meaning that the individual attribute information does not proscribe the possibilities for co-occurrence.
2. It should indicate direction (sign) in addition to extent of alignment.
3. The maximum co-occurrence should equal that of an attribute with itself.
4. The minimum co-occurrence should equal that of an attribute with its exact opposite (negative).

It follows from the first property that co-occurrence must be invariant to a simple scaling of $\frac{1}{2}(d(x_{i,A}, x_{j,A}) + d(x_{i,B}, x_{j,B}))$, because if it were not, then the sum of individual information would convey information about co-occurrence, and they would be partly redundant. Properties 2 and 4 suggest a symmetry whereby the co-occurrence of one attribute with another's opposite should equal the opposite of the co-occurrence of the original pair. Thus, the metric should allow both positive and negative values. Next, we note that the existence of a maximum and a symmetric minimum, from 3 and 4, together with magnitude invariance, implies that co-occurrence may be standardized to range between -1 and $+1$.

To solve this puzzle, we must retain the signs of the spreads. Previously, the signs were discarded when the values were squared, as we did not need to distinguish between positive and negative direction. But we need this context to compare attributes. With this goal in mind, it is helpful to express the information distance as the square of a signed quantity:

$$d(x_{i,A}, x_{j,A}) = z_{ij,A}^2 \tag{30}$$

Here, $z_{ij,A}$ is a normalized distance between $x_{i,A}$ and $x_{j,A}$, which we call a z-score.[1]

$$z_{ij,A} = \frac{\frac{1}{\sqrt{2}}(x_{i,A} - x_{j,A})}{\sigma_{x_A}} \tag{31}$$

In this expression, σ_{x_A} (the square root of the variance) is the standard deviation of x_A. Note that the multiple $\frac{1}{\sqrt{2}}$ carries over from the multiple of $\frac{1}{2}$ that is contained within the expression for $d(x_{i,A}, x_{j,A})$, as required for pairwise measurements. Whereas $\frac{1}{2}$ canceled out the implicit $\frac{1}{2}$ contained in the variance $\sigma_{x_A}^2$, $\frac{1}{\sqrt{2}}$ cancels out the implicit $\frac{1}{\sqrt{2}}$ that is contained in the standard deviation σ_{x_A}.

Like the information distance itself, the signed value before squaring (which we call the z-score) does not depend on the units of measurement. Thus, these values are comparable across attributes, no matter their underlying units. We now multiply the signed values for two attributes, A and B, and divide by the average of their information distance to arrive at a measure of co-occurrence:

$$c = \frac{z_{ij,A} z_{ij,B}}{\frac{1}{2}(d(x_{i,A}, x_{j,A}) + d(x_{i,B}, x_{j,B}))} \tag{32}$$

---

[1] Traditionally, a z-score is defined relative to the average of the attribute, rather than the spread between two observations, as we have done here. We will soon relate this definition to the version that involves an average.

Or equivalently:

$$c = \frac{z_{ij,A}z_{ij,B}}{\frac{1}{2}(z_{ij,A}^2 + z_{ij,B}^2)} \tag{33}$$

This definition satisfies our requirements. It is invariant to a scaling of the denominator because the same scaling factor will apply to the product of $z_{ij,A}$ and $z_{ij,B}$. The scale invariance holds for negative multiples too, so any mirror image outcomes will be judged the same. The measure is also bounded between -1 and $+1$. Whenever $z_{ij,A}$ and $z_{ij,B}$ take the same value, $c = 1$, and if they take the same values but with opposite signs, $c = -1$. Any value between these extremes is possible. As a result, co-occurrence has a direct interpretation as the direction and strength of alignment.

We next summarize the typical co-occurrence for a pair of attributes by taking an average across every pair of observations:

$$\rho(x_A, x_B) = \frac{1}{N(N-1)} \sum_i \sum_j info_{ij} obj_{ij} \tag{34}$$

Where:

$$info_{ij} = \frac{1}{2}(z_{ij,A}^2 + z_{ij,B}^2) \tag{35}$$

$$obj_{ij} = \frac{z_{ij,A}z_{ij,B}}{\frac{1}{2}(z_{ij,A}^2 + z_{ij,B}^2)} \tag{36}$$

Therefore:

$$\rho(x_A, x_B) = \frac{1}{N(N-1)} \sum_i \sum_j z_{ij,A}z_{ij,B} \tag{37}$$

Even though the denominator of obj_{ij} cancels out $info_{ij}$ when they are combined, our definition of these quantities is not arbitrary, nor is it trivial. The co-occurrence represents information we have yet to learn, even after we know how much information is contained in the collection of the individual attribute values.

We have suggestively labeled the informativeness-weighted average co-occurrence as ρ, and we will now show that it is identical to the well-known Pearson correlation coefficient. First, we extract the factor of $\frac{1}{2}$ and the standard deviations σ_{x_A} and σ_{x_B} from the pairwise z-score definitions to get:

$$\rho(x_A, x_B)\sigma_{x_A}\sigma_{x_B} = \frac{1}{N(N-1)} \sum_i \sum_j \frac{1}{2}(x_{i,A} - x_{j,A})(x_{i,B} - x_{j,B}) \quad (38)$$

As before, the spread of each observation with itself is zero and conveys no information, so we must remove these diagonal elements from our normalization factor, leaving $N(N-1)$ informative pairs. Following the same logic as Equations 10 through 16 from Chapter 2, we collapse this pairwise sum into a sum across observations, relative to the averages $\overline{x}_A$ and $\overline{x}_B$ to obtain:

$$\rho(x_A, x_B)\sigma_{x_A}\sigma_{x_B} = \frac{1}{N-1} \sum_i (x_{i,A} - \overline{x}_A)(x_{i,B} - \overline{x}_B) \quad (39)$$

The relationship may be expressed as the covariance divided by the respective standard deviations of the attributes:

$$\rho(x_A, x_B) = \frac{\frac{1}{N-1} \sum_i (x_{i,A} - \overline{x}_A)(x_{i,B} - \overline{x}_B)}{\sigma_{x_A}\sigma_{x_B}} \quad (40)$$

Or it may be expressed as the averaged product of z-scores relative to the respective averages $\overline{x}_A$ and $\overline{x}_B$ of the attributes:

$$\rho(x_A, x_B) = \frac{1}{N-1} \sum_i z_{i,A} z_{i,B} \quad (41)$$

Here we should emphasize that these z-scores with a single index i do not contain the scaling factor of $\frac{1}{\sqrt{2}}$ because they are relative to the attributes' respective averages:

$$z_{i,A} = \frac{x_{i,A} - \overline{x}}{\sigma_{x_A}} \quad (42)$$

As should now be apparent, the scaling factors of $\frac{1}{2}$ or $\frac{1}{\sqrt{2}}$ are needed to translate the definitions of quantities that are measured as pairwise spreads to those that are measured as deviations from the sample average.

Correlations are a common workhorse of statistical analysis, but single-observation co-occurrences are rarely, if ever, studied. The connection between the two concepts is core to our observation-centric approach. We have shown that the correlation coefficient $\rho(x_A, x_B)$

represents the typical co-occurrence of two attributes. This will prove useful in Chapter 4, when we need to evaluate the co-occurrence of attributes against the backdrop of their typical behavior.

The Covariance Matrix

To assess multivariate observations collectively, we need a concise way to capture all the pairwise correlations across a collection of K attributes. We form a correlation matrix with K rows and K columns:

$$P = \begin{pmatrix} 1 & \rho(x_A, x_B) & \rho(x_A, x_C) & \cdots \\ \rho(x_A, x_B) & 1 & \rho(x_B, x_C) & \\ \rho(x_A, x_C) & \rho(x_B, x_C) & 1 & \\ \vdots & & & \ddots \end{pmatrix} \tag{43}$$

Throughout this book, we will continue to express averages using the notation of traditional sums. We will not use much matrix notation, but it is extremely helpful to convey the many sums involved in evaluating pairwise correlations across attributes with matrices. We will include limited amounts of matrix notation to represent such sums in short form.

We can combine the alignment in the correlation matrix with the individual attribute variances to form a covariance matrix. One cell's entry in the covariance matrix equals:

$$\text{Cov}(x_A, x_B) = \rho(x_A, x_B)\sigma_{x_A}\sigma_{x_B} \tag{44}$$

The entire matrix is:

$$\Omega = \begin{pmatrix} \sigma_{x_A}^2 & \text{Cov}(x_A, x_B) & \text{Cov}(x_A, x_C) & \cdots \\ \text{Cov}(x_A, x_B) & \sigma_{x_B}^2 & \text{Cov}(x_B, x_C) & \\ \text{Cov}(x_A, x_C) & \text{Cov}(x_B, x_C) & \sigma_{x_C}^2 & \\ \vdots & & & \ddots \end{pmatrix} \tag{45}$$

The covariance matrix contains the information we need to evaluate observations using many attributes at the same time.

Co-occurrence Applied

In this section, we will use the economic data we introduced in Chapter 2 to illustrate the co-occurrence of pairs of attributes. To start, let us consider the first two attributes in the dataset: industrial production and nonfarm payrolls. If we select an observation at random, how do we know if the attributes' joint occurrence is unusual? To answer this question, we must understand the typical sign and strength of their relationship, which is known as their correlation. The conventional approach to measuring the correlation of two attributes is to compute the average product of the attributes' normalized deviations from average. An alternative, but equivalent, approach is to estimate correlation as a function of pairwise co-occurrences between observations.

In the conceptual section of this chapter, we presented co-occurrence and correlation based on deviations from average for expository convenience. However, in the mathematical section we considered pairs of observations described by pairs of attributes. In this empirical section we will carry on with this pairs perspective.

First, let us review what we mean by a pairs of pairs approach. Exhibit 3.5 offers a simple illustration. The first notion of pairs refers to pairs of observations. For a single attribute, such as industrial production, we select a pair of observations and record the normalized distance, or pairwise z-score, between its two values. Then, we repeat this process for a second attribute, such as nonfarm payrolls, for the same pair of observations. The second notion of pairs refers to pairs of attributes. For a given pair of attributes—in this case industrial production and nonfarm

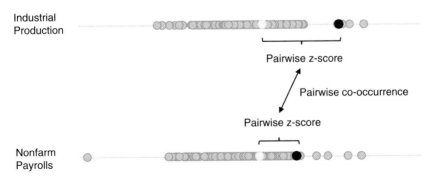

Exhibit 3.5 Pairs of Pairs Approach for Estimating Co-occurrence

payrolls—we compare their respective pairwise z-scores. The result is a measure of co-occurrence that is specific to this pair of attributes, and this pair of observations. It tells us the extent to which the z-scores are aligned.

The following exhibits summarize our empirical analysis of co-occurrence. To start, we consider each attribute in isolation. We compute the pairwise z-scores for every possible pair of observations. This corresponds to the first pairwise comparison described in Exhibit 3.5 (indicated by the brackets between shaded observations).

Exhibit 3.6 reports pairwise z-scores for industrial production in the top panel and nonfarm payrolls in the bottom panel. As before, we only show values for pairs formed from the first four and last four observations in the sample. Recall from Equation 31 that the definition of a pairwise

Exhibit 3.6 Pairwise z-scores for Individual Attributes

Attribute 1: Industrial Production

		1	2	3	4	• • •	291	292	293	294
1	Q1 1947	0.0	0.6	2.4	2.5		3.4	3.4	3.3	5.1
2	Q2 1947	−0.6	0.0	1.7	1.9		2.7	2.8	2.7	4.5
3	Q3 1947	−2.4	−1.7	0.0	0.2		1.0	1.1	1.0	2.7
4	Q4 1947	−2.5	−1.9	−0.2	0.0		0.8	0.9	0.8	2.6
	•									
	•									
	•									
291	Q3 2019	−3.4	−2.7	−1.0	−0.8		0.0	0.1	0.0	1.7
292	Q4 2019	−3.4	−2.8	−1.1	−0.9		−0.1	0.0	−0.1	1.7
293	Q1 2020	−3.3	−2.7	−1.0	−0.8		0.0	0.1	0.0	1.7
294	Q2 2020	−5.1	−4.5	−2.7	−2.6		−1.7	−1.7	−1.7	0.0

Attribute 2: Nonfarm Payrolls

		1	2	3	4	• • •	291	292	293	294
1	Q1 1947	0.0	1.6	2.4	2.5		2.9	2.9	2.8	6.8
2	Q2 1947	−1.6	0.0	0.7	0.9		1.3	1.2	1.2	5.2
3	Q3 1947	−2.4	−0.7	0.0	0.2		0.6	0.5	0.4	4.4
4	Q4 1947	−2.5	−0.9	−0.2	0.0		0.4	0.3	0.3	4.3
	•									
	•									
	•									
291	Q3 2019	−2.9	−1.3	−0.6	−0.4		0.0	0.0	−0.1	3.9
292	Q4 2019	−2.9	−1.2	−0.5	−0.3		0.0	0.0	−0.1	3.9
293	Q1 2020	−2.8	−1.2	−0.4	−0.3		0.1	0.1	0.0	4.0
294	Q2 2020	−6.8	−5.2	−4.4	−4.3		−3.9	−3.9	−4.0	0.0

z-score is different from a traditional z-score: it has no notion of the attribute's average. Moreover, some of the pairwise z-scores are negative, while others are positive. These signs are important because they indicate which observation in the pair is larger than the other, and we will need to account for this fact when we measure co-occurrence. We did not encounter signs like this in Chapter 2 because all the pairwise distances were squared. Lastly, we should stress that these distances are unitless, as each pairwise spread is normalized by its attribute's standard deviation. Normalized values are essential when we compare two attributes that might be measured in different units.

Now we are ready to compare pairs of attributes for pairs of observations. This corresponds to the second pairwise comparison in Exhibit 3.5 (indicated by the arrow between z-scores).

Exhibit 3.7 shows the grid of co-occurrences for our attribute pair. Each cell's value follows from the corresponding cells in Exhibit 3.6. Per Equation 33, we multiply the values across attributes and divide by the average of their squared values. In other words, co-occurrence is the product of the attributes' pairwise z-scores divided by the average of their squared z-scores.

Notice that co-occurrence is a signed quantity. Mathematically, this is because its numerator equals the product of the attributes' z-scores, which are themselves signed. The sign will be positive if the observation that is larger for the first attribute is also larger for the second attribute. An observation that is larger for one attribute and smaller for the other attribute will register a negative co-occurrence.

Exhibit 3.7 Pairwise Co-occurrence—Industrial Production and Nonfarm Payrolls

		1	2	3	4	• • •	291	292	293	294
1	Q1 1947	0.0	0.7	1.0	1.0		1.0	1.0	1.0	1.0
2	Q2 1947	0.7	0.0	0.7	0.8		0.8	0.7	0.7	1.0
3	Q3 1947	1.0	0.7	0.0	1.0		0.8	0.8	0.7	0.9
4	Q4 1947	1.0	0.8	1.0	0.0		0.7	0.7	0.6	0.9
	•									
	•									
	•									
291	Q3 2019	1.0	0.8	0.8	0.7		0.0	−1.0	0.1	0.7
292	Q4 2019	1.0	0.7	0.8	0.7		−1.0	0.0	1.0	0.7
293	Q1 2020	1.0	0.7	0.7	0.6		0.1	1.0	0.0	0.7
294	Q2 2020	1.0	1.0	0.9	0.9		0.7	0.7	0.7	0.0

Exhibit 3.7 illustrates the fact that co-occurrence is bounded between −1 and 1. For example, it approaches 1.0 (we have rounded to one decimal place) for both the Q1 1947/Q3 2019 observation pair (row 1, column 291) and the Q1 1947/Q2 2020 observation pair (row 1, column 294 in Exhibit 3.7). The upper bound prevails even though the pairwise z-scores of the latter example were about 1.5 times larger than the former. Mathematically, co-occurrence is bounded because of its denominator, which equals the average of the attributes' squared z-scores. Conceptually, it is bounded because it measures not the size, but rather the degree of sameness for an observation pair across attributes.

Next, we want to summarize co-occurrence across all pairs of observations. Once again, we will turn to the average as a powerful aggregator.

However, before we estimate average co-occurrence, we must acknowledge that some pairwise co-occurrences are more informative than others. Let us recall how to compute the information distance between two observations of a single attribute. As shown in Equation 30, it equals the pairwise z-score, squared. Put simply, unusual pairs contain more information than common ones. For co-occurrence we have not one but two attributes, and thus two sources of information, and we take their average. In other words, the informativeness of one cell in our co-occurrence grid equals the average of the squared z-scores for that cell.

Exhibit 3.8 shows the informativeness of each element for industrial production and nonfarm payrolls. By happenstance, the first and last observations in our dataset are quite extreme, and hence we are

Exhibit 3.8 Information Distance of Pairwise Co-occurrence—Industrial Production and Nonfarm Payrolls

		1	2	3	4	• • •	291	292	293	294
1	Q1 1947	0.0	1.5	5.6	6.4		9.9	9.9	9.6	36.1
2	Q2 1947	1.5	0.0	1.8	2.2		4.6	4.7	4.4	23.3
3	Q3 1947	5.6	1.8	0.0	0.0		0.7	0.7	0.6	13.6
4	Q4 1947	6.4	2.2	0.0	0.0		0.4	0.5	0.4	12.4
	•									
	•									
	•									
291	Q3 2019	9.9	4.6	0.7	0.4		0.0	0.0	0.0	9.0
292	Q4 2019	9.9	4.7	0.7	0.5		0.0	0.0	0.0	9.1
293	Q1 2020	9.6	4.4	0.6	0.4		0.0	0.0	0.0	9.5
294	Q2 2020	36.1	23.3	13.6	12.4		9.0	9.1	9.5	0.0

Exhibit 3.9 Pairwise Correlation Calculation—Industrial Production and Nonfarm Payrolls

		1	2	3	4	• • •	291	292	293	294
1	Q1 1947	0.0	1.0	5.6	6.4		9.8	9.8	9.4	34.6
2	Q2 1947	1.0	0.0	1.3	1.7		3.5	3.5	3.2	23.1
3	Q3 1947	5.6	1.3	0.0	0.0		0.6	0.5	0.4	12.1
4	Q4 1947	6.4	1.7	0.0	0.0		0.3	0.3	0.2	11.0
	•									
	•									
	•									
291	Q3 2019	9.8	3.5	0.6	0.3		0.0	0.0	0.0	6.7
292	Q4 2019	9.8	3.5	0.5	0.3		0.0	0.0	0.0	6.6
293	Q1 2020	9.4	3.2	0.4	0.2		0.0	0.0	0.0	7.0
294	Q2 2020	34.6	23.1	12.1	11.0		6.7	6.6	7.0	0.0

Sum of information-weighted co-occurrence	71005
Number of pairs excluding pairs of observations with themselves	86,142
Correlation	0.82

instructed to pay a great deal of attention (informativeness of 36.1) to their co-occurrence (which was high, approaching 1).

The next step is to summarize the typical alignment, or correlation, of these two attributes. We accomplish this by taking an information-weighted average of all their pairwise co-occurrences. Exhibit 3.9 shows the information-weighted co-occurrences in each cell (the numbers from Exhibit 3.7 times those of Exhibit 3.8), along with their sum, the number of pairs, and the resulting correlation that follows from applying Equation 37. This process emphasizes co-occurrences from the most informative pairs of observations. Again, keep in mind that this calculation includes all 86,436 pairs of observations.

Exhibit 3.10 illustrates pairwise co-occurrence graphically. Here, we show a scatter plot of pairwise z-scores, sticking with the same example of industrial production and nonfarm payrolls. Each dot represents a pair of observations. The coordinates of this plot are the pairwise z-scores that give rise to co-occurrence. A dot's position from left to right reflects its z-score for industrial production, and the dot's height reflects the z-score for payrolls. This chart would be very crowded if we were to plot all of the more than 86,000 pairs, so we show only the 64 pairs from Exhibit 3.6.

Now let us visualize the geometry of co-occurrence for the highlighted observation pair, which corresponds to Q3 2019 and Q2 2020. To start, we draw a line from the origin to the observation pair.

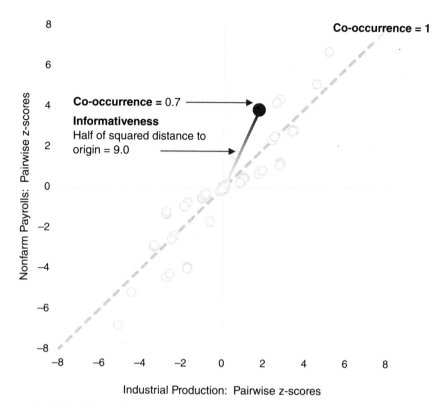

Exhibit 3.10 Pairwise Co-occurrence—Industrial Production and Nonfarm Payrolls

The direction of this line reveals the pair's co-occurrence. Its upward slope indicates a positive relationship. However, it is located away from the 45-degree line, indicating less than perfect alignment; in this instance, co-occurrence is positive but less than 1. In fact, it is 0.7, as previously reported in Exhibit 3.7.

The length of the line from the origin to the point is related to informativeness. Specifically, the informativeness of an observation pair equals half its squared distance from the origin. This pair has an informativeness of 9.0, as previously reported in Exhibit 3.8.

Imagine, now, that we could swing the highlighted dot around in a circle, as if the line connecting it to the origin were a string that always remained stretched to this length. (This exercise is similar to Exhibit 3.2 in the conceptual section of this chapter.) Any point along this circle will have the same informativeness of 9.0. If, however, we chose a random point on the circle, its informativeness alone would tell us nothing of co-occurrence. The essence of co-occurrence is to know the location on this circle, the direction of travel from the center. This example makes clear geometrically why co-occurrence and informativeness are distinct. Informativeness tells us how far from the origin an observation pair lies. Co-occurrence tells us its radial direction, as if on a compass.

Finally, imagine measuring the distance (informativeness) and direction (co-occurrence) of every other dot in this chart, and for that matter the more than 86,000 that are not shown. The correlation statistic is nothing other than the average co-occurrence across all these pairs, where each pair is weighted according to half the squared distance from the origin (informativeness).

For comparison, Exhibit 3.11 illustrates the conventional approach to calculating the same correlation figure (Equation 41), which is equivalent. Note, here, that z-scores reflect normalized deviations from the attributes' respective average, as in Equation 42.

Exhibit 3.12 presents the correlations for all pairs of attributes in the dataset (Equation 43). And, using Equation 44, we combine the

Exhibit 3.11 Conventional Correlation Calculation—Industrial Production and Nonfarm Payrolls

		Deviation from Average		Z-score from Average		
		Industrial Production	Nonfarm Payrolls	Industrial Production	Nonfarm Payrolls	Product of z-scores
1	Q1 1947	24.1%	9.2%	4.0	3.9	15.7
2	Q2 1947	18.8%	3.8%	3.1	1.6	5.0
3	Q3 1947	4.1%	1.3%	0.7	0.6	0.4
4	Q4 1947	2.8%	0.8%	0.5	0.3	0.1
	•	•	•	•	•	•
	•	•	•	•	•	•
	•	•	•	•	•	•
291	Q3 2019	−4.5%	−0.5%	−0.7	−0.2	0.2
292	Q4 2019	−4.9%	−0.4%	−0.8	−0.2	0.1
293	Q1 2020	−4.4%	−0.1%	−0.7	−0.1	0.0
294	Q2 2020	−19.3%	−13.4%	−3.2	−5.7	18.2

Sum of product of z-scores	241.5
Number of observations − 1	293
Correlation	0.82

Exhibit 3.12 Correlation Matrix

		A	B	C	D
A	Industrial Production	1.00	0.82	0.18	0.15
B	Nonfarm Payrolls	0.82	1.00	0.05	−0.05
C	Stock Market Return	0.18	0.05	1.00	0.20
D	Slope of the Yield Curve	0.15	−0.05	0.20	1.00

Exhibit 3.13 Covariance Matrix

		A	B	C	D
A	Industrial Production	0.36%	0.12%	0.18%	0.01%
B	Nonfarm Payrolls	0.12%	0.06%	0.02%	0.00%
C	Stock Market Return	0.18%	0.02%	2.61%	0.04%
D	Slope of the Yield Curve	0.01%	0.00%	0.04%	0.02%

information about typical alignment (correlation) with typical spreads (variance) to form the covariance matrix shown in Exhibit 3.13. We will use the covariance matrix extensively in Chapter 4.

References

Czasonis, M., M. Kritzman, and D. Turkington. 2021. "The Stock-Bond Correlation." *The Journal of Portfolio Management* 47 (3): 1–10.

Galton, F. 1889. "Co-relations and Their Measurement, Chiefly from Anthropometric Data." *Proceedings of the Royal Society of London* 45 (273–279).

Galton, F. 1889. *Natural Inheritance.* London: Macmillan.

Galton, F. 1890. "Kinship and Correlation." *North American Review* 150: 419–431.

Magnello, and M. Eileen. 2009. "Karl Pearson and the Establishment of Mathematical Statistics." *International Statistical Review* 1 (1): 3–29.

Pearson, K. 1920. "Notes on the History of Correlation." *Biometrika* 13 (1, October): 2–45.

Stigler, S. M. 1989. "Francis Galton's Account of the Invention of Correlation." *Statistical Science* 4 (2): 73–86.

4

Relevance

In Chapter 2, we reconsidered the distribution of individual attributes through the lens of pairs, and we used this lens to illuminate the connection between probability and informativeness. In Chapter 3, we reconsidered the association between pairs of attributes within the context of informativeness. Now we show how to combine informativeness with similarity to determine the relevance of observations. In addition, we reveal how relevance is related to linear regression analysis and how this relationship enables us to improve predictions.

Relevance Conceptually

By now we have learned what is typical for the attributes in our dataset: how much they vary and the extent to which pairs tend to vary together. Most importantly, we have become more knowledgeable historians, able to pinpoint the notable events in each attribute's history. The next step is to consider circumstances more holistically. By circumstances, we mean patterns that occur across many attributes at the same time. Put differently, circumstances are the collection of values that we choose to define an observation. They are more colorful, more descriptive, and more informative than any one attribute on its own. What if we can refine our historical understanding to identify the circumstances that truly matter: those that inform us about outcomes yet to be observed? To do this properly, we need all the richness of understanding we have developed up to this point.

Informativeness

Remember that information is a measure of surprise; unusual events are more informative than common events. Informativeness depends on all that we have discussed so far, but we need to take another step forward. Thanks to Chapter 3, we know the typical pattern of comovement. Now we can observe whether two attributes that usually move in tandem suddenly diverge, for example. If so, something unusual has happened. Moreover, we should recognize that while divergence is slightly surprising for two loosely correlated attributes, it is remarkable for those that almost never separate. Size still matters too, of course. The more dramatic these effects, the more attention we should pay to them. But how, exactly, should we extend our notion of informativeness to account for interactions? To make matters even trickier, we would like to evaluate more than two attributes at the same time.

The answer comes from an Indian statistician named Prasanta Chandra Mahalanobis, who studied human skulls in the 1920s. In service to a colleague, Mahalanobis assembled various measurements of skull samples from available data. His interest was not born of a passion for skulls or a fascination with death, but rather from a desire to understand the dynamics of marriage between native Indians and English settlers in the caste system of the times. He wanted to know if interracial marriage had been more prevalent among the wealthy compared to lower castes in Bengalese society. This work required sorting unclassified skulls into groups by caste based on their resemblance to samples known to have come from a homogenous group, such as those obtained from graveyards and battlefields.

The many features of skulls made the problem multidimensional. Mahalanobis's idea was to measure the distance of a given skull from the center of each known cluster. The nearest group would be the most likely match. For this he needed a multivariate distance, akin to the hypotenuse of a triangle on graph paper that may have three or even more dimensions, which is hard to visualize though not hard to compute. The Pythagorean theorem, $a^2 + b^2 = c^2$, dating back more than 2,000 years, dictates the length of a triangle's hypotenuse as the square root of the sum of its squared sides. The familiar Euclidean distance works the same way for many dimensions; you just sum as many squared items as you please before taking the square root. For five dimensions, $f = \sqrt{a^2 + b^2 + c^2 + d^2 + e^2}$.

Mahalanobis could have stopped here, but there is an obvious problem. A skull whose head is one centimeter longer than a group's average will be judged equally distant as a skull whose nose is one centimeter longer. But is one centimeter not more meaningful for a nose than an entire head? The nose measurement is more unusual—more informative—because the typical variation in nose size is smaller. Thus, in a 1927 article, before squaring and summing the items, Mahalanobis divided each measurement's distance from average by the standard deviation of the attribute. The result is a sum of squared z-scores, reminiscent of Chapter 3.

In our everyday three-dimensional world, we can measure the Euclidean distance between any two points using a ruler. That is no longer true after we adjust for the variation of each attribute. Sadly, there is no physical ruler that measures information. And yet the refined measure of information distance is still, conceptually, a distance. It is as if you can run north and south normally, but to go east or west you must run through molasses. Nobody makes it very far. Even short distances left or right are noteworthy.

By 1936, Mahalanobis had advanced his distance measure by one more crucial step; he accounted for co-occurrence. The result became his namesake measure, the Mahalanobis distance—a more accurate way to evaluate statistical proximity and organize observations, whether skulls or anything else, into self-similar groups.

The Mahalanobis distance improves the sum of squared z-scores by considering every pairwise relationship among the attributes. Keeping track of every pair is daunting, which is where matrix math comes in. We make use of the covariance matrix that we described in Chapter 3 to proceed in an orderly fashion.

The covariance matrix is rich with information. It captures the typical information spread for each attribute and the degree to which deviations tend to be aligned. We want to know, for any set of values we observe, whether they conform to the archetype of typical behavior. Conceptually, we want to take our vector of observed circumstances and divide it by the normal amount of fluctuation. Are the values we observe equal to one dose of surprise? Two doses? Or perhaps much more or much less? This is precisely what the Mahalanobis distance tells us, but since we cannot divide by a matrix, we must calculate its inverse instead.

Inverting a matrix is like inverting a fraction, only more complicated. To invert 1/2, we flip it to get 2. To invert 3, we flip it to get 1/3. These are inversions because their product equals 1. They cancel out.

To invert a matrix, we must find another matrix by which we multiply it to cancel it out, leaving behind a nearly empty shell of 1s on the diagonal and 0s everywhere else. Finding a matrix inverse is not a simple task for pen and paper. It requires one to apply a complex algorithm or to conduct a lengthy trial-and-error search which, thankfully, is trivial for today's computers. The reward of finding the inverse covariance matrix is that it holds the key to computing the informativeness of any observation.

The recipe for informativeness includes every average, variance, and correlation, together with every attribute value for the observation we want to assess. These are multiplied and summed in many permutations, and though they could be written out or described at length, doing so is no more enlightening than just referring to the matrices that carry out these rules. At the end of it all, the resulting distance is a single number. It is a concise summary of the information distance of one observation from another. Rather than dwell on the math here, let us explore the intuition for some simple cases.

An observation that is average in every dimension has a distance of zero, and thus an informativeness score of zero. A Mahalanobis distance of 1 indicates an observation that lies an average distance away from the center, taking all this nuance into account. The distance may be arbitrarily large, as collective unusualness rises. As always, large distances mean greater unusualness and more information. Remember, there is only one way to be average, but there are many ways to be eccentric.

If we choose just one attribute, the Mahalanobis distance collapses to the one-dimensional squared z-score we discussed earlier. It computes the difference of the observation from average, squares it, and divides by the variance. The squared z-scores we used in Chapter 3 were simple forms of Mahalanobis distances. They implicitly assumed no correlation, but we cannot blame them for that because their entire purpose was to compute the correlation in the first place! More generally, if correlations are zero, the Mahalanobis distance simplifies to a sum of squared z-scores no matter how many attributes we include. If correlations are zero, it means there are no regular patterns in the data, and no pattern should surprise us more than any other. All the information comes from magnitudes in that case. To wit, the scatter plot on the left of Exhibit 4.1 shows two attributes that are uncorrelated. The circles represent distances from the centroid of the data; that is, their average values. All points on a given circle, such as points A and B, have the same Mahalanobis distance from the centroid. In this case they also have the same Euclidean distance.

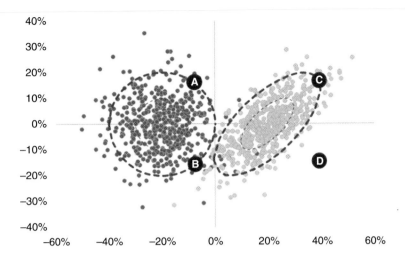

Exhibit 4.1 Scatter Plot of Two Hypothetical Attributes

The scatter plot on the right helps us visualize the Mahalanobis distance when correlations are not zero. This plot shows two attributes that are positively correlated. Now, tilted ellipses centered on the average values trace out all the points with the same Mahalanobis distance. Observations with the same Euclidean distance no longer share the same Mahalanobis distance. Consider, for example, points C and D. They both have the same Euclidean distance from the centroid, but C is closer in Mahalanobis distance than D. C is statistically closer because it is consistent with a positive correlation, whereas D represents an interaction that violates this norm.

We may now characterize observations based on their circumstances, using the attributes we prefer. We can identify the most unusual circumstances from the past, which are also the most informative. The constant buzz of random noise weighs less heavily on these observations. Hopefully, a more interesting truth about the structure of occurrences will shine through. Our measure of informativeness, which is precisely the Mahalanobis distance, serves as a guide to experience. There is no judgment or bias in its logic, just a straight reading of the facts. This thought process is intuitive and familiar: we seek occurrences so we can learn from them, and we prefer interesting stories to boring ones.

The whole point of building our knowledge about circumstances is to study outcomes that might depend on them. In other words, there is an outcome, called Y, that is informed by attributes, collectively called X.

To predict Y in the future, it stands to reason that we should overweight what happened during the most informative times, according to X. But there is still one missing piece to the puzzle. Predictions are not made in a vacuum; they are made in the context of whatever conditions prevail. Therefore, we must consider the similarity of past observations to current circumstances. Then, we will have an intuitive algorithm for extrapolating from the past.

Similarity

A frequent phrase in TV show courtrooms is "Objection! ... Relevance." Only relevant evidence is admissible at trial. The U.S. legal definition of relevance is nuanced, but it requires two parts. Evidence must have probative value, which means it could raise or lower the probability of a fact. And it must also be material to the issue at hand.[1]

There are parallels to prediction. The notion of probative value relates to informativeness. Unusual observations carry more value because they are less likely to occur by accident. In a murder trial, for instance, it is notable if the defendant has never missed a day of work but went mysteriously missing on the day of the killing.

What about materiality? If the murder suspect previously interacted with the victim or went to the same part of town, we want to know about it. But do we care about the suspect's grocery shopping from three weeks prior, or his high school reunion? Probably not. We are looking for circumstances like those of the crime.

We introduce a statistical measure of similarity by once again using the Mahalanobis distance. Anchoring to the time of prediction, we compare present circumstances to everything that came before. Larger distances mean conditions are less similar, and vice versa. Similarity operates in the same way as informativeness, with the same inverse covariance matrix and set of observed attributes. The only difference is that instead of computing the distance from average conditions, we compute the distance from the conditions that prevail at the time of prediction.

Some facts about similarity may help:

- Any observation is most like itself and is awarded the highest possible score: zero.
- All other observations will take negative values.

---

[1] Please keep in mind that we are not lawyers.

- The more distant the circumstances, the more negative the value, and the less similar the observation.
- There is no limit on how dissimilar an observation can be.

Remember that the variances and correlations of each attribute are embedded in the inverse covariance matrix. That matrix does the hard work. It holds these facts as it judges each observation in turn.

Relevance and Prediction

Relevance measures the importance of an observation to a prediction. It is equal to a sum of two parts: informativeness and similarity. Simply put, observations that are different from average but like present circumstances are more relevant than those that are not. For reasons that we will elucidate in the forthcoming section on partial sample regression, we add an observation's similarity to current circumstances to one half of the observation's informativeness. The result tells us how to weight historical observations intelligently.

Filtering experience in this way is intuitive. Faced with a new situation, we automatically scour our memory for noteworthy experiences that bear some resemblance to the one we face. A pending snowstorm might recall past storms while stuck at home, plus some from ski trips, and maybe even other types of severe weather events. A new illness might conjure images of people our age who recently struggled with a similar disease. A new product launch might spark comparison to a company's history and to related products from competitors. Relevance is a matter of degree. We might include less relevant experiences along with highly relevant ones, but we acknowledge the difference.

Exhibit 4.2 depicts two observations that, based on two attributes, are equally similar to current circumstances. But observation B is more informative, and therefore more relevant, because it is more distant from the average conditions that lie at the center of the chart.

Predictions arise from this view almost effortlessly. Just take the relevance-weighted average of what occurred in each case, where the occurrence we care about can be anything we wish to predict.

To be more precise, we start with a baseline prediction, which is the simple average of the Y outcome we want to predict (something we cannot yet observe, to be informed by past outcomes that we can observe). Next, we multiply each deviation of Y from its average by the relevance of that observation, where relevance is determined by the

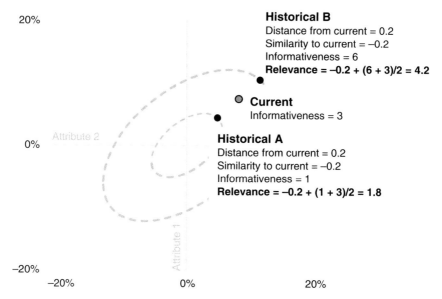

Exhibit 4.2 Similarity, Informativeness, and Relevance of Hypothetical Observations

circumstances we define as X. And in keeping with a pattern that you might by now recognize, we simply average these weighted deviations, dividing by $N - 1$ instead of N. This tilts our naïve prediction away from the average based on past deviations that we observe. Deviations that correspond to relevant observations have the most influence.

How Much Have You Regressed?

You may be wondering whether the predictions that come from relevance-weighted outcomes are any good. The most direct answer, of course, would come from testing them in a live real-world setting and evaluating the track record. Unfortunately, for many applications, you may need to wait years before a compelling answer emerges one way or the other. In the meantime, we can at least demonstrate that the approach is sensible.

It turns out that our relevance-weighted predictions are exactly equivalent to the predictions that come from a traditional linear regression model. We have derived them differently, but they will match a regression model's prediction to as many decimal places as you wish.

This is great news because linear regression analysis is credible. In fact, it has many virtues.

Briefly, the typical view of a linear regression model is as follows. Assume the outcome Y emanates from a weighted sum of the attributes X, plus a random error term. Solve for the weights on the attributes (the beta coefficients) that minimize the sum of squared prediction errors for your dataset. Apply these coefficients to the attributes' current values to render a prediction for the future.

Technically speaking, the procedure is to specify a linear model, estimate its unknown coefficients using the method of Ordinary Least Squares, and apply the resulting linear sum across variables to a new set of inputs to arrive at a prediction. This approach is a centerpiece of any "Introduction to Statistics" course. The fact that it equals the relevance-weighted average occurrence across observations is intriguing to say the least.

Carl Friedrich Gauss, who originated the method of least squares (which we now call linear regression analysis) circa 1795, realized that this approach is by no means arbitrary. In fact, he proved that it is a perfectly efficient use of information in the following sense. If there is a linear relationship between a set of X attributes and the Y outcomes, and if we want an unbiased prediction of Y in the future, the least squares solution provides the most reliable answer.[2] By reliable, we mean that its expected variance from the truth is lower than any other linear and unbiased estimate. To drive the error down more, we would have to accept a systematic over- or underprediction bias. Or, we would have to add complexity such as nonlinearity. There is no free lunch here—we must sacrifice something to buy further improvement. Gauss proved that this supremacy holds when errors are normally distributed and independent across observations. Decades later, the Russian mathematician Andrey Markov showed that it holds even more generally, so long as errors are uncorrelated and have equal variance. All these benefits accrue to relevance as well, owing to its equivalence with linear regression.

Does the world need a new interpretation of linear regression? After all, the way classical regression stores estimated relationships as beta coefficients is admirably concise. There may be thousands of observations, N, but linear regression boils them down to a handful of coefficients

---

[2] The method of least squares provides the best linear unbiased estimate of the slope parameters in a linear regression, and by extension a linear combination of those slopes to form a prediction $\hat{y}_t$.

(one for each of the K attributes, to be precise). We can see which attributes matter most and evaluate their statistical properties. By contrast, our relevance-weighting procedure asks you to revisit the sprawling well of data for every prediction. Is that necessary?

Let us be clear that these two views of regression prediction are not mutually exclusive; they are complementary. There are many benefits to studying model coefficients and generalizing knowledge from the key relationships that emerge. But we argue that reorienting one's perspective to observations offers many advantages, too. One advantage is ease of interpretation, because most people naturally process experience in terms of narratives rather than variables. The observation-centric view allows people to overlay subjective judgment in a more intuitive way. A second advantage of relevance is that it provides a simple, yet profoundly powerful, tool with which to improve the forecasting process. By merely sharpening our focus on the most relevant subset of observations, we can make the prediction process more sensitive to changes in circumstances. The observations we rely on will not remain static—they will depend on the prediction task. After this tweak, the relevance-weighted prediction can no longer be described by a static set of beta coefficients. The logic is more sophisticated and conditional now, but in a way that pays homage to the foundations of linear regression. This approach is called partial sample regression.

Partial Sample Regression

The equivalence of relevance-weighted prediction to classical regression analysis reveals an intriguing feature of linear regression. Owing to the inherently symmetric nature of a best-fit line, regression analysis places equal importance on relevant and nonrelevant observations—it just flips the sign of the effect of the nonrelevant observations on the prediction. In other words, linear regression tells us to expect the opposite of what occurred in past events that are the most unlike current circumstances. This feature of regression analysis invites a fundamental question about prediction: Are nonrelevant observations as useful in forming a prediction as relevant ones? In some cases, they may be, but not always, and perhaps not usually. It is this feature of regression analysis that led us earlier to question how regression analysis processes historical observations to predict the future. And it provides the insight about how we can use relevance to improve prediction.

Suppose, for example, we would like to predict the impact on economic growth from a decrease in interest rates when the rates are currently above average. Should we attach as much importance to past rate reductions when interest rates were below average (assuming the effect will be the mirror image) as we do to past reductions when interest rates were above average? Most market analysts would say no. They would instinctively pay more attention to past episodes of monetary easing when rates were similarly above average, reasoning that the effect of this policy shift on a previously booming economy with high rates should be quite different from the effect on an economy that is already on monetary life support. A drop in already-low interest rates would likely have a more muted effect on growth. The essential point is that differences in the values of attributes do not always have a symmetric effect on the outcome we wish to predict, which leads us to propose a new way to assign importance to observations.

Before we describe partial sample regression, we must take a brief detour. We said earlier that the relevance of an observation is a sum of two major parts: informativeness and similarity. The informativeness part should, in fact, reflect both the informativeness of the historical observation and the informativeness of current circumstances. In particular, we should take their average. When we put it all together, this means that an observation's relevance contains three distinct elements: the similarity of the observation to current circumstances, the informativeness of the observation, and the informativeness of current circumstances. We have neglected this third element until now because it turns out to have no impact on the predictions that come from a full-sample linear regression. It remains silent in the full sample because for any given prediction, it is a constant. Recall that our prediction is a weighted average of how prior outcomes for Y deviate from their own average. By definition, the average deviation of Y from its average is zero, and it will not budge no matter what constant we throw at it. This term does matter, though, when we no longer include every observation in the average.

How should we think about this expanded conception of relevance? For starters, it has the attractive property that it is symmetric for any pair of observations, meaning that the relevance of A to B equals the relevance of B to A. We will make use of this fact in Chapter 6. But there are other more immediate benefits, too. The symmetric definition of relevance recenters it so that the average is zero across all the observations in any sample. As a result, it is natural to use a threshold of zero to partition observations that are relevant (positive values) from those that are not (negative values). If, instead, we ignore the informative-ness of current circumstances, relevance may sum to an arbitrarily large positive or negative value, and we would struggle to distinguish clearly between relevant and nonrelevant observations. By including this seem-ingly innocuous term, the meaning of relevance shifts from a relative quantity to an absolute quantity.

The second benefit is to preserve linearity with respect to the cir-cumstances of prediction. Let us unpack what this means. Returning to our economic example, suppose we predict that economic growth will rise by 0.5 of a percentage point if interest rates are reduced by 0.5 of a percentage point from a starting value of 3%. Now imagine that we want to predict a circumstance that is doubly extreme—reducing interest rates by one percentage point from a level of 6%—and let us assume, for the sake of argument, that this circumstance has never occurred before. We would like to extrapolate that the outcome will also double to a one-percentage-point rise in growth. It is important to stress, however, that the linearity we are talking about here is a mere shadow of the lin-earity that applies to full-sample regression. If we scale the prediction circumstances by a constant, we will get a corresponding linear effect in the prediction, even for partial sample regression. But the instant we change our circumstances in any other way, partial sample regression recalibrates its subset based on a new assessment of relevance, and the linearity breaks.

Partial sample regression prescribes a two-step approach. First, we create a subset of observations that are relevant to our prediction task. And second, drawing upon the mathematical equivalence regarding rel-evance and regressions, we form our prediction as a relevance-weighted average of the historical outcomes in the subset. The relevance weights assigned to each observation stay the same no matter what we attempt to predict, but the sample we use to compute the weighted average changes from large N, which includes every observation, to small n, which is the relevant subset. By censoring nonrelevant observations, the process becomes dynamic, and it is conditional on the prediction task. Recall that the prediction is anchored to the full-sample average and tilts around it using relevance-weighted deviations of Y. Partial sample regression keeps its anchor fixed at the full-sample average. This means that in an extreme case in which we restrict attention to a small subset of the most relevant observations, our prediction would echo whatever occurred in those instances, times their relevance, which is presumably quite large. This creates a problem that we must address, and it might be different from the problem you suspect.

We mentioned earlier that our newly expanded definition of relevance may be positive or negative, and it sums to zero across all observations. Therefore, as we zoom into small subsets of highly relevant observations, our weighted average prediction involves elements of very high relevance. It turns out that we do not need to worry about the fact that relevance no longer sums to zero. The skew toward positive relevance does not impose a bias. To see why, note that we could arbitrarily flip both X and Y for half of the highly relevant observations to be a negative mirror image of themselves. This flipping would place the average relevance close to zero, but it would not change the prediction at all because the negative signs of relevance and outcomes would cancel each other out. Instead, the problem we face is that observations of modest relevance no longer temper the extreme few. Our predictions become more erratic as a result. The solution is to scale our weighted average predictions by a measure of how extreme the relevant subset has become. Specifically, we compute the average squared relevance of the full sample divided by the average squared relevance of the subset (often called a semi-variance). In a full-sample regression, of course, this ratio is equal to 1, and the adjustment has no effect. The ratio is likely to remain close to 1 in a partial sample regression that splits a sample in half, since both positively signed and negatively signed relevance contain small, medium, and large values. When we zoom into a more targeted subset, however, the ratio increases. Multiplying by this ratio counteracts the inflationary bias of subset relevance.

After all this, you might question why we do not simply apply regression analysis to the subset of relevant observations. Why do we instead rely on a mathematical equivalence and use a weighted average of the values of the historical outcomes? The answer is that the weights preserve valuable information about relevance in the context of the full sample. If we were to apply regression analysis to the relevant subset, it would consider some of the relevant observations to be nonrelevant and interpret them opposite to the way they should be used to inform the prediction. No matter how narrowly we want to filter experience, we should not lose sight of how the chosen events compare to the full range of experience.

To summarize, when we form a prediction from historical observations, we should consider the relevance of the observations, which consists of two fundamental components: informativeness and similarity.

We use a statistic called the Mahalanobis distance to measure informativeness and similarity, because it considers how the variables of an observation behave independently as well as how they interact with one another. This notion of relevance, as we define it, is hardly arbitrary. As we will show in our mathematical description of relevance, the prediction from a linear regression equation is mathematically equivalent to a relevance-weighted average of the historical values of the outcomes. This equivalence reveals that the prediction from a fitted regression line places as much importance on nonrelevant observations as it does on relevant observations; it just flips the sign of the effect. This insight about regression analysis leads to an alternative approach for forming predictions from historical observations called partial sample regression, which is first to create a subset of relevant observations, and then to form a prediction as a relevance-weighted average of the historical values of the outcomes.

Asymmetry

Let us compare partial sample regression to classical linear regression. Recall that with partial sample regression, we sharpen our focus on a subset of relevant observations. This introduces conditionality to our prediction because the subset of relevant observations depends on current circumstances. As those circumstances change, so do the observations we rely upon. Compared to classical regression, this dynamic process of selecting observations will generate more reliable predictions when the relationship between attributes and outcomes is asymmetric, because linear regression always assumes symmetry, whether it exists or not. It assumes that opposite circumstances should have opposite outcomes. By contrast, partial sample regression is more flexible. It recognizes that the relationship between attributes and outcomes might change depending on the circumstances. This is useful for dealing with asymmetric processes.

If partial sample regression is a medicine, asymmetric relationships are the disease. How can we diagnose asymmetry in data? We should start by recognizing that asymmetry pertains to the relationship between outcomes and circumstances. To give the data of X and Y a clean bill of symmetric health, we need to show that it does not matter if we predict with the most relevant observations or the least relevant observations. If instead the prediction differs when drawn from the most relevant subset than when drawn from the least relevant subset, we have evidence of asymmetry. We quantify the difference using a measure we have already introduced: dissimilarity (the negative of similarity).

Our diagnostic test for asymmetry requires just one more tweak. To the extent asymmetry exists, we should expect more extreme circumstances to reveal proportionately more of it. So, to create a standardized measure for a given prediction, we divide by the informativeness of its circumstances. At the same time, it remains as true here as in Chapter 3 that more informative observations should carry more weight. Therefore, to summarize asymmetry across every prediction task we take an informativeness-weighted average of the standardized measure. The result tells us the degree of asymmetry for a collection of attributes and outcomes, X and Y. We can compute this number for different thresholds of relevance, comparing the top and bottom 50% of relevance, the top and bottom 20% of relevance, or any other threshold.

It may be helpful to walk through some simple examples, starting with the case of just a single attribute. Assume that we have an attribute whose influence on outcomes is strongly positive and symmetric. In other words, when the attribute value is highly positive, the outcome is highly positive too, and vice versa. And, for any two opposing observations of the attribute, their outcomes are opposing too. We simulate 1,000 observations with a strong symmetric relationship, as shown in Exhibit 4.3.

How well do observations predict actual outcomes in this example? Our first contender is classical linear regression, which we may think of as fitting a line through the cluster of points, or, equivalently, taking relevance-weighted averages of every point to form predictions. Our second contender is partial sample regression, armed with the power of conditionality. The partial sample method discards observations it deems nonrelevant because they are too far away on the horizontal axis.

Exhibit 4.4 shows the result of this contest. In short, it is a draw. Partial sample regression, shown on the right, is nearly indistinguishable from classical regression, shown on the left. Both sets of predictions are 90% correlated with actual outcomes. This finding is not surprising. Rather, it confirms our statement from earlier that partial sample regression helps only if there is an asymmetric relationship.

Now let us change the game by introducing extreme asymmetry and explore this matchup again. The example we contrive, shown in Exhibit 4.5, has a positive relationship when the attribute is positive, and an inverse relationship when the attribute is negative.

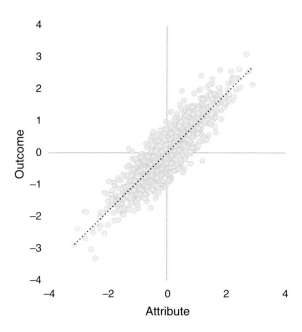

Exhibit 4.3 Simulated Symmetric Relationship

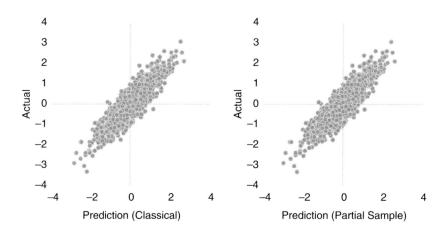

Exhibit 4.4 Predictions versus Actual Outcomes

The fact that the linear best-fit line is flat does not bode well for traditional regression. It is blind to the actual relationships, rendering it effectively immobile and doomed to predict the same outcome no matter the circumstance. On the other hand, partial sample regression performs deftly. Exhibit 4.6 shows the results.

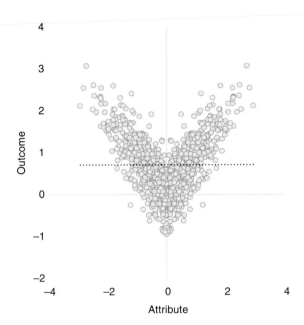

Exhibit 4.5 Simulated Asymmetric Relationship

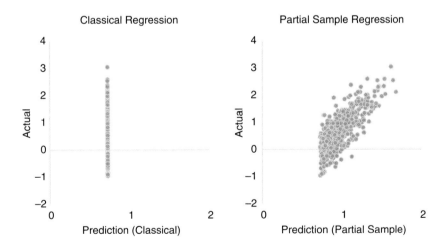

Exhibit 4.6 Predictions versus Actual Outcomes

Consider the process of predicting an outcome in the top right cor-ner of Exhibit 4.5, where the attribute is highly positive. In this case, the most relevant observations will fall to the right side of the distribu-tion because they are similar to the positive circumstance from which we aim to predict. Conversely, the nonrelevant observations will fall to the left side of the distribution because they are highly dissimilar. When the traditional regression generates its prediction, it flips the sign of the nonrelevant outcomes, erroneously offsetting the outcomes of the relevant subset. As a result, the full-sample prediction collapses to the equally weighted average.

As we saw in the first example, the full-sample flipping of opposites is quite reasonable for a symmetric relationship. In fact, it is helpful, because it delivers additional data points that bring genuine insight. But this flipping becomes harmful in the presence of asymmetry. In this case, relying on nonrelevant outcomes contaminates the prediction. By using only relevant observations, partial sample regression overcomes this limitation. Its predictions are 80% correlated with actual outcomes. By tailoring its focus to current conditions, it generates better predictions.

This conditionality becomes even more powerful when we describe the world with more than one attribute. A single dimension leaves only a few ways for observations to be relevant or not. Informativeness and similarity are entirely defined by magnitudes, and there are no interesting patterns to consider. Thus, relevant observations are those with extreme values in the same direction as the current environment. As we include more attributes, we start to see much more interesting variation in circumstances.

For example, consider circumstances that are defined by two attributes instead of just one. The two attributes might look something like the constellation of points in Exhibit 4.7. Unlike the previous simpler example, Exhibit 4.7 does not show the outcomes; they would have to be plotted in a third dimension that would rise off the page. Our key point here is that defining circumstances in two dimensions is far more interesting than just one dimension. There are now many ways an observation can be informative. In fact, for a given level of informativeness there is an entire ellipse of possible observations that have precisely the same level (the large ellipse in the chart). And there are many ways an observation can be like current conditions (the smaller ellipses show four examples).

If we imagine the outcomes plotted on an axis that jumps out from the page, there are many more ways that asymmetry could occur. To predict a circumstance close to point A, we would judge A as highly relevant and C as notably nonrelevant (opposite). B and D might be

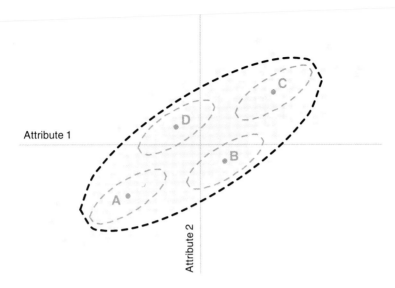

Attribute 1

Attribute 2

Exhibit 4.7 Informativeness and Similarity with Two Attributes

tied in between. Observations B and D share the same degree of relevance with respect to predicting A, so we cannot discriminate how we use them. Therefore, even if there is asymmetry between B and D, it is not material to predicting A. On the other hand, asymmetry between A and C could have a large influence because partial sample regression is able to treat observations in their respective neighborhoods differently. Interestingly, if we set out to predict a circumstance close to point B, the dominant asymmetry would fall on the diagonal axis that joins B and D, and asymmetry between A and C would not matter. More generally, any line through the center could be associated with more or less asymmetry than another.

The possibilities multiply with each new attribute we add. Instead of scatter plots, which become hard to visualize in many dimensions, it may be helpful to view circumstances as sets of bars, sort of akin to a rudimentary fingerprint. Exhibit 4.8 shows three circumstances that could exist for five hypothetical attributes. They are equally informative, yet highly dissimilar. Each set of bars also corresponds to an observed outcome, which for simplicity we could write next to each chart. Because the three examples are equally informative, if we predict circumstances that look a lot like one of them, it might be best to include the most

Exhibit 4.8 Equally Informative Observations with Five Attributes

relevant runner-up and to censor the irrelevant third observation. These configurations will change for each prediction, effectively conditioning on current circumstances. Whether or not we gain an advantage depends on the degree of asymmetry, just as it did in our simpler examples. The point we wish to emphasize is that with more attributes, there are more ways to be relevant and more ways not to be relevant. The information is vast.

Sensitivity

An observation-centric approach may also soothe some classical anxieties about regression prediction. Analysts often worry about collinearity, which is when several attributes that are highly correlated with each other are used collectively in a model. The biggest problem is that such high correlation clouds the influence of both attributes, and it is hard to draw clean inferences about which of them truly matter and how. This concern, however, does not extend to prediction; we care more about the prediction itself and the observations that inform it than about the attribution of individual effects. Relevance is certainly aware of the tight bond between two correlated attributes, but it does not bias the result. As we have seen, relevance is indeed highly sensitive to breakdowns in hypercorrelated attributes, but these events are bound to be rare. They are also likely to be meaningful.

The bottom line is that when two attributes are highly correlated, they will almost always point to the same observations as relevant. They are redundant, yes, but not harmful. In a traditional regression setting, one might say that the beta coefficients assigned to these attributes reflect mostly errors. That may be true, but we should remember that these errors largely self-correct when it comes time to predict. The attributes are so similar that they automatically function as a group.

Memory and Bias

The natural way people process information has advantages, but it is far from perfect. Yes, the human brain can forecast the likely outcomes of hundreds of possible actions in an instant to inform our actions, and it can remember a huge quantity of information. But there are tasks it does not handle well. These likely come from the losing side of evolutionary tradeoffs. If our ancestors' survival tens of thousands of years ago had depended on multiplying five-digit numbers together quickly, perhaps we could all do so effortlessly. Instead, nature tuned our minds to flee in the face of physical threats and to collaborate socially.

In their seminal 1974 paper, two pioneers in the field of decision study, Daniel Kahneman and Amos Tversky, outline three decision-making heuristics that result in undesirable biases. The first is representativeness, the tendency to form predictions based on group similarity, while potentially ignoring other relevant information. As we have seen, similarity is a key part of a rigorous and unbiased prediction from data. In this case, applying the intuitive approach to data holistically may help overcome some natural prediction errors.

The second heuristic they describe is availability, whereby people overextrapolate from the most salient examples they can recall. This heuristic leads to errors in judgment such as subjectively believing a car or plane crash is more likely after seeing one in the news, even if it has no rational effect on the probability faced by an individual. We have shown why extreme or unusual events do indeed contain more information, and that it is proper to overweight them in an unbiased forecast. Here, too, a data-driven approach might help overcome human bias by considering events dispassionately. People may fail to recall distant events that are genuinely relevant, or they may lack enough personal experience in a topic to extrapolate intelligently. Data-driven algorithms do not necessarily suffer from these problems.

The third heuristic is adjustment and anchoring; that is, the way people use new evidence to revise their own prior estimates. Typically, people err by adjusting too little. By considering the relevance of observations, it becomes clear what degree of adjustment makes sense.

Key Takeaways

- Circumstances are patterns that occur across many attributes at the same time; they are the collection of values we select to define an observation.

- We use a statistic called the Mahalanobis distance to measure the distance between collections of values; that is, the distance between circumstances.

- Like the z-score, the Mahalanobis distance is a standardized measure of surprise that considers average variation. But it is more than a summation of squared z-scores. It also considers every pairwise relationship among the attributes.

- Relevance measures the importance of a set of prior circumstances to forming a prediction. Its components are the informativeness of past circumstances, the informativeness of current circumstances, and the similarity of past circumstances to current circumstances.

- We measure the informativeness of a past circumstance as its Mahalanobis distance from average. Likewise, we measure the informativeness of current circumstances as its Mahalanobis distance from average. We measure the similarity of a past circumstance to current circumstances as the negative of half the Mahalanobis distance between the two. Relevance equals similarity plus the average of these two informativeness values.

- By including the informativeness of current circumstances in our calculation of relevance, we convert relevance from a relative measure to an absolute measure for which positive values are relevant and negative values are not relevant. The sum of relevance across observations equals zero.

- Relevance is hardly an arbitrary measure. It follows from information theory, and it rests on a mathematical equivalence—that a relevance-weighted average of the historical values of the outcomes computed over the full-sample of observations equals the prediction from a linear regression equation.

- This equivalence reveals that linear regression analysis places as much importance on nonrelevant observations as it does on relevant observations; it just flips the sign of the effect nonrelevant observations have on the prediction.

- This insight about linear regression analysis, together with the notion of relevance, invites researchers to consider an alternative prediction technique called partial sample regression.

- Partial sample regression prescribes a two-step approach. First, we create a subset of relevant observations. And, second, drawing upon the mathematical equivalence regarding relevance and regressions, we form our prediction as a relevance-weighted average of the past values of the dependent variable in the relevant subset.

- Partial sample regression will produce a more reliable prediction than full-sample linear regression if outcomes have an asymmetric relationship with the attributes used to predict the outcomes. Full-sample linear regression always assumes a symmetric relationship, whereas partial sample regression recognizes that the relationship between outcomes and attributes could change depending on the circumstances.

- If the benefit gained from responding to asymmetry outweighs the additional noise that arises from shrinking the sample of observations, partial sample regression will produce a more reliable prediction than full-sample linear regression.

- We measure the asymmetry of a given prediction as the dissimilarity of the predictions that arise from subsets of the most and least relevant observations divided by the informativeness of current circumstances. Equivalently, asymmetry equals the average fit of the two subsets minus the cross-fit between them (we discuss fit in more detail in Chapter 5).

Relevance Mathematically

We now turn to the practical issue of prediction within a more formal, mathematical context. We denote the object of our prediction as y. It could be any of the M measurements in our dataset. Our specific task is to predict an unknown future outcome of y, which we call y_t. We use the subscript t to emphasize the dimension of time, because the outcome we want to predict is not observable at the time we make the prediction; it will be revealed at some point in the future.

The historical observations y_i for $i = 1, 2, \ldots, N$ provide the basis of our knowledge about y. We may use these values to inform our prediction. As a simple but reasonable starting point, we might take as our prediction the average of observed values of y, as defined in Chapter 2:

$$\bar{y} = \frac{1}{N} \sum_i y_i \qquad (46)$$

This choice assumes that every observation is equally relevant to our task. Put differently, the simple average does not account for the circumstances of the prediction. The spread of y, when interpreted as the average squared difference of y_i from $\bar{y}$, suggests that if we were to use this prediction approach to project the previously observed values we would frequently err by an amount related to the size of the spread. To improve the accuracy of our forecast, we consider circumstances that are known at the time of prediction and use them to refine our assessment of each observation's relevance.

We may use any set of K attributes to describe the circumstances of prediction. We arrange these attribute values into a row vector with K elements:

$$x_t = \begin{bmatrix} x_{t,A}, x_{t,B}, \ldots \end{bmatrix} \qquad (47)$$

From this point forward, any reference to x_t without reference to a letter subscript such as A or B should be taken to be a row vector containing a total of K attributes. Likewise, we define the values of the same set of K attributes for observation i as a row vector:

$$x_i = \begin{bmatrix} x_{i,A}, x_{i,B}, \ldots \end{bmatrix} \qquad (48)$$

We define the information distance between x_i and x_t (or more generally, any two vectors i and t) as:

$$d(x_i, x_t) = \frac{1}{2}(x_i - x_t)\Omega^{-1}(x_i - x_t)' \tag{49}$$

In this expression, the symbol $'$ indicates vector (or matrix) transpose from a row to a column and vice versa, and Ω^{-1} is the inverse of the covariance matrix such that $\Omega\Omega^{-1} = I$, where I is the identity matrix with 1s on the diagonal and 0s elsewhere. This measure is a form of the Mahalanobis distance, which is often defined as Mahal $(x_i, x_t) = \sqrt{(x_i - x_t)\Omega^{-1}(x_i - x_t)'}$. This expression converges to a physical distance in the sense that for the special case when $\Omega = I$ (the identity matrix), the resulting Euclidean distance Euclid$(x_i, x_t) = \sqrt{(x_i - x_t)(x_i - x_t)'}$ is a length we could measure on graph paper or in the real three-dimensional world with a ruler. However, as discussed in Chapter 2, we are interested in the amount of surprise, or information, contained in the difference between observations, which means we should record distances in squared form.

The multivariate distance measure embeds a range of simpler cases that are worth noting. If we include only one attribute, then $\Omega^{-1} = \left(\sigma_{x_A}^2\right)^{-1}$ and $d(x_i, x_t) = \frac{1}{2}\left(\frac{x_i - x_t}{\sigma_x}\right)^2$. In this case, the pairwise distance is also equal to the squared pairwise z-score z_{it}^2 that we defined in Chapter 3. If we include multiple attributes but they are uncorrelated to one another, Ω^{-1} is a diagonal matrix, and the distance equals half the sum of squared z-scores across the attributes. If we include multiple attributes with nonzero correlations, the distance reflects both the variance of attributes in isolation and the correlations between them. All else equal, two multivariate observations are statistically more distant if their patterns of co-occurrence across attributes depart from what is typical.

We define the similarity between two observations as the opposite (negative) of distance:

$$sim(x_i, x_t) = -d(x_i, x_t) = -\frac{1}{2}(x_i - x_t)\Omega^{-1}(x_i - x_t)' \tag{50}$$

With this definition, identical observations have a similarity of zero. Other pairs have negative values, and the more negative the less similar. All else equal, we might expect prior observations that are more like x_t are more relevant to the prediction of y_t. There is, however, another important component of relevance. We define the multivariate informativeness of an observation as its distance from average:

$$info\,(x_i) = d\,(x_i, \bar{x}) = (x_i - \bar{x})\,\Omega^{-1}(x_i - \bar{x})' \qquad (51)$$

In direct analogy to Equation 21, when we measure distances from average we must no longer scale by one half. This choice preserves the important equivalence that we discuss in Chapter 2.

All else equal, observations that are more informative are more relevant to any prediction. This is because they are more likely to reflect genuine events as opposed to noise.

As an aside, it is interesting to note that multivariate informativeness may be expressed in terms of surprise (the z-scores of Chapter 3 again, but this time versus the average) and the correlation matrix P from Equation 43, instead of the covariance matrix Ω.

$$d\,(x_i, \bar{x}) = z_{x_i} P^{-1} z'_{x_i} \qquad (52)$$

Here, z_{x_i} is a row vector of z-scores for the attributes, akin to x_i but with each item centered to its average and divided by its standard deviation.

$$z_{x_i} = \left[\frac{x_{iA} - \bar{x}_A}{\sigma_A}, \frac{x_{iB} - \bar{x}_B}{\sigma_B}, \ldots\right] \qquad (53)$$

It is clear from this formulation that if correlations are zero, the Mahalanobis distance is a sum of squared z-scores. This view also reinforces the incremental nature of accounting for correlations. In what follows, we will proceed with the expressions in terms of the covariance matrix and the x_i values.

We now define the relevance between any two observations as their similarity plus their average informativeness. Though we will return to the notation of x_t soon, we express relevance here in terms of x_i and x_j to stress the symmetry of the definition:

$$r_{ij} = r\,(x_i, x_j) = sim\,(x_i, x_j) + \frac{1}{2}\,\big(info\,(x_i) + info\,(x_j)\big) \qquad (54)$$

Similarity is never positive, and informativeness is never negative. The value of r_{ij} may be positive, negative, or zero. It identifies the relevance between observations i and j based on the attributes chosen to represent them. We may consolidate the complete formula for relevance as follows:

$$r_{ij} = -\frac{1}{2}(x_i - x_j)\Omega^{-1}(x_i - x_j)' + \frac{1}{2}(x_i - \bar{x})\Omega^{-1}(x_i - \bar{x})'$$
$$+ \frac{1}{2}\left(x_j - \bar{x}\right)\Omega^{-1}(x_j - \bar{x})' \tag{55}$$

$$r_{ij} = \frac{1}{2}\left(2x_i\Omega^{-1}x_j' + 2\bar{x}\Omega^{-1}\bar{x}' - 2x_i\Omega^{-1}\bar{x}' - 2\bar{x}\Omega^{-1}x_j'\right) \tag{56}$$

$$r_{ij} = (x_i - \bar{x})\Omega^{-1}\left(x_j - \bar{x}\right)' \tag{57}$$

We note some useful properties. First, the measure is symmetric because $r_{ij} = r_{ji}$. Second, the relevance of an observation with itself equals its informativeness:

$$r_{ii} = info\,(x_i) \tag{58}$$

We also derive identities for the sum of relevance, which hold as long as the sum spans the same N observations that are used to compute $\bar{x}$ and Ω. The first identity is that relevance sums to zero under these conditions, which can be seen by factoring out the terms that do not depend on i, and noting that their deviations sum to zero by definition:

$$\sum_i r_{ij} = \left(\sum_i (x_i - \bar{x})\right)\Omega^{-1}(x_j - \bar{x})' = 0 \tag{59}$$

Now, let us compute the variance of r_{ij} across every observation i, holding j constant. Because average relevance is zero:

$$\sigma^2_{r_{i|j}} = \frac{1}{N-1}\sum_i r_{ij}^2 \tag{60}$$

$$\sigma^2_{r_{i|j}} = \frac{1}{N-1}\sum_i (x_j - \bar{x})\Omega^{-1}(x_i - \bar{x})'(x_i - \bar{x})\Omega^{-1}(x_j - \bar{x})' \tag{61}$$

$$\sigma^2_{r_{i|j}} = (x_j - \bar{x})\Omega^{-1}\Omega\Omega^{-1}(x_j - \bar{x})' \tag{62}$$

$$\sigma^2_{r_{i|j}} = (x_j - \bar{x})\Omega^{-1}(x_j - \bar{x})' = r_{jj} = info(x_j) \tag{63}$$

The next identity is about the sum of each observation's relevance with itself, which we begin by expressing as follows:

$$\sum_i r_{ii} = \sum_i info\,(x_i) \tag{64}$$

$$\sum_i r_{ii} = \sum_i (x_i - \bar{x})\,\Omega^{-1}\,(x_i - \bar{x})' \tag{65}$$

Next, we rewrite the covariance matrix as $\Omega = \frac{1}{N-1}X_d'X_d$, where X_d is a matrix of N observations in rows by K chosen attributes in columns. We subtract each column's average by multiplying a column of N ones, 1_N, by $\bar{x}$, and call this demeaned matrix $X_d = (X - 1_N\bar{x})$ to keep the notation concise.

$$\sum_i r_{ii} = (N-1)\sum_i (x_i - \bar{x})\left(X_d'X_d\right)^{-1}(x_i - \bar{x})' \tag{66}$$

In matrix notation, the sum equals the trace (sum of diagonal elements) of a broader matrix product:

$$\sum_i r_{ii} = (N-1)\,\mathrm{tr}\!\left[X_d\left(X_d'X_d\right)^{-1}X_d'\right] \tag{67}$$

In matrix algebra the trace is known to be invariant to cyclic permutations, so we use the identity $\mathrm{tr}\,[ABCD] = \mathrm{tr}\,[DABC]$ to simplify this expression to I_K, the K-by-K identity matrix with ones on the diagonal and zeros elsewhere:

$$\sum_i r_{ii} = (N-1)\,\mathrm{tr}\left[X_d'\,X_d\left(X_d'\,X_d\right)^{-1}\right] \tag{68}$$

$$\sum_i r_{ii} = (N-1)\,\mathrm{tr}\,[I_K] = (N-1)\,K \tag{69}$$

Later in this chapter, we will use the fact that relevance sums to zero to develop intuition and extensions to the use of relevance for prediction. Also in this chapter, as well as in Chapter 5, we will use the fact that the variance of relevance equals the informativeness of the fixed circumstances under consideration to measure asymmetry and fit. In Chapter 6, we will use the fact that the sum of observations' relevance to themselves equals $(N-1)\,K$ to modify and interpret our measure of predictive reliability.

Prediction

We are now able to augment our baseline prediction of $\bar{y}$ by applying nonequal weights to the deviations of y around its average. As before, we use the term *weight* loosely—it is a scalar multiple that can be positive, negative, or zero. In fact, the weight of each deviation $(y_i - \bar{y})$ is that observation's relevance.

$$\hat{y}_t = \bar{y} + \frac{1}{N-1} \sum_i r_{it} obj_i \tag{70}$$

Where:

$$obj_i = (y_i - \bar{y}) \tag{71}$$

Therefore:

$$\hat{y}_t = \bar{y} + \frac{1}{N-1} \sum_i r_{it} (y_i - \bar{y}) \tag{72}$$

In Chapters 2 and 3, we defined objects of interest and weighted them by informativeness. Our current approach to prediction is the same, but we have expanded the notion of informativeness. The weights are now equal to relevance, which subsumes informativeness but also includes similarity, a quantity that varies according to the circumstances of prediction, x_t.

The use of $N - 1$ rather than N in the denominator follows from the same logic we described in Chapter 2 and which we also applied in Chapter 3. Whenever we have a sum of differences from average, we may convert it to an equivalent sum across pairs of observations indexed as i and j (the arithmetic is simpler here than before, because the average is not squared in the formula).

$$\hat{y}_t = \bar{y} + \frac{1}{N-1} \sum_i r_{it} \left(y_i - \frac{1}{N} \sum_j y_j \right) \tag{73}$$

$$\hat{y}_t = \bar{y} + \frac{1}{N(N-1)} \sum_i \sum_j r_{it}(y_i - y_j) \tag{74}$$

From this logic it is once again apparent that $y_i - y_j$ is trivially zero when $i = j$, so the normalization must equal the complement of informative pairs.

This relevance-based prediction formula, which we derived as a weighted average of historically observed outcomes, yields precisely the same prediction as Ordinary Least Squares linear regression. But before we demonstrate that equivalence let us review a few additional points.

We noted earlier that relevance is a symmetric measure. Therefore, it includes the informativeness of each observation i as well as the informativeness of the conditions x_t that prevail at the time of prediction. When we expand r_{it} into its component parts, we notice that the informativeness of x_t does not depend on i, so it is a constant from the prediction's point of view. Moreover, it multiplies the sum of y deviations from average, which equals zero when all N observations are included:

$$\hat{y}_t = \bar{y} + \frac{1}{N-1} \sum_i \left(sim\,(x_i, x_t) + \frac{1}{2} info\,(x_i) \right)$$

$$\times\, (y_i - \bar{y}) + \frac{\frac{1}{2} info\,(x_t)}{N-1} \sum_i (y_i - \bar{y}) \tag{75}$$

$$\hat{y}_t = \bar{y} + \frac{1}{N-1} \sum_i \left(sim\,(x_i, x_t) + \frac{1}{2} info\,(x_i) \right) (y_i - \bar{y}) \tag{76}$$

Even though the informativeness of t has no effect on the present prediction, we should not be in a rush to discard it. This term still serves a valuable purpose. As we saw earlier, the sum (or average) relevance equals zero. This is not true of $\left(sim\,(x_i, x_t) + \frac{1}{2} info\,(x_i) \right)$, which will sum to a negative amount that varies depending on t (to be precise, it will sum to $-\frac{1}{2} info\,(x_t)$). It is easier to interpret the weights when they include $info\,(x_t)$ and are centered on zero. Even more importantly, the informativeness of t plays an essential role when we extend relevance-weighted prediction to a partial sample. But before we get to that, let us continue to explore the properties and intuition of this approach applied to the full-sample of N observations.

Another interesting perspective comes from rearranging the prediction formula to remove reference to $\bar{y}$. It can be embedded in the main summation. These manipulations lead to:

$$\hat{y}_t = \frac{1}{N} \sum_i \left(1 + \frac{N}{N-1} (r_{it} - \bar{r}) \right) y_i \tag{77}$$

We have recast the prediction as a weighted average across y_i. The $\bar{y}$ that fell outside of the sum is now reflected by the 1 in the parentheses, and the $\bar{y}$ that was inside the sum has been effectively replaced by $\bar{r}$. We showed earlier that $\bar{r} = 0$, so we have:

$$\hat{y}_t = \frac{1}{N} \sum_i \left(1 + \frac{N}{N-1} r_{it} \right) y_i \tag{78}$$

The scaling factor $\frac{N}{N-1}$ approaches 1 when N is large. This equation reveals that the weight on each observation of y_i is essentially 1 plus relevance. An observation with the average level of relevance (equal to zero) will contribute y_i exactly. Those observations with above-average relevance will contribute a multiple of y_i greater than 1. Keep in mind that for some observations to be more relevant than average, others must be less relevant than average. Those that are less relevant receive a multiple of y_i less than 1. Whenever we overweight some observations, we must underweight others. To see why, imagine we want to dramatically overweight one observation, holding all else constant. We would multiply that observation's y_i by a large number. The fact that this observation is more relevant, however, does not mean that we want to extrapolate a large multiple of that y_i occurrence. Rather, it means that we want to include more of that occurrence compared to others. We must effectively "borrow" from the other observations to accommodate this larger weight.

When the variation in relevance is modest, the weights that multiply y_i might all be positive numbers, both above and below 1. As the variation in relevance grows, however, we may end up with some net negative weights.

Equivalence to Linear Regression

It turns out that the relevance-weighted predictions are equivalent to those of a traditional linear regression model. This equivalence holds when we sum across every i from 1 to N, which we emphasize in the following summation notation. For this discussion, we return to the form of the prediction that references $\bar{y}$:

$$\hat{y}_t = \bar{y} + \frac{1}{N-1} \sum_{i=1}^{N} r_{it} (y_i - \bar{y}) \tag{79}$$

Applying Equation 57, we get:

$$\hat{y}_t = \bar{y} + (x_t - \bar{x}) \frac{1}{N-1} \sum_{i=1}^{N} \Omega^{-1} (x_i - \bar{x})' (y_i - \bar{y}) \qquad (80)$$

Let us now recast the formula and its sum over i in matrix notation, using the definition of $X_d = (X - 1_N \bar{x})$ from earlier:

$$\hat{y}_t = \bar{y} + (x_t - \bar{x}) \frac{1}{N-1} \Omega^{-1} X_d' (Y - 1_N \bar{y}) \qquad (81)$$

Substituting the definition $\Omega = \frac{1}{N-1} (X - 1_N \bar{x})' (X - 1_N \bar{x})$ inside the matrix inverse gives:

$$\hat{y}_t = \bar{y} + (x_t - \bar{x}) \left(X_d' X_d \right)^{-1} X_d' (Y - 1_N \bar{y}) \qquad (82)$$

We now define a column vector $\beta = \left(X_d' X_d \right)^{-1} X_d' Y$ and rearrange to get:

$$\hat{y}_t = \bar{y} - \bar{x}\beta + x_t\beta - (x_t - \bar{x}) \left(X_d' X_d \right)^{-1} X_d' 1_N \bar{y} \qquad (83)$$

Noting that each element of $X_d' 1_N$ equals zero because it is the sum of deviations from average, we are left with:

$$\hat{y}_t = (\bar{y} - \bar{x}\beta) + x_t\beta \qquad (84)$$

The second term, $x_t\beta$, shows that the predictions are linear with respect to x_t, where β provides the set of linear coefficients. The first term, $(\bar{y} - \bar{x}\beta) = \alpha$, is a constant that does not depend on x_t, and is typically described as the regression's intercept. It is also worth noting that β does not depend on $\bar{x}$, because we have defined it in terms of the demeaned attributes, X_d.

Traditional linear regression arrives at the same formula via a different logical route. The typical derivation of the coefficient estimate starts by presuming the following model:

$$Y_t = \alpha + x_t\beta + \varepsilon_t \qquad (85)$$

In this expression, ε_t is an error term that is assumed to be normally distributed and centered around zero. The method of Ordinary Least Squares solves for the parameters α and β that minimize the sum of squared prediction errors for the available observations, defined as SqErr $= (Y - \alpha 1_N - X\beta)' (Y - \alpha 1_N - X\beta)$. Here, we intentionally separate the intercept term α from the vector of coefficients β for clarity in comparing it to our prior result.[3] Setting the derivatives of the squared errors with respect to both alpha and beta equal to zero yields:

$$\frac{\partial SqErr}{\partial \alpha} = 1'_N (Y - 1_N \alpha - X\beta) = 0 \tag{86}$$

$$\alpha = \bar{y} - \bar{x}\beta \tag{87}$$

$$\frac{\partial SqErr}{\partial \beta} = X' (Y - 1_N \alpha - X\beta) = 0 \tag{88}$$

$$X' (Y - 1_N (\bar{y} - \bar{x}\beta) - X\beta) = 0 \tag{89}$$

$$X' (Y - 1_N \bar{y}) - X' (X - 1_N \bar{x}) \beta = 0 \tag{90}$$

$$(X_d + 1_N \bar{x})' (Y - 1_N \bar{y}) - (X_d + 1_N \bar{x})' X_d \beta = 0 \tag{91}$$

$$(X_d + 1_N \bar{x})' X_d \beta = (X_d + 1_N \bar{x})' (Y - 1_N \bar{y}) \tag{92}$$

Noting as before that each element of $1'_N X_d$ equals zero because it is the sum of deviations from average, we have:

$$X'_d X_d \beta = (X_d + 1_N \bar{x})' (Y - 1_N \bar{y}) \tag{93}$$

$$\beta = \left(X'_d X_d \right)^{-1} (X_d + 1_N \bar{x})' (Y - 1_N \bar{y}) \tag{94}$$

$$\beta = \left(X'_d X_d \right)^{-1} \left(X'_d Y + X'_d 1_N \bar{y} + \bar{x}\bar{y}N - \bar{x}\bar{y}N \right) \tag{95}$$

$$\beta = \left(X'_d X_d \right)^{-1} X'_d Y \tag{96}$$

Filling in the linear model from Equation 85 with the result for α from Equation 87 and noting the definition of β from Equation 96 leads to:

$$\hat{y}_t = (\bar{y} - \bar{x}\beta) + x_t \beta \tag{97}$$

This expression for linear regression prediction is equal to the relevance-weighted prediction from Equation 84, despite both having been derived from very different perspectives.

---

[3] Our representation is mathematically identical to the common practice of prepending a column of 1s to the X matrix. It is concise in terms of notation to consider the intercept as part of the vector of all coefficients. However, it becomes difficult to track the effect of the intercept term that is contained within the operation of a matrix inverse. Treating the intercept as a separate entity makes it simpler to see the impact of nonzero averages for X and Y.

Partial Sample Regression

A careful look at the relevance of the observations reveals that many of them are substantially negative (even while their average is zero). This means that the linear regression's prediction puts as much emphasis on the least relevant observations as it does on the most relevant ones; it just flips the sign of the effect. If we believe that the more relevant data is also more pertinent to the prediction task at hand, we may wish to censor the nonrelevant observations. We do this by restricting the sum to a subset of the relevant observations. In other words, a partial sample prediction is the same prediction formula applied to a filtered set of n observations that have relevance above some chosen threshold r^*. We use a lowercase n to stress that this new prediction does not sum across all N observations. Importantly, though, we still compute $\bar{y}$ and the covariance matrix Ω (within the relevance formula) using all N observations.

$$\hat{y}_t = \bar{y} + \left(\frac{\sigma^2_{r,full}}{\sigma^2_{r,partial}} \right) \frac{1}{n-1} \sum_{\substack{i \text{ where} \\ r_{it} > r^*}} r_{it} (y_i - \bar{y}) \tag{98}$$

In Equation 98, we have introduced an additional scaling term, which is the ratio of the full-sample variance of r to its variance in the partial sample. Here, variance is always defined in reference to the full-sample average of r, which is zero:

$$\sigma^2_{r,partial} = \frac{1}{n-1} \sum_{\substack{i \text{ where} \\ r_{it} > r^*}} r_{it}^2 \tag{99}$$

For concision, we introduce the notation λ as follows, along with abbreviations for *full* and *partial,* which we use going forward:

$$\lambda^2 = \frac{\sigma^2_{r,full}}{\sigma^2_{r,partial}} = \frac{\sigma^2_{r,f}}{\sigma^2_{r,p}} \tag{100}$$

Therefore, we may write the partial sample regression prediction as:

$$\hat{y}_t = \bar{y} + \frac{\lambda^2}{n-1} \sum_{\substack{i \text{ where} \\ r_{it} > r^*}} r_{it} (y_i - \bar{y}) \tag{101}$$

Note that the ratio of variances collapses to $\lambda^2 = 1$ when we include all N observations, so it has no effect on the full-sample regression. Interestingly, it also has a negligible effect when r^* is near the center of the distribution, such as $r^* = 0$. The variance of relevance values reflects the fact that most values are close to zero, while a minority represent large negative or positive deviations. The magnitudes (though not the signs) tend to be similar in the negative and positive domains, so focusing on the more relevant half of the observations preserves the same balance as the full sample. The adjustment becomes important, though, when we choose more extreme thresholds. For example, if we only include a subset of observations with extremely positive relevance, the effect within the sum is to overweight them compared to the weight they would have received in the presence of many more moderate observations. In this case, our new adjustment term would equal a fraction less than one to counteract the bias.

Let us now consider an appealing derivation of the λ^2 term based on the familiar principle of minimizing squared errors.[4] In the previous section, we showed that for a given prediction task, x_t, full-sample regression only needs to know one number per observation: its relevance. In other words, the formula for relevance compresses the multivariate attribute values of each observation into just one highly articulate dimension. Remarkably, we arrive at the same prediction by performing a simple linear regression of outcomes on these relevance values. This simple regression minimizes the following sum of squared errors:

$$b = \min_{b} \left(\sum_{i=1}^{N} (y_i - a - r_{it}b)^2 \right) \quad (102)$$

Here, b is a coefficient on relevance for the prediction task at hand. Unlike the vector of coefficients β from earlier, b is a single number. The solution, which follows as a one-dimensional simplification of the conventional result from Equations 95 and 86, is:

$$b = \frac{\sum_{i=1}^{N} r_{it} y_i}{\sum_{i=1}^{N} r_{it}^2} \quad (103)$$

$$b = \left(\frac{1}{\sigma_{r,f}^2} \right) \frac{1}{N-1} \sum_{i=1}^{N} r_{it} y_i \quad (104)$$

$$a = \bar{y} \quad (105)$$

---

[4] We thank Bruce Turkington for providing us with this insight.

The prediction follows from applying a and b to the relevance of current circumstances (to themselves), r_{tt}. Recalling from earlier that $r_{tt} = \sigma^2_{r,f}$ and that $\sum_i r_{it} = 0$ over the full sample, the prediction thereby matches the full-sample prediction from Equation 72:

$$\hat{y}_t = a + b r_{tt} = \bar{y} + \left(\frac{\sigma^2_{r,f}}{\sigma^2_{r,f}} \right) \frac{1}{N-1} \sum_i r_{it} (y_i - \bar{y}) \qquad (106)$$

If, instead, we minimize squared errors over the partial sample—while importantly still retaining the measurements of $\bar{x}$, Ω, and $\bar{y}$ from the full sample—we end up with the following least squares problem and solution, matching our definition of λ^2:

$$b = \min_b \left(\sum_{\substack{i \text{ where} \\ r_{it} > r^*}} (y_i - \bar{y} - r_{it} b)^2 \right) \qquad (107)$$

$$b = \frac{\sum_{\substack{i \text{ where} \\ r_{it} > r^*}} r_{it} (y_i - \bar{y})}{\sum_{\substack{i \text{ where} \\ r_{it} > r^*}} r_{it}^2} \qquad (108)$$

$$b = \left(\frac{1}{\sigma^2_{r,p}} \right) \frac{1}{n-1} \sum_{\substack{i \text{ where} \\ r_{it} > r^*}} r_{it} (y_i - \bar{y}) \qquad (109)$$

$$\hat{y}_t = \bar{y} + b r_{tt} = \bar{y} + \left(\frac{\sigma^2_{r,f}}{\sigma^2_{r,p}} \right) \frac{1}{n-1} \sum_{\substack{i \text{ where} \\ r_{it} > r^*}} r_{it} (y_i - \bar{y}) \qquad (110)$$

As further support for λ^2, we will illustrate in Chapter 5 that this scaling maintains proper proportions by containing fit to its required range of 0 to 1.

Asymmetry

Partial sample regression will generate more reliable predictions than traditional linear regression when the relationship between circumstances and outcomes is asymmetric. This is because partial sample regression conditionally focuses on a subset of observations that depends on the current environment. In doing so, it allows the relationship between attributes and outcomes to change depending on the circumstances. By contrast, classical regression assumes that opposite circumstances will always experience opposite outcomes. The conditionality introduced by partial sample regression becomes more powerful as we describe circumstances with more attributes, which allows for greater variation across conditional subsets.

We say that the relationship between attributes and outcomes is asymmetric with respect to circumstance x_t if there is a difference between a partial sample prediction based on a subset of relevant observations, $\hat{y}_{t,most}(x_t)$, and one based on a subset of nonrelevant observations, $\hat{y}_{t,least}(x_t)$. We will refer to the subset of relevant observations as $\mathscr{M}_t$ and the equal-sized subset of the nonrelevant observations as $\mathscr{L}_t$. The distance between the two predictions is given by their dissimilarity (the negative or opposite of similarity) divided by the informativeness of current conditions.

$$asymmetry_t = \frac{-sim\left(\hat{y}_{t,most}, \hat{y}_{t,least}\right)}{info\left(x_t\right)} \tag{111}$$

$$asymmetry_t = \frac{d\left(\hat{y}_{t,most}, \hat{y}_{t,least}\right)}{info\left(x_t\right)} \tag{112}$$

$$asymmetry_t = \frac{1}{2info\left(x_t\right)\sigma_y^2}\left(\hat{y}_{t,most} - \hat{y}_{t,least}\right)^2 \tag{113}$$

For notational brevity we use $y_{i,d}$ (d for de-meaned) to stand in for the longer form ($y_i - \bar{y}$). Expanding on the definitions of the two partial sample predictions based on their form from Equation 98, and using $\sigma_{y,f}^2$ to stress that the variance of y is assessed over the full-sample, we obtain:

$$asymmetry_t = \frac{1}{2info\left(x_t\right)\sigma_{y,f}^2}\left(\frac{\lambda_{\mathscr{M}_t}^2}{n-1}\sum_{i\in\mathscr{M}_t}r_{it}y_{i,d} - \frac{\lambda_{\mathscr{L}_t}^2}{n-1}\sum_{i\in\mathscr{L}_t}r_{it}y_{i,d}\right)^2 \tag{114}$$

As a reminder, following the definition from earlier:

$$\lambda_{\mathscr{M}_t}^2 = \frac{\sigma_{r,f}^2}{\sigma_{r,\mathscr{M}_t}^2} \tag{115}$$

As in Equation 99, we define subset variance as a semi-variance, where relevance values are compared to their full-sample average, which is always zero, even when we only include terms for a subset of observations. Therefore, in the case of $\mathscr{M}_t$, for example:

$$\sigma^2_{r,\mathscr{M}_t} = \frac{1}{n-1} \sum_{i \in \mathscr{M}_t} r^2_{it} \tag{116}$$

Squaring the quantity in parentheses in Equation 114 and replacing the $\mathit{info}(x_t)$ in the denominator with the equivalent $\sigma^2_{r,f}$ gives:

$$\mathit{asymmetry}_t = \frac{1}{2(n-1)^2 \sigma^2_{r,f} \sigma^2_{y,f}} \left(\left(\lambda^2_{\mathscr{M}_t} \sum_{i \in \mathscr{M}_t} r_{it} y_{i,d} \right)^2 + \left(\lambda^2_{\mathscr{L}_t} \sum_{i \in \mathscr{L}_t} r_{it} y_{i,d} \right)^2 \right.$$
$$\left. - 2\lambda^2_{\mathscr{M}_t} \lambda^2_{\mathscr{L}_t} \left(\sum_{i \in \mathscr{M}_t} r_{it} y_{i,d} \right) \left(\sum_{i \in \mathscr{L}_t} r_{it} y_{i,d} \right) \right) \tag{117}$$

Next, we express each multiple (or square) of a sum as a sum across pairs, and we pull the variances of r and y into the summations to obtain an expression we can write using full-sample z-scores for r and y:

$\mathit{asymmetry}_t$

$$= \frac{1}{2(n-1)^2} \left(\lambda^2_{\mathscr{M}_t} \sum_{i \in \mathscr{M}_t} \sum_{j \in \mathscr{M}_t} \frac{r_{it} r_{jt}}{\sigma^2_{r,f}} \frac{y_{i,d} y_{j,d}}{\sigma^2_{y,f}} + \lambda^2_{\mathscr{L}_t} \sum_{i \in \mathscr{L}_t} \sum_{j \in \mathscr{L}_t} \frac{r_{it} r_{jt}}{\sigma^2_{r,f}} \frac{y_{i,d} y_{j,d}}{\sigma^2_{y,f}} \right.$$
$$\left. - 2\lambda_{\mathscr{M}_t} \lambda_{\mathscr{L}_t} \sum_{i \in \mathscr{M}_t} \sum_{j \in \mathscr{L}_t} \frac{r_{it} r_{jt}}{\sigma^2_{r,f}} \frac{y_{i,d} y_{j,d}}{\sigma^2_{y,f}} \right) \tag{118}$$

$\mathit{asymmetry}_t$

$$= \frac{1}{2(n-1)^2} \left(\lambda^2_{\mathscr{M}_t} \sum_{i \in \mathscr{M}_t} \sum_{j \in \mathscr{M}_t} z_{r_{it}} z_{r_{jt}} z_{y_i} z_{y_j} + \lambda^2_{\mathscr{L}_t} \sum_{i \in \mathscr{L}_t} \sum_{j \in \mathscr{L}_t} z_{r_{it}} z_{r_{jt}} z_{y_i} z_{y_j} \right.$$
$$\left. - 2\lambda_{\mathscr{M}_t} \lambda_{\mathscr{L}_t} \sum_{i \in \mathscr{M}_t} \sum_{j \in \mathscr{L}_t} z_{r_{it}} z_{r_{jt}} z_{y_i} z_{y_j} \right) \tag{119}$$

In the next chapter, we introduce the concept of fit, which lends further intuition to these expressions. The first two terms represent the co-alignment of relevance and outcomes. The final term is called the cross-fit. It captures the co-alignment of relevance and outcomes when we pair each of the observations in the nonrelevant subset with each of the observations in the relevant subset.

$$asymmetry_t = \frac{1}{2}\left(fit_t\left(\mathcal{M}_t\right) + fit_t\left(\mathcal{L}_t\right)\right) - crossfit_t\left(\mathcal{M}_t, \mathcal{L}_t\right) \quad (120)$$

In summary, asymmetry is the extent to which the average of two subsets' fits exceeds their cross-fit. To take an extreme example, imagine a sample of highly asymmetric data with one attribute and one outcome that, when plotted, looks like a V-shaped graph. In this case, the average subset fit for the left and right sides will be high. The relationships that exist in the left and right subsets are opposite, though, and we will find that the cross-fit is negative. In this case, asymmetry is large. The opposite extreme is perfect symmetry, where asymmetry equals its smallest possible value of zero. This occurs when the average of the subset fits is equal to the cross-fit.

Asymmetry pertains to a single prediction, t. To characterize the asymmetry of X and Y over all available observations, we compute the average asymmetry across observations, weighted by informativeness:

$$\text{Aggregate asymmetry} = \frac{1}{N-1}\sum_{t=1}^{N} info_t obj_t \quad (121)$$

Where:

$$obj_t = asymmetry_t \quad (122)$$
$$info_t = info\left(x_t\right) \quad (123)$$

Therefore:

$$\text{Aggregate asymmetry} = \frac{1}{N-1}\sum_{t=1}^{N} info\left(x_t\right) asymmetry_t \quad (124)$$

Note that we take the sum across all N observations, even for partial sample regression. We will encounter this approach again when we discuss reliability as the information-weighted average fit in Chapter 6. Also, borrowing a concept that we introduce at the end of Chapter 6, it is possible to express this weighted average formulation in terms of explicit

nonnegative weights $w_t \geq 0$ that sum to 1, $\sum_{t=1}^{N} w_t = 1$, by distributing
a term for the number of predictive attributes K as follows:

$$\text{Aggregate asymmetry} = \sum_{t=1}^{N} w_t \left(K \times asymmetry_t \right) \qquad (125)$$

Where:

$$w_t = \frac{info\left(x_t\right)}{K\left(N-1\right)} \qquad (126)$$

These normalized weights are precisely the same as those we will
introduce for reliability later. The normalized conception of weights
may be more intuitive to view empirically, as we will soon show in our
numerical illustration.

Relevance Applied

Armed with the averages from Chapter 2 and the covariance matrix from Chapter 3, we are ready to apply this chapter's predictive formulas to our economic example. As we stated earlier, our goal is to predict the year-ahead growth of the U.S. economy, defined as the percentage change in GDP. Our prediction will be informed by the circumstances we observe at the end of 2020, shown in the top panel of Exhibit 4.9. The calendar year of 2020, roiled by the Covid pandemic, was certainly notable by historic standards. Though the full year included both acute economic pain and a partial recovery, payrolls decreased substantially, and industrial production fell nearly 5%. The stock market still ended the year up by double digits, and the yield curve still sloped up.

We apply Equation 51 to learn that the informativeness of these prediction circumstances equals 18.7. Next, we assess the relevance of

Exhibit 4.9 Observations and Their Relevance to x_t

Predicting the Outcome for x_i:

	Industrial Production	Nonfarm Payrolls	Stock Market Return	Slope of the Yield Curve	$Info(x_t)$
Q4 2020	−4.7%	5.9%	16.3%	0.5%	18.7

Historical Data:

	Industrial Production	Nonfarm Payrolls	Stock Market Return	Slope of the Yield Curve	$Info(x_i)$	$Info(x_t)$	$sim(x_i,x_t)$	$r(x_i,x_t)$
Q1 1947	27.1%	11.0%	−13.5%	1.9%	21.5	18.7	−30.4	−10.3
Q2 1947	21.9%	5.5%	−20.1%	1.9%	20.5	18.7	−16.9	2.7
Q3 1947	7.1%	3.1%	−0.2%	1.9%	1.4	18.7	−12.0	−1.9
Q4 1947	5.8%	2.5%	−0.7%	1.8%	1.1	18.7	−11.0	−1.1
•	•	•	•	•	•	•	•	•
•	•	•	•	•	•	•	•	•
•	•	•	•	•	•	•	•	•
Q3 2019	−1.4%	1.2%	2.2%	0.2%	1.2	18.7	−11.1	−1.1
Q4 2019	−1.9%	1.4%	28.9%	0.0%	4.6	18.7	−13.2	−1.5
Q1 2020	−1.4%	1.6%	−8.8%	0.0%	2.2	18.7	−12.7	−2.2
Q2 2020	−16.2%	−11.7%	5.4%	0.1%	43.5	18.7	−3.3	27.8

every historical observation to these present circumstances. We do this without any knowledge of the outcomes for GDP; relevance is based exclusively on the four attributes shown in Exhibit 4.9. One component is the informativeness of x_t, which only requires us to repeat the 18.7 for every observation. More interesting, though, is the informativeness of each observation x_i, which also comes from Equation 51. Recall that informativeness equals the difference of an observation from average, times the inverse covariance matrix of the attributes, times the transpose of the difference from average. These values are never negative. We see examples of small and large values in the first four and last four observations in the table.

The third component of relevance is similarity, which is the negative of half of the Mahalanobis distance, as shown in Equation 50. A perfect replica of current circumstances would have a similarity of zero. Barring a perfect match, smaller negative numbers are desirable. Of the eight observations in the table, the most recent one is the most similar. The four quarters ending in June 2020 shared dismal economic fundamentals, albeit more extreme than at the year's end. And stock market performance was still positive. As a heuristic for similarity, though, a recency rule quickly falters. Q4 of 1947 is more similar to current circumstances than any of the next-most-recent episodes. Relevance, shown in the final column, is the sum of similarity and average informativeness from the preceding columns (Equation 54).

Exhibit 4.10 plots the relevance of each observation. By coincidence, the first and last observations bookend this sample as the least and the most relevant observations. Clusters of relevant observations are evident in the chart. They appear to coincide with turning points following

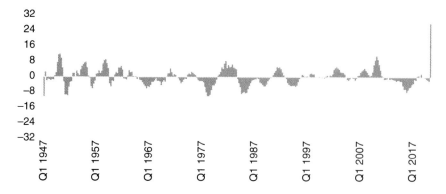

Exhibit 4.10 Relevance of Observations to x_t

economic slowdowns in industrial production and payrolls where the stock market had begun to pick up steam; examples include periods around 1950, 1958, 1982, 1991, and, notably, the global financial crisis recovery in 2009.

We may now apply Equation 72 to form a prediction. We proceed in two steps, as shown in Exhibit 4.11. First, we apply equal weights to compute the average outcome for subsequent GDP growth, which is 6.3%, as we discovered long ago in Exhibit 2.6. Next, we compute the difference between each historical outcome and the average, as shown in the final column. We compute a weighted average of these outcomes following Equation 72. The weights are equal to the relevance from Exhibit 4.9, divided by $N - 1 = 293$. Relevance serves two purposes. First, it may flip the sign of the impact a given outcome has on the result, as is the case for the first observation, for example. Future GDP growth for Q1 1947 was 2.9% above average, but this observation is dissimilar enough to current circumstances that it has negative relevance, so we should in fact project that GDP growth will behave opposite to its deviation in Q1 1947. Second, relevance also scales the influence of

Exhibit 4.11 Relevance-Weighted Outcomes and Full-Sample Regression Prediction

		Equal Weight	Outcome	Relevance Weight	Outcome Deviation from Average
1	Q1 1947	1/294	9.3%	−10.3/293	2.9%
2	Q2 1947	1/294	10.8%	2.7/293	4.5%
3	Q3 1947	1/294	11.9%	−1.9/293	5.5%
4	Q4 1947	1/294	7.9%	−1.1/293	1.6%
	•	•	•	•	•
	•	•	•	•	•
	•	•	•	•	•
291	Q3 2019	1/294	−1.7%	−1.1/293	−8.0%
292	Q4 2019	1/294	−1.0%	−1.5/293	−7.3%
293	Q1 2020	1/294	2.6%	−2.2/293	−3.7%
294	Q2 2020	1/294	16.7%	27.8/293	10.4%
	Weighted average:		6.3%		1.8%

Average outcome	6.3%
Average relevance-weighted deviation	1.8%
Full-sample prediction	8.2%

each observed outcome. Some observations are more important than others. For example, Q2 2020 has about 10 times as much relevance as Q2 1947. The net effect will be to rely about 10 times more heavily on the future GDP growth observed after the second quarter of 2020 compared to that of 1947. The weighted average deviation equals 1.8%, which we add to 6.3% for a total prediction of 8.2%.

Exhibit 4.12 repeats relevance (on the axis at left) and overlays as dots the series of outcome deviations from average (on the axis at right). It is apparent that some of the most extreme positive outcomes belong to some of the most relevant observations in the early and the late part of the sample. Many other highly relevant episodes had above-average growth, although that of 2009 still fell below average. In observing Exhibit 4.12, remember that negative relevance bars will flip the projected impact of the outcome dots that accompany them. This view makes clear how the lens of relevance interprets each historical outcome.

Exhibit 4.13 applies the conventional linear regression logic of Equation 85, which focuses on a set of beta coefficients (Equation 96). We find the same 8.2% prediction from a beta-weighted sum across attributes.

From this traditional view, which rests on a linear combination of attribute values, we see that the substantial fall in nonfarm payrolls contributes the bulk of the prediction that the following year's GDP growth will exceed average. The classical perspective allows us to critique and apply the finding that payroll growth is inversely related to future growth, holding all other factors constant. However, it does not grant us the ability to inspect which historical observations contribute to the

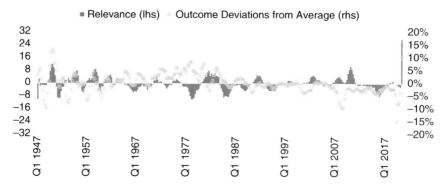

Exhibit 4.12 Outcome Deviations from Average

Exhibit 4.13 Conventional Full-Sample Regression Prediction

	Intercept	Industrial Production	Nonfarm Payrolls	Stock Market Return	Slope of the Yield Curve
x_t	1	−4.7%	−5.9%	16.3%	0.5%
Beta	0.07	0.12	−0.31	0.03	−0.35
Beta-weighted x_t	6.6%	−0.6%	1.8%	0.5%	−0.2%
Full-sample prediction = Sum of beta-weighted x_t					8.2%

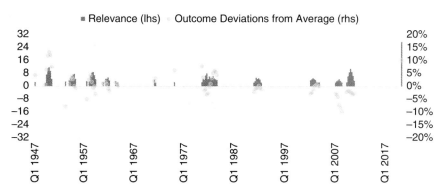

Exhibit 4.14 Relevance and Outcome Deviations—25% Most Relevant Observations

prediction. Moreover, it does not allow us to distinguish past conditions in which falling payrolls might have had a different effect. What if the stock market had suffered large losses in the prior year, indicating a potentially more severe blow to investor confidence and economic activity? Would a subset of observations that share this pattern point to a different result? To address this question, we turn to partial sample regression.

The easiest way to visualize the partial sample prediction is to censor the undesired observations and keep only those that are sufficiently relevant. We choose to keep the top 25%. Exhibit 4.14 shows the surviving observations. The weight of the evidence appears to skew toward positive outcomes for the most relevant observations in this focused subset.

Exhibit 4.15 shows the calculations that lead to the partial sample prediction, following Equation 98.

The reason the partial sample prediction differs from the full-sample prediction is due to asymmetry. It is helpful to evaluate the asymmetry of a prediction directly, using Equation 111. Exhibit 4.16

Exhibit 4.15 Partial Sample Prediction Calculation

		Equal Weight	Outcome	Relevance Weight	Outcome Deviation from Average
1	Q1 1947	1/294	9.3%	Not Relevant	Not Relevant
2	Q2 1947	1/294	10.8%	2.7/73	4.5%
3	Q3 1947	1/294	11.9%	Not Relevant	Not Relevant
4	Q4 1947	1/294	7.9%	Not Relevant	Not Relevant
	•	•	•	•	•
	•	•	•	•	•
	•	•	•	•	•
291	Q3 2019	1/294	−1.7%	Not Relevant	Not Relevant
292	Q4 2019	1/294	−1.0%	Not Relevant	Not Relevant
293	Q1 2020	1/294	2.6%	Not Relevant	Not Relevant
294	Q2 2020	1/294	16.7%	27.8/73	10.4%
	Weighted average:		6.3%		10.3%

Average outcome	6.3%
Average relevance-weighted deviation	10.3%
Lambda	0.45
Partial sample prediction	11.0%

Exhibit 4.16 Asymmetry Calculation for x_t Prediction

Partial Sample Prediction – 25% Most Relevant	11.0%
Partial Sample Prediction – 25% Least Relevant	4.5%
Distance between Predictions	1.6
Informativeness of x_t	18.7
Asymmetry	0.08

details this calculation. First, we input the partial sample prediction we have already generated. Second, we create an alternate prediction using the polar opposite observations—the 25% that are least relevant to our prediction task. We compute the Mahalanobis distance between these two observations and divide it by the informativeness of the prediction circumstances to arrive at an asymmetry of 0.08.

It is important to recognize that asymmetry depends on the prediction task, and what we have measured here is particular to the prediction formed at the end of 2020. To gauge aggregate asymmetry across our entire dataset, we consider every prediction task motivated by history, and we repeat the calculations from Exhibit 4.16. This exercise results in

294 assessments of asymmetry. In Exhibit 4.17, we apply Equation 125 to form explicit weights that sum to 1 across the 294 prediction tasks. Obtaining this more intuitive accounting only requires a benign adjustment: dividing the weights by the number of attributes $K = 4$ and multiplying the asymmetry values by the same amount. We do this adjustment before taking a weighted average, although clearly we will obtain the same result without it. The main benefit of this adjustment is a more direct visualization of the weighted average process, as shown for every observation in Exhibit 4.18.

Exhibit 4.17 Aggregate Asymmetry Calculation

		$info(x_t)$ Weight	Asymmetry	Asymmetry × K
1	Q1 1947	21.5/1172	0.22	0.89
2	Q2 1947	20.5/1172	0.04	0.18
3	Q3 1947	1.4/1172	0.13	0.53
4	Q4 1947	1.1/1172	0.06	0.25
•	•	•	•	•
•	•	•	•	•
•	•	•	•	•
291	Q3 2019	1.2/1172	0.04	0.17
292	Q4 2019	4.6/1172	0.02	0.09
293	Q1 2020	2.2/1172	0.03	0.12
294	Q2 2020	43.5/1172	0.10	0.40
			Weighted average:	0.18

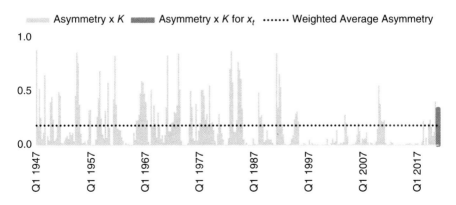

Exhibit 4.18 Asymmetry

Appendix 4.1: Predicting Binary Outcomes

Predicting Binary Outcomes Conceptually

So far, our goal has been to predict outcomes that are distributed across a wide range of values and that, in principle, could be arbitrarily large. What if we want to predict a simple binary outcome instead? In this case, we are predicting true or false: 1 or 0. Our historical observations tell us whether outcomes have been true or false in the past. This sounds straightforward, but when we apply the formula for relevance-weighted prediction to a binary target we confront two new problems.

The first problem is that, as a weighted average of the observed 1s and 0s, our prediction will almost certainly produce a value that is neither 1 nor 0. To take a simple example, suppose we are interested in outcomes that were historically true half of the time. Without any special insight, our baseline prediction is the average of an equal number of 1s and 0s: 0.5. When the outcome is revealed, it will be binary, so 0.5 is not a literal prediction for what will happen. Still, 0.5 has meaning. It is a prediction of the probability that the outcome will equal 1.

This brings us to the second problem. Probabilities only make sense for values between 0 and 1, but our prediction formula can produce values outside that range. This is most likely to happen when circumstances are extreme. To fix this issue, we need to transform the raw predictions, essentially compressing them to fall between 0 and 1 no matter what. We do this by using a so-called sigmoid function that curves like an S. Raw predictions that are exceptionally large should approach a value of 1, but never quite reach it. Large negative values should approach 0. A curve called the logistic function has these features, and it is a popular choice to confront this issue.

We can plug the output of our relevance-weighted prediction formula into the logistic function. Administering this functional medicine ensures that our new predictions never fall outside of 0 and 1. But as with most medicines, there are side effects we must address. We mentioned earlier that in the absence of an informed view, the simple average is a good forecast for probability (0.5 in the previous example). Unfortunately, if this average enters the logistic function, it will come out as something else. To preserve the baseline forecast, we need to shift all the values before they enter the logistic function.

The other side effect of the logistic curve's compression is that it may compress too much. If we do nothing, our probability forecasts may be too timid, hugging the simple average. If we scale by too much, our probability forecasts will convey too much confidence, suggesting near certainties when they are prone to error. We need to amplify the predictive deviations from our relevance formula before we put them into the logistic function. But by how much?

There is a direct, if inelegant, answer. We could use a numerical search (an intelligent form of trial and error) to find the best scaling factor, which is the one that minimizes the distance between our probability predictions and the 0s and 1s that occurred. This approach is called logistic regression, and it is classical statistics' answer to our question. However, we want to dig a bit deeper here, if only to make certain that the concept of relevance, and its extension to partial sample regression, applies as much to categorical prediction as it does to predicting outcomes that are distributed across a wide range.

We can gain insight by flipping the problem around. Instead of computing the typical value of Y during relevant observations of X, we ask: What are the typical values of X when Y is true and when it is false? And then: Which of these X conditions is more like the present? Because a binary Y identifies two groups unambiguously, we can treat the average X values as characteristics of each group. Moreover, we might imagine that X values emanate from one normal distribution when Y is true, and another when it is false. We do not know the current value of Y, but we can consider the likelihood of X under both possibilities. As we mentioned before, likelihood is the conceptual inverse of information distance. As a result, the Mahalanobis distance is the key to this calculation, just as it is for relevance. This procedure is also well known. It is called linear discriminant analysis.

After some mathematical wrangling (which we present in the math section that follows), we find that the linear discriminant's prediction is nearly identical to the relevance-weighted answer that came out of the logistic function. The main difference is the scaling factor we have been looking for. It amounts to dividing the predictive deviations of Y by the variance of Y. Conveniently, there is a simple way to compute the variance of a series of binary outcomes. It is the fraction of true outcomes times the fraction of false outcomes. For example, a process that was true 50% of the time would have a variance of $0.5 \times 0.5 = 0.25$, while one that was true 80% of the time would have a variance of $0.8 \times 0.2 = 0.16$. When one outcome is more frequent than the other, variance is low, and we are often right to predict the more common occurrence. Dividing by these fractions acts as a multiplier for the predictions we put into our logistic function. And the more skewed the outcomes are to one side or the other, the more confident our predictions will appear, as the boosted inputs to the logistic function will press toward the extremes of 0 and 1. It is intuitive to imagine that these predictions will more often match the realities of a skewed set of outcomes.

To summarize, it is perfectly acceptable to apply relevance-weighted prediction to a binary outcome. It requires some contortions, though, if we want to force the result to lie within the probability bounds of 0 and 1. We can run our prediction through the logistic function, but we should shift and scale it first. By applying some simple transformations—which we can prescribe in advance—the predictions behave the way we expect. Though the results will not perfectly match those of a logistic regression search, they are nearly indistinguishable in practice. Moreover, the fact that a simple change in multiple explains most of the difference means that relevance-weighted outcomes are at the heart of logistic regression just as they are for conventional regression analysis. Thus, we can benefit from the intuition of relevance and its extension to partial sample regression even when we wish to predict binary outcomes.

Predicting Binary Outcomes Mathematically

We now turn our attention to the mathematics of predicting binary outcomes, which we code as 1 or 0. If we apply the formula in Equation 72 with y values of this sort, we will get values other than 1 and 0, which, moreover, need not lie between them. It is convenient and intuitive to use the same approach as before, but to interpret the result as a probability forecast. However, we need to transform the output so that it lies within the bounds of a valid probability. The logistic function is a relatively simple choice that meets our needs:

$$logistic(a) = \frac{1}{1 + e^{-a}} \tag{127}$$

For example, we might define $\hat{y}_{t,prob}$ as a modified version of the relevance-weighted prediction $\hat{y}_t$ from earlier:

$$\hat{y}_{t,prob} = logistic(\hat{y}_t) = \frac{1}{1 + e^{-\hat{y}_t}} \tag{128}$$

This formulation by itself is not particularly compelling, though, because the range of raw predictions tends to cluster between 0 and 1 (although as noted, it is not guaranteed). Therefore, our transformed values will only fall between approximately 0.5 and 0.7 on the vertical axis as shown in Exhibit 4.19. The first obvious remedy is to shift the average to accord with the baseline prediction of $\bar{y}$ that we would make in the absence of any further information. We should shift the values so that:

$$logistic\,(\bar{y}^*) = \bar{y} \tag{129}$$

The inverse of the logistic function is the so-called logit function as shown in Exhibit 4.20 (short for logistic unit):

$$\bar{y}^* = logit\,(\bar{y}) = \ln\left(\frac{\bar{y}}{1-\bar{y}}\right) \tag{130}$$

This logic implies the following adjustment to the formula:

$$\hat{y}_t = \ln\left(\frac{\bar{y}}{1-\bar{y}}\right) + \frac{1}{N-1}\sum_i r_{it}\,(y_i - \bar{y}) \tag{131}$$

Now, in the absence of circumstantial information coming from X, our baseline prediction for $\hat{y}_{t,prob}$ will still equal $\bar{y}$. But we are not done. We must still determine a proper scaling factor for the second term. It turns out that a reasonable choice is to divide by the variance of y, which for a binary variable is given by $\sigma_y^2 = \frac{N}{N-1}\bar{y}\,(1-\bar{y})$. To justify this choice, let us consider a different perspective on the problem.

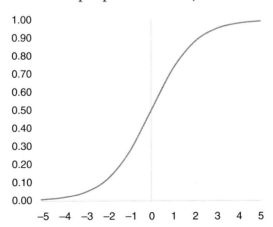

Exhibit 4.19 Logistic Function

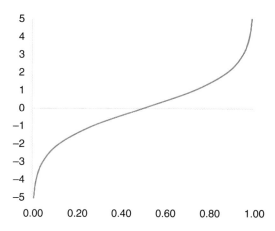

Exhibit 4.20 Logit Function (inverse of the logistic function)

Suppose that our observations come from one of two groups, cor-responding to Y values of 1 and 0, respectively. Each observation has its attributes, x_i. Using Bayes' rule of probabilities, we can recast this classification problem as the probability that x_t emanates from the group corresponding to values of 1 rather than the group corresponding to values of 0. Bayes' rule stated generically is:

$$P(A|B) = \frac{P(B|A)\,P(A)}{P(B)} \tag{132}$$

Where $P(A|B)$ denotes the probability of event A conditional on event B. In the case of our specific interest, we have:

$$P(Y=1|X=x_t) = \frac{P(X=x_t|Y=1)\,P(Y=1)}{P(X=x_t)} \tag{133}$$

Because 1 and 0 are the only options for Y, we can express the denominator as a comprehensive sum over all its possibilities:

$$P(X=x_t) = P(X=x_t|Y=1)P(Y=1) + P(X=x_t|Y=0)P(Y=0) \tag{134}$$

Therefore:

$$P(Y=1|X=x_t)$$
$$= \frac{P(X=x_t|Y=1)\,P(Y=1)}{P(X=x_t|Y=1)\,P(Y=1) + P(X=x_t|Y=0)\,P(Y=0)} \tag{135}$$

If we assume that the attributes in X follow a joint normal distribution with a different center when $Y = 1$ and when $Y = 0$ but continue to obey a common covariance matrix, we can express our probabilistic forecast in terms of x_t's similarity to the center (average) of these two groups, the row vectors μ_0 and μ_1. Note also that $P(Y = 1) = \bar{y}$.

$$\hat{y}_{t,prob} = P(Y = 1 | X = x_t) = \frac{e^{sim(x_t, \mu_1)} \bar{y}}{e^{sim(x_t, \mu_1)} \bar{y} + e^{sim(x_t, \mu_0)}(1 - \bar{y})} \qquad (136)$$

$$\hat{y}_{t,prob} = \frac{e^{sim(x_t, \mu_1) + \ln(\bar{y})}}{e^{sim(x_t, \mu_1) + \ln(\bar{y})} + e^{sim(x_t, \mu_0) + \ln(1 - \bar{y})}} \qquad (137)$$

$$\hat{y}_{t,prob} = \frac{1}{1 + e^{sim(x_t, \mu_0) - sim(x_t, \mu_1) + \ln(1 - \bar{y}) - \ln(\bar{y})}} \qquad (138)$$

$$\hat{y}_{t,prob} = \frac{1}{1 + e^{-\left\{ sim(x_t, \mu_1) - sim(x_t, \mu_0) + \ln\left(\frac{\bar{y}}{1 - \bar{y}}\right) \right\}}} \qquad (139)$$

$$\hat{y}_{t,prob} = logistic\left(sim(x_t, \mu_1) - sim(x_t, \mu_0) + \ln\left(\frac{\bar{y}}{1 - \bar{y}}\right) \right) \qquad (140)$$

Using our notation from earlier, the input to the logistic function is:

$$\hat{y}_t = sim(x_t, \mu_1) - sim(x_t, \mu_0) + \ln\left(\frac{\bar{y}}{1 - \bar{y}}\right) \qquad (141)$$

Note that we can define the row vector of average attribute values using y as an indicator for whether to include an observation in a given average. In other words, each element of the average vector is the sum of x_A for attribute A including, as appropriate, the observations where $y = 1$ or those where $y = 0$ (in which case $1 - y = 1$).

$$\mu_1 = \frac{Y'X}{Y'1_N} = \frac{Y'X}{n_1} \qquad (142)$$

$$\mu_0 = \frac{(1_N - Y)'X}{(1_N - Y)'1_N} = \frac{(1_N - Y)'X}{n_0} \qquad (143)$$

We also note the relationship between μ_1 and μ_0:

$$\mu_0 = \frac{1_N'X - Y'X}{1_N'1_N - Y'1_N} = \frac{n_1(\bar{x} - \mu_1)}{N - n_1} = -\frac{n_1}{n_0}(\mu_1 - \bar{x}) = -\frac{\bar{y}}{1 - \bar{y}}(\mu_1 - \bar{x}) \qquad (144)$$

We write out and rearrange Equation 141 as follows:

$$\hat{y}_t = \frac{1}{2}\left(x_t - \mu_0\right)\Omega^{-1}\left(x_t - \mu_0\right)'$$

$$-\frac{1}{2}\left(x_t - \mu_1\right)\Omega^{-1}\left(x_t - \mu_1\right)' + \ln\left(\frac{\bar{y}}{1-\bar{y}}\right) \qquad (145)$$

$$\hat{y}_t = x_t\Omega^{-1}\left(\mu_1 - \mu_0\right)' + \frac{1}{2}\mu_0\Omega^{-1}\mu_0' - \frac{1}{2}\mu_1\Omega^{-1}\mu_1' + \ln\left(\frac{\bar{y}}{1-\bar{y}}\right) \qquad (146)$$

Now, putting everything in terms of μ_1 gives:

$$\hat{y}_t = x_t\Omega^{-1}\mu_1'\left(1 + \frac{\bar{y}}{1-\bar{y}}\right) + x_t\Omega^{-1}\bar{x}'\frac{\bar{y}}{1-\bar{y}}$$

$$+ \frac{1}{2}\left(\mu_1 - \bar{x}\right)\Omega^{-1}\left(\mu_1 - \bar{x}\right)\left(\left(\frac{\bar{y}}{1-\bar{y}}\right)^2 - 1\right) + \ln\left(\frac{\bar{y}}{1-\bar{y}}\right) \qquad (147)$$

Noting that $\mu_1 = \frac{Y'X}{N\bar{y}}$ for purposes of the first term above and that $\bar{x} = \frac{1'X}{N}$ for purposes of the second term, we have:

$$\hat{y}_t = \left(\frac{1}{N\bar{y}\left(1-\bar{y}\right)}\right)\sum_i r_{it}y_i + \left(\frac{\bar{y}}{N\left(1-\bar{y}\right)}\right)\sum_i r_{it}$$

$$+ \left(\left(\frac{\bar{y}}{1-\bar{y}}\right)^2 - 1\right)\frac{1}{2}\left(\mu_1 - \bar{x}\right)\Omega^{-1}\left(\mu_1 - \bar{x}\right)' + \ln\left(\frac{\bar{y}}{1-\bar{y}}\right) \qquad (148)$$

Lastly, recall that for the full-sample $\frac{1}{N}\sum_i r_{it} = 0$, which means that the second term disappears. It also means we can include $\bar{y}$ (a constant with respect to i) inside the main sum with no effect on the prediction. We include it here to facilitate comparison to the relevance-weighted formulas from earlier.

$$\hat{y}_t = \ln\left(\frac{\bar{y}}{1-\bar{y}}\right) + \left(\frac{1}{\bar{y}\left(1-\bar{y}\right)}\right)\frac{1}{N}\sum_i r_{it}\left(y_i - \bar{y}\right)$$

$$+ \left(\left(\frac{\bar{y}}{1-\bar{y}}\right)^2 - 1\right)info\left(\mu_1\right) \qquad (149)$$

Equation 149 yields multiple insights. First, it shows that when evaluating relative probabilities that we arrange into a logistic function, the relevance-weighted average is divided by the variance $\sigma_y^2 = \frac{N}{N-1}\bar{y}(1-\bar{y})$ as compared to Equation 72. The variance is largest when $\bar{y} = 0.5$ and smallest when it is close to 0 or 1. Intuitively, when the variance is large there is greater uncertainty, and predictions that often fall close to the center are appropriate. If the outcomes are often skewed to one side or the other, we may want to express greater confidence in the typical occurrence. This means we should amplify the predictive deviations within $\hat{y}_t$.

Second, there is an additional constant term in the formula that further shifts the baseline prediction away from $\bar{y}$. This additional shift equals zero when $\bar{y} = 0.5$, but it amounts to a multiple of the informativeness of μ_1 otherwise. This term is large (either negative or positive) when y is skewed toward taking on just one of its possible values most of the time, and when the conditions μ_1 that coincide with that common value are highly distinct from average. In these cases, it is wise to furnish extreme positive or negative answers most of the time, resulting in probabilistic predictions that rarely deviate from 0 or 1, as the case may be.

The key takeaway is that relevance-weighted average predictions are just as important and applicable to binary predictions as they are to predictions of values that cover a broader range. The results may be interpreted as probabilities, which demand a transformation and, as a result, require additional shifting and scaling of the prediction logic.

The probability-based approach we derived earlier is known as linear discriminant analysis. For practical purposes, it is nearly identical to logistic regression (or its close cousin, probit regression), which is perhaps the most common approach to predicting categorical variables as probabilities. Logistic regression assumes the same form as Equation 149, where $\hat{y}_t$ is a linear function of x_t. It is not identical, though, because it calibrates the scaling factor in a slightly different manner, but the differences tend to be immaterial for practical purposes.

References

Czasonis, M., M. Kritzman, and D. Turkington. 2020. "Addition by Subtraction: A Better Way to Forecast Factor Returns (and Everything Else)." *The Journal of Portfolio Management* 46 (8).

Czasonis, M., M. Kritzman, and D. Turkington. 2022. "Relevance." *Journal of Investment Management* 20 (1): 37–47.

Rudra, A. 1996. *Prasanta Chandra Mahalanobis: A Biography.* Oxford University Press.

Tversky, A., and D. Kahneman. 1974. "Judgment Under Uncertainty: Heuristics and Biases." *Science, New Series* 185 (4157): 1124–1131.

5

Fit

I n Chapter 4, we described how to predict an unknown outcome by taking a relevance-weighted average of its past values. This process will always yield a prediction, whether the data is useful for predicting the unknown outcome or not. Therefore, it is important to evaluate the relationships underlying a prediction to determine its quality, using a measure we call fit. In general, higher fit indicates greater consistency, and should inspire more confidence in a prediction.

Fit Conceptually

Your predictions will most likely be wrong. If you are good, they will not be wrong by much. Professional forecasters and pundits have an incentive to hide their doubts. But for the rest of us, it is usually better to confront our uncertainty head-on.

Recall that a single prediction is a weighted average of many observations. We can think of each observation as a vote for the unknown outcome, reflecting both the relevance of the attributes, X, and the value of the observed outcome, Y. If relevance and outcomes are aligned, the final tally probably reflects an underlying truth. But if relevance and outcomes are inconsistent, their aggregate tally could be meaningless. In general, we should be more confident in a prediction if its observations display consistency.

Imagine planning a trip to Paris and asking your friends how much they think it will cost. You are likely to get a range of estimates, which

123

reflects uncertainty. But if some of your friends have traveled to Paris before—which means their views are the most relevant among the group—and they offer similar estimates, there is more wisdom in their combined suggestion. This same idea applies to data-driven predictions. A consistent alignment between relevance and outcomes increases our confidence in the prediction they generate. We refer to this alignment as a prediction's fit.

To measure the fit for a single prediction, we consider every pair of observations that comprises it. We sum across every pair in the same way we did to estimate variance in Chapter 2, but rather than focusing on the spread of a single attribute, we now measure the alignment between the relevance and outcome for each pair. The notion of alignment is like that of co-occurrence from Chapter 3. Each observation in a pair has a relevance value based on X and an outcome value based on Y for a total of four numbers. We are interested in the alignment of these four numbers. We can interpret this alignment in two ways, depending on how we group the components mentally.

In the first interpretation, we focus on the alignment of relevance and the alignment of outcomes, and finally, the alignment of these alignments. This warrants some more explanation. We ask: Are the two observations similarly relevant? If they are both highly relevant, highly not relevant, or moderately relevant, the answer is yes. If not, the answer is no. And in the extreme case where one is highly relevant and the other is highly nonrelevant, we consider the observations to be opposites. We then ask a similar question of their outcomes: Do observations A and B have similar outcomes? Again, the answer is yes, no, or opposites, based on the same reasoning. Finally, we consider whether the observations have similar answers to these two questions. Are they similarly relevant (yes, no, opposites) and do they have similar outcomes (yes, no, opposites)? The answer to this final question takes the same form as the others and indicates the alignment between the pair's predictive components. If the final answer is yes, the pair of observations has similar relevance and similar outcomes. This result is desirable, and it builds confidence. It was the case in our earlier example, in which our knowledgeable friends gave similar estimates about the cost of a trip to Paris. If, however, the answer is no, or worse yet, opposites, then our confidence decays quickly. It would be like asking two equally knowledgeable people the same question but receiving opposite answers. How would you know whom to trust?

A second interpretation focuses on the vote from each observation in which a vote is the product of the observation's relevance and its outcome. A vote can be positive, negative, or zero. Then, we ask whether the two observations in a pair cast similar votes. If both are positive, or both are negative, the answer is yes. If one is close to zero while the other is not, the answer is no. And if one is positive while the other is negative, the answer is opposites.

Both interpretations always reach the same conclusion, but through a different sequence of questions. Ultimately, the answer stems from the product of four numbers for each observation pair.

To measure fit precisely, we apply concepts from Chapter 3. Recall that to measure the co-occurrence between a pair of attributes, we transformed the attributes into units of surprise, or z-scores, so that we could compare values that might otherwise have different units. To determine the alignment between a pair of attributes, we multiplied their z-scores. We are going to do the same thing for fit. For each observation in a pair, we multiply four numbers: the z-scores of their respective relevance values with the z-scores of their respective outcomes. The sign of the result indicates the direction of the relationship (positive or negative), and the magnitude indicates its strength. A positive result is welcome; it means that a pair of observations is similarly relevant and has similar outcomes. A negative result means that observations are similarly relevant but have dissimilar outcomes, or vice versa. Inconsistency breeds doubt.

Fit pertains to a single prediction, but to get it we must average the alignment across every pair of observations that contribute to that prediction. We wish to stress three important points. First, although the alignment for any given pair of observations may be positive or negative, the average across all pairs never falls below zero nor rises above one. Second the fit varies across prediction tasks, as we will soon explore. And third, it is derived exclusively from the information that goes into the prediction, without any knowledge of the eventual outcome that will be revealed later. The fit helps us calibrate our confidence in advance. Whether or not the prediction is successful is a separate question.

Failing Gracefully

What if there is no relationship between the attributes we have selected and the outcome we are trying to predict? In this rather unfortunate case, a fortunate dynamic takes place. Rather than charging ahead with bold and misguided pronouncements, our prediction routine will soften its bets; they will fall closer to the average. To see why, consider that when there is no real relationship, the observations' votes will be erratic and random. They will often cancel each other out, and the combined effect will be muted. This natural diversification accords with our earlier example of asking two equally knowledgeable people the same question but receiving contradictory answers. Your best guess of the correct answer is the average response, which would equal zero. This means that in the worst-case scenario, where your data has no predictive power, the forecast tends to degrade gracefully toward the equally weighted average outcome across observations. The fit becomes zero—or close to it. Thankfully, the worst possible fit is no fit.

As an interesting side note, we can flip this logic on its head to deduce that only strong fits produce dramatic predictions. The size of a prediction relates directly to its fit. The measure of size that is appropriate here is, once again, informativeness. It turns out that the informativeness of a prediction (how far it is from average in information units) divided by the informativeness of its circumstances provides an equivalent definition of fit.

As we discuss in more detail in Chapter 6, our definition of fit accords with the commonly used R-squared statistic. If we average the fit across every prediction task for a full-sample regression, we end up with the regression's R-squared statistic. The advantage of fit is that we can pinpoint how much confidence we should have in a single prediction. Fit is an individual element of model reliability, just as information distance is an element of variance, and co-occurrence is an element of correlation. Fit depends on the specific prediction circumstance, whereas reliability (or R-squared) describes a prediction model more generally. Our observation-centric view of prediction relies on these elemental components. Let us now explore why fit varies from one prediction to another, even if we use the same model and data in each case.

Why Fit Varies

It is commonly assumed that every prediction a model generates is of equal quality. Is this view warranted? The answer is fascinating and nuanced. Put simply, the magnitude of prediction circumstances does not affect fit, but the pattern does. Let us start by considering a prediction based on just one attribute, X. Further, let us assume that we include the full sample of observations, so that our relevance-weighted predictions match those of traditional linear regression. Suppose we carry out this exercise and find that the prediction is 10 when $X = 1$. If we make the circumstances twice as extreme, so $X = 2$, the prediction will also double, to 20.[1] In fact, we can multiply the circumstances by any number and the prediction will scale in perfect proportion. In other words, the prediction is linear with respect to the circumstances. This linearity reveals that observations are used in the same way no matter the magnitude of our current circumstances. The result is merely scaled, and fit is unaffected by such scaling. This means that when X is defined by a single attribute, every prediction does indeed carry the same fit.

This convenient finding does not hold, however, for multivariate inputs. Suppose we expand our definition of circumstances to include two attributes. Linearity still guarantees that any multiple of circumstances merely multiplies the prediction: the predictions for inputs where X equals $(1, 1)$, $(2, 2)$ or $(3, 3)$ will form a line. They will also share the same fit. In fact, the fit of any input vector will have the same scale invariance; take $(-1, 6)$ and $(1.5, -9)$, for instance, where the scaling factor equals -1.5. On a graph of two-dimensional inputs, any circumstances that fall on the same line through the center will have the same fit. What differs for these points is their informativeness. Now, it is with respect to orientation that things get interesting. Recall from Chapter 4 that the set of points with a given level of informativeness trace an ellipse around the center of X. As we move along this ellipse, what differs for these points is their orientation. Except for each point's opposite, none of these points are scalar multiples of another. It turns out that fit varies, often quite dramatically, for the circumstances along this curve.

To see why, it is best to visualize an elongated oval tilted on a 45-degree diagonal. Imagine that this ellipse encompasses the bulk of the observations for two correlated attributes. Any observation that falls on the ellipse will have the same Mahalanobis distance from the center. As a measure of informativeness, the Mahalanobis distance recognizes that for two correlated attributes, an observation that lies up and to the right, on the 45-degree diagonal line, is only unusual if it is extreme in size. Meanwhile, an observation that breaks from tradition and tends toward the bottom right of our scatter plot does not need to move far

---

[1] For simplicity, we implicitly assume for this example that the averages of X and Y equal zero.

to qualify as an outlier. If such an observation falls on the same ellipse, it is unusual not because of its size, but because of its orientation. The northeast and southwest extremities have the most unusual magnitude but the most common orientation. The southeast and northwest extremities are the opposite; they have the most unusual orientation but the most common magnitude (compared to other points on that ellipse). Everything in between has its own blend of peculiarities, just enough to earn a spot on the same unusualness ellipse.

As we discussed at length in Chapter 4, any kind of unusual observation is informative because it is more likely to reflect a genuine event rather than noise. But when the unusualness pertains to our current prediction circumstances, another dynamic enters the picture. The crux of the issue is that correlated attributes contain overlapping information. Some attributes are only slightly correlated, so they have something in common but perhaps more that is distinct. Other attributes might be highly correlated and therefore less driven by noise. As an example, imagine measuring traffic in New York City using cameras at two different intersections. The broad trends will be closely correlated, picking up on common factors like rush hour timing, day of the week, season of the year, construction projects, and special events that are about to take place. Anyway, it is comforting when two overlapping sources of information coincide, because they logically reinforce each other. The argument is probabilistic. The attributes' agreement is more likely to result from mutual information than from pure chance, so we should expect that we are witnessing more signal than noise. On the flip side, a sharp divergence of values for two attributes that normally move together calls their mutual information into question. Maybe the underlying source of mutual information has broken. Or maybe it is overwhelmed by a tsunami of noise. Our conviction drops either way. The stronger the correlation, the stronger a cautionary signal we get from divergence. This is why fit varies according to circumstance, even for full-sample regression.

What happens when we have more than two attributes? Fortunately, the same logic applies. Our conviction falls when circumstances defy their average behavior, and it rises when patterns are more common. There is, in fact, a feature of circumstances that governs this process, and we can measure it. We need only take the informativeness of the prediction circumstances and divide it by the informativeness that would prevail in the absence of correlations. The denominator is equal to a sum of squared z-scores, so it reflects only magnitude. The ratio is a scale-independent measure of surprise that reflects orientation alone.

Mechanically speaking, the comparisons we described earlier for two attributes are repeated many times over to capture every pair in the covariance matrix, which fuels the Mahalanobis distance and, therefore, informativeness. With many attributes, the range of possibilities is vast. Fit tells us a lot.

Lastly, we would be remiss not to mention an even more obvious, although no less important, reason for fit to vary: partial sample regression. As we feed our prediction routine new tasks, it filters observations down to relevant subsets that are each different from the last. Any asymmetry will cause fit to differ across circumstances above and beyond the issues we have already discussed.

We should not underestimate the importance of the point that each prediction task has its own specific fit. It follows that a prediction model with better average fit could produce a less reliable prediction, given a specific circumstance, than a model with lower average fit. The crucial message is that we should look beyond the confidence we have in a particular prediction model to the confidence we have in a particular prediction task.

Avoiding Bias

There is one remaining aspect to note regarding fit. Because fit is measured over every pair of observations, it includes the alignment of each observation with itself. This self-alignment artificially inflates fit because an observation's self-alignment is always positive. To understand why, consider asking our earlier questions of an observation with itself. Do the two observations have similar relevance? Yes, they are identical. Do they have similar outcomes? Yes, they are also identical. Do these two answers agree? Yes. For each observation with itself, the final answer will always be yes.

We address this bias by decomposing model fit into two components: the fit of observations with themselves, which we call outlier influence (for reasons that will soon become apparent), and the fit of observations with their peers, which we call agreement. The outlier influence component is guaranteed to be positive. Its size indicates whether observations with notable relevance tend to have notable outcomes. When this is the case, it acts as a form of leverage in the prediction. In our continuing example, outlier influence tells you whether your most knowledgeable friends offered the most extreme estimates. However, this calculation does not indicate whether there is agreement among your friends. You would not know whether your most extreme friends said the same thing or whether they submitted opposite views. Here, the agreement component comes to the rescue. It reveals whether there is alignment between relevance and outcomes across observations. In other words, did your similarly knowledgeable friends offer similar projections? If the data contains nothing useful, agreement can reach pure zero. It can even be negative.

To inspire confidence, we should look for a high value of agreement. To be fair, overall fit is still worth considering; in fact, it tends mostly to reflect agreement anyway, as there are far fewer dubious self-comparisons (n) than distinct pairwise comparisons (n times $n-1$). We will continue to refer to fit as a measure of the quality of a prediction. But as we now turn to the topic of precision, it will be important to distinguish between the two components of fit.

Precision

Our recipe for prediction gives a single number. The fact that we must predict at all means that we face uncertainty, so we should imagine a cloud of uncertainty around our estimate. So far in this chapter, we have shown that a prediction's fit conveys the informativeness of the prediction itself, and that the answer depends on the circumstances of the prediction as well as the relationships we observe in the data. We turn now to the notion of precision, which is distinct from fit.

Suppose we could travel back in time to repeat all the experiences that are recorded in our dataset. Each round trip creates an alternative universe in which core relationships persist, but chance outcomes turn out differently. What range of predictions would our alternate selves come up with if they all faced the same challenge we do today? In other words, we acknowledge that if history had taken a different turn, we would produce a different prediction. To what extent does historical noise cloud our prediction?

If we could collect data from each alternate universe, we could easily compute the spread in predictions. But, for better or worse, we are confined to our current universe, and we have already used all the information to render our one and only prediction. This exercise differs from the sample variance we computed before, because the variation we ponder now is completely hypothetical; we cannot observe it directly.

We have no choice but to infer it from the variance of the components that underlie our prediction.

As it turns out, precision depends on four features of our data. Our prediction is more precise when:

1. The number of observations, n, is large, because noise is random and cancels out over many observations.
2. The variance of relevance across observations is small, because relevance could act as a multiplier for noise. (In a full-sample regression, the variance of relevance equals the informativeness of the prediction circumstances.)
3. The influence of outliers is small, because undue influence from a minority of observations leaves the estimate vulnerable.
4. The agreement among observations is large, because widespread alignment is unlikely to be swayed by noise-driven disruptions.

As we detail in the mathematical section of this chapter, the expected variance of a prediction's deviation from average is equal to the product of the first two items in this list, times a slightly modified difference between items 3 and 4, times the variance of Y. To estimate precision, however, we divide this expected variance by the variance of Y to normalize it, and then we take its inverse. We normalize by the variance of Y so that we can compare precision when we make different predictions. Low variance means high precision and vice versa.

Let us explore the intuition behind these ideas more thoroughly. Taken together, our cloud of uncertainty depends on whether the votes that comprise a prediction are dispersed or compact. After we asked our friends to project the cost of a trip to Paris, we should have noted the variety in their responses. If all five estimates are in the same ballpark, we should be reasonably confident in their validity. If they deviate a lot, it is a sign either that this prediction task is quite difficult, or these people are not very good at it. Perhaps both are true. The greater the dispersion, the greater the uncertainty and the lower the precision. With this in mind, we measure the spread in votes across observations, as in Chapter 2, and we extrapolate to the expected variance for a single prediction using known properties of variance (as a concept).

We must not confuse precision with accuracy. Consider a naïve prediction equal to the full-sample average of an outcome, which we mentioned so long ago that it now seems quaint. This prediction is stable and thus admirably precise, yet it lacks informative power. Its fit equals zero. It is probably not accurate, because it fails to hit its target most of the time. Accuracy requires both precision and fit. As the naïve average makes clear, these two concepts are complementary. It is possible, of course, for both measures to be mutually aligned, and a high value for both is desirable. A crystal ball that cannot err would have perfect fit (equal to one) and infinite precision (each prediction would repeat itself in alternative universes). The predictions would vary across prediction tasks, of course, as this is what makes it useful and impressive. But they would not vary across alternative universes. We would believe this to be true because the predictive components would line up perfectly across an expansive set of observations. We would have no grounds to doubt it. This perfect scenario can never really exist, of course.

Previously, we showed that amplifying current conditions by using a multiple larger than 1 has no effect on fit. Such a transformation does reduce precision, however, because to predict more extreme circumstances of the same variety we have no choice but to scale up the noise along with the signal. It is like turning up the volume on an old AM or FM radio for a channel that does not come in clearly. After you turn up the volume you will hear even more static.

It is also true that if we found a treasure trove of new data and it confirmed the same patterns as our original observations, fit would remain unchanged. But our data discovery would be favorable for precision because more observations would cancel out more noise. We would have more confidence in the prediction's robustness.

The area where fit and precision diverge the most pertains to the influence of outliers. Remember that outlier influence represents the alignment of each observation's predictive component with itself. It is always positive, and it is larger to the extent that extreme occurrences dominate the predictive sum. Fit views outlier influence as a good thing, because if relevance and outcomes are strongly aligned for some observations, this is evidence that a relationship exists. Nevertheless, we have argued that it may be wise to discount this component of fit because it introduces bias. Put simply, comparing observations to themselves lends an unfair advantage that can lead to spurious results. Precision goes even further and views outlier influence as a source of risk. The higher the outlier influence, the lower the precision, because all else being equal, outliers dominate a result—which means that the relationship's support is more tenuous. Interestingly, precision views agreement among peer observations as a positive feature, just as fit does. But it places comparatively less emphasis on agreement and more on outliers.

Focus

Let us now return to the case of partial sample regression. Here we form a prediction from a subset of relevant observations based on the belief that these observations are more useful than nonrelevant ones. The degree to which we tighten our view around a more exclusive subset is what we call focus.

A narrower focus results in fewer observations. Ideally, we would like to have many observations to reduce noise. Consider our earlier thought experiment in which we observe alternative paths through history. With each alternative new path, an observation's outcome would differ by chance, and this in turn would lead to a different prediction. If we only included the single most relevant observation, its noise would pass directly into the prediction. If, however, our prediction routine took a broader focus, relying on a greater number of observations, noise across observations would be diversified, and the prediction would be more stable.

So why, as in the case of partial sample regression, would we intentionally narrow a model's focus? We would do so if it improved our confidence, even after accounting for the increased effect of noise. And what would improve our confidence? Greater consistency among the subset of relevant observations. Exhibit 5.1 shows an impressionistic view of the data underlying a prediction. In this example, the nonrelevant observations have outcomes that straddle the average, whereas the relevant subset has a decisive positive tilt.

We must also recognize a fundamental tradeoff between the accuracy of a subset in the presence of asymmetry and the precision from including as many observations as possible. The bar for success is not merely that an asymmetric relationship exists, but that its salience outweighs the reduced noise of a larger sample. We determine the optimal solution empirically.

Continuing with the theme of our hypothetical excursion to France, imagine asking 1,000 people to estimate the price of a bottle of wine based on a few facts and a taste test. You are likely to receive a wide range of estimates, including some dubious ones. Now let us suppose that prior to conducting the experiment, you survey each participant about their

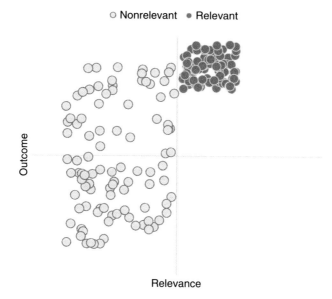

Exhibit 5.1 Relevance and Outcomes for a Very Good Partial Fit

wine expertise. You find that 100 people are true wine aficionados or experts. They are your relevant subset. Should we be more confident in their average estimate than the average across all 1,000 participants? If the group of 100 experts tends to agree more than the full group of 1,000 people, we should feel more confident in their collective wisdom, especially if their range of estimates is narrower than the range across all participants. It indicates that the experts know more than the average person; therefore, we should feel comfortable relying on their expertise.

Key Takeaways

- We measure fit for a single prediction. It depends on the specific circumstances from which we are predicting.
- We obtain the fit for a single prediction by taking an average across all the pairs of observations that comprise the prediction. For each pair we record the product of the observations' z-scores for relevance and their z-scores for outcomes. A positive product indicates that when observations are similarly relevant, they have similar outcomes, in which case we should have confidence in the prediction.

A negative product indicates that relevance does not line up with outcomes, in which case we should view our prediction more cautiously.

- We may calculate fit equivalently as a ratio of the informativeness of the prediction (how different it is from average) to the informativeness of the prediction circumstances.

- A weighted average fit across all predictions gives a general measure of a model's reliability and is equal to a regression's R-squared. (Chapter 6 explores this relationship in more detail.)

- Fit is biased upward because it includes the alignment of observations with themselves. We therefore decompose fit into two components: the fit of observations with themselves, which we call outlier influence, and the fit of observations with their peers, which we call agreement.

- Noise impairs the precision of a prediction, but it is less consequential if the number of observations is large, the variance of relevance across observations is small, the influence of outliers is small, and the agreement among observations is large.

- When we focus on a subset of relevant observations to form our prediction, as we do with partial sample regression, we must consider the tradeoff between noise and confidence, which comes from consistency among the relevant observations.

Fit Mathematically

The formulas in Chapter 4 will always render predictions, extrapolating from observations as best they can. However, the data will support some predictions better than others. We would like to know the extent to which a prediction stems from consistent patterns across observations as opposed to noise. For this purpose, we introduce a measure of fit.

Fit is equal to the ratio of the informativeness of the prediction $\hat{y}_t$ to the informativeness of the circumstances x_t:

$$fit_t = \frac{info(\hat{y}_t)}{info(x_t)} \tag{150}$$

$$fit_t = \frac{d(\hat{y}_t, \bar{y})}{info(x_t)} \tag{151}$$

$$fit_t = \left(\frac{\hat{y}_t - \bar{y}}{\sigma_y} \right)^2 \left(\frac{1}{info(x_t)} \right) \tag{152}$$

We want fit to be invariant to the scale of x_t, which this definition satisfies. A scalar multiple a applied to x_t will multiply both the denominator and the numerator by a^2, the latter by way of x_t's influence on $\hat{y}_t$ via the r_{it} terms inside the prediction sum. The smallest possible fit is zero, and it occurs when the prediction is equal to the full-sample average. In such a case, the relationship between circumstances and outcomes is not even trustworthy enough to depart from the naïve baseline prediction of $\bar{y}$.

The intuition for the numerator, $info(\hat{y}_t)$, is that close relationships between prior outcomes and circumstances will lead to a large prediction, because the most relevant observations will have the most positive outcomes and vice versa. The intuition for the denominator, $info(x_t)$, is that we should expect more extreme circumstances to yield more extreme predictions, all else being equal, so we must control for this effect.

The formula for fit bears a close resemblance to the formula for asymmetry, which we presented in Chapter 4. Whereas asymmetry measures the dissimilarity of a relevant prediction to a nonrelevant one, fit measures the dissimilarity of a prediction to the average. And dissimilarity from average equals informativeness. The manipulations that follow are closely related to those we applied to asymmetry in Chapter 4. In fact, they are a simplified version of the same logic.

We start by expressing $\hat{y}_t$ as a sum across observations:

$$fit_t = \frac{1}{info(x_t)\sigma_{y,f}^2}\left(\frac{\lambda^2}{n-1}\sum_i r_{it}(y_i - \bar{y})\right)^2 \qquad (153)$$

As before, $\sigma_{r,f}$ is the full-sample standard deviation of relevance for the prediction in question. Note that the sum over i may include a subset of the observations, as in partial sample regression where $n < N$, or it may include all $n = N$ observations. Expressing the squared term as a double sum, and recalling from Chapter 4 that $\sigma_{r,f}^2 = info(x_t)$, we have:

$$fit_t = \frac{\lambda^4}{(n-1)^2}\sum_i\sum_j \frac{r_{it}r_{jt}}{\sigma_{r,f}^2}\frac{(y_i - \bar{y})(y_j - \bar{y})}{\sigma_{y,f}^2} \qquad (154)$$

Next, we include the average relevance for conceptual emphasis, even though $\bar{r} = 0$, as always. We write this expression suggestively to make clear that fit is based on a product of four z-scores. Keep in mind that $\lambda = 1$ when $n = N$ for the full-sample.

$$fit_t = \frac{\lambda^4}{(n-1)^2}\sum_i\sum_j \left(\frac{r_{it}-\bar{r}}{\sigma_{r,f}}\right)\left(\frac{r_{jt}-\bar{r}}{\sigma_{r,f}}\right)\left(\frac{y_i-\bar{y}}{\sigma_{y,f}}\right)\left(\frac{y_j-\bar{y}}{\sigma_{y,f}}\right) \qquad (155)$$

$$fit_t = \frac{\lambda^4}{(n-1)^2}\sum_i\sum_j z_{r_{it}}z_{r_{jt}}z_{y_i}z_{y_j} \qquad (156)$$

Fit captures whether the alignment of relevance accords with the alignment of outcomes. In other words, if two observations are both relevant, do they have similar outcomes? Or, if one observation is relevant and the other is not, do they have divergent outcomes? If so, the fit is strong. If not, the fit is weak or possibly nonexistent.

In fact, taking the product of two z-scores is equivalent to computing the relevance between two observations:

$$r(r_{it}, r_{jt}) = (r_{it} - \bar{r})\left(\frac{1}{\sigma_{r,f}^2}\right)(r_{jt} - \bar{r}) = z_{r_{it}}z_{r_{jt}} \qquad (157)$$

$$r(y_i, y_j) = (y_i - \bar{y})\left(\frac{1}{\sigma_{y,f}^2}\right)(r_{jt} - \bar{y}) = z_{y_i}z_{y_j} \qquad (158)$$

Therefore, we may also write fit as:

$$fit_t = \frac{\lambda^4}{(n-1)^2} \sum_i \sum_j r(r_{it}, r_{jt}) r(y_i, y_j) \tag{159}$$

We realize that some may find it esoteric to ponder the relevance between two relevance values. However, it shows the versatility of the concept of relevance and connects it to other uses. Above all, it provides a concise expression of fit. (As an aside, the fact that a product of z-scores equates to relevance gives us yet another way to interpret the product of z-scores we used to define co-occurrence in Chapter 3.)

These formulas help reveal the upper bound for fit. If we assume that y_i precisely matches r_{it} for every i—the perfect alignment—then we can write everything in terms of r:

$$fit_{t,y=r} = \frac{\lambda^4}{(n-1)^2 \sigma_{r,f}^4} \sum_i \sum_j r_{it}^2 r_{ij}^2 \tag{160}$$

$$fit_{t,y=r} = \frac{\lambda^4}{\sigma_{r,f}^4} \left(\frac{1}{n-1} \sum_i r_{it}^2 \right)^2 = \lambda^4 \frac{(\sigma_{r,p}^2)^2}{\sigma_{r,f}^4} = \frac{\lambda^4}{\lambda^4} = 1 \tag{161}$$

Fit is thus bounded between 0 and 1 for both full-sample and partial sample predictions.

Components of Fit

Next, it is helpful to isolate the elements of the sum within the fit equation that pertain to observations with themselves:

$$fit_t = \frac{\lambda^4}{(n-1)^2} \sum_i \sum_{j \neq i} r(r_{it}, r_{jt}) r(y_i, y_j) + \frac{\lambda^4}{(n-1)^2} \sum_i r(r_{it}, r_{it}) r(y_i, y_i) \tag{162}$$

The first term in this expression now represents an average of non-diagonal pairs. If there is truly no empirical relationship between X and Y in the prediction sample, this term will equal zero. The second term reflects the extent to which notable circumstances (relevant or not) coincide with notable outcomes (positive or negative). It stands to reason that the weight of evidence is stronger if more notable circumstances correspond to more notable outcomes. However, we must keep in mind that, even in the absence of a genuine relationship, this term will not equal zero. Hence, it may make more sense to eliminate this inherent measurement bias by focusing on the first term only, which we call the agreement:

$$agreement_t = \frac{\lambda^4}{(n-1)^2} \sum_i \sum_{j \neq i} r(r_{it}, r_{jt}) r(y_i, y_j) \qquad (163)$$

$$agreement_t = \frac{\lambda^4}{(n-1)^2} \sum_i \sum_{j \neq i} z_{r_{it}} z_{r_{jt}} z_{y_i} z_{y_j} \qquad (164)$$

We call the second term the outlier influence, because it increases when extreme outcomes tend to coincide with extreme circumstances. It does not retain any information about the sign of these occurrences, so it is quite possible that it measures alignments of magnitude that often diverge in direction.

$$outlier\ influence_t = \frac{\lambda^4}{(n-1)^2} \sum_i r(r_{it}, r_{it}) r(y_i, y_i) \qquad (165)$$

$$outlier\ influence_t = \frac{\lambda^4}{(n-1)^2} \sum_i z_{r_{it}}^2 z_{y_i}^2 \qquad (166)$$

It is worth noting that the outlier influence is summed across n observations, yet is divided by a much larger number, $(n-1)^2$. As a result, this term contributes a greater proportion of total fit when there are few observations, and a relatively small proportion of total fit when observations are plentiful.

Precision

We would now like to assess the prediction's precision, still using only the information that is available prior to the occurrence of a future outcome. Recall that the prediction is given by:

$$\hat{y}_t = \bar{y} + \frac{\lambda^2}{n-1} \sum_i r_{it}(y_i - \bar{y}) \qquad (167)$$

Precision is inversely related to variance. The expected variance of the prediction around the baseline (equal weights) average is:

$$Var(\hat{y}_t) = Var\left(\bar{y} + \frac{\lambda^2}{n-1} \sum_i r_{it}(y_i - \bar{y}) \right) \qquad (168)$$

As an aside, it is very important to recognize that we are contemplating the expected variance for just a single prediction, the one corresponding to circumstances x_t. We are not considering the variation of the prediction across different prediction tasks, which is a more common exercise in traditional statistics. We use the term *expected variance* for clarity here, because there is only one observed value for $\hat{y}_t$; therefore, the variance that results from random noise is not something we observe for the single estimate of $\hat{y}_t$. Rather, it is something we deduce from the properties of variance as a concept, together with the observed variance of the individual components inside the predictive sum. Using the identity $\text{Var}(ax) = a^2\text{Var}(x)$:

$$\text{Var}(\hat{y}_t) = \frac{\lambda^4}{(n-1)^2} \sum_i \text{Var}\left(r_{it}(y_i - \bar{y})\right) \tag{169}$$

We must now compute the variance of the terms, $r_{it}(y_i - \bar{y})$. Using the identity from Chapter 2, we rewrite $\text{Var}(r_{it}(y_i - \bar{y})) = \sigma^2_{r(y-\bar{y})}$ equivalently as a double sum across pairs of predictive components:

$$\sigma^2_{r(y-\bar{y})} = \frac{1}{n(n-1)} \sum_i \sum_j \frac{1}{2}\left(r_{it}(y_i - \bar{y}) - r_{jt}(y_j - \bar{y})\right)^2 \tag{170}$$

$$\sigma^2_{r(y-\bar{y})} = \frac{1}{n(n-1)} \sum_i \sum_j \frac{1}{2}\left(r_{it}^2 (y_i - \bar{y})^2 + r_{jt}^2(y_j - \bar{y})^2\right.$$
$$\left. -2r_{it}r_{jt}(y_i - \bar{y})(y_j - \bar{y})\right) \tag{171}$$

Because the first two sums in the parentheses are identical and the third term has a factor of 2:

$$\sigma^2_{r(y-\bar{y})} = \frac{n}{n(n-1)} \sum_i r_{it}^2(y_i - \bar{y})^2 - \frac{1}{n(n-1)} \sum_i \sum_j r_{it}r_{jt}(y_i - \bar{y})(y_j - \bar{y}) \tag{172}$$

Now we transfer the diagonal terms from the second sum to the first:

$$\sigma^2_{r(y-\bar{y})} = \frac{n-1}{n(n-1)} \sum_i r_{it}^2(y_i - \bar{y})^2 - \frac{1}{n(n-1)} \sum_i \sum_{j \neq i} r_{it}r_{jt}(y_i - \bar{y})(y_j - \bar{y}) \tag{173}$$

And finally, to align with the definitions of outlier influence and agreement, we multiply by λ^4, $1/\sigma^2_{y,f}$, and $1/\sigma^2_{r,f}$ inside the parentheses and their reciprocals outside, to arrive at:

$$\sigma^2_{r(y-\bar{y})} = \frac{\sigma^2_{y,f}\sigma^2_{r,f}}{\lambda^4}\left((n-1)\text{outlier influence}_t - \left(\frac{n-1}{n}\right)\text{agreement}_t\right) \quad (174)$$

All else equal, the variance of the predictive components increases with the variance of y, the variance of r, and the influence of outliers that occurs if extreme values of y tend to happen at the same time as extreme values of r. The variance decreases with the agreement across observations. This relationship is intuitive because agreement means that many observations imply similar outcomes for similar circumstances (we use the term *similar* loosely, as the precise relationship is one of relevance).

Substituting Equation (174) into Equation (169), we get:

$$\text{Var}(\hat{y}_t) = \frac{\sigma^2_{y,f}\sigma^2_{r,f}}{(n-1)^2}\sum_i\left((n-1)\text{outlier influence}_t - \left(\frac{n-1}{n}\right)\text{agreement}_t\right)$$
$$(175)$$

$$\text{Var}(\hat{y}_t) = \frac{1}{n-1}\sigma^2_{y,f}\sigma^2_{r,f}(n \times \text{outlier influence}_t - \text{agreement}_t) \quad (176)$$

Keep in mind that the impact of a partial sample will be reflected in the outlier influence and agreement terms, as the explicit variance terms always pertain to the full-sample.

The expected variance of $\hat{y}_t$ is in units of squared deviations of $\hat{y}_t$. One way to apply this value is to take its square root to arrive at the standard deviation measured in direct units of $\hat{y}_t$:

$$\sigma_{\hat{y}_t} = \sqrt{\text{Var}(\hat{y}_t)} \quad (177)$$

We may then compute lower and upper bounds on the prediction as $\hat{y}_t - \eta\sigma_{\hat{y}_t}$ and $\hat{y}_t + \eta\sigma_{\hat{y}_t}$, respectively, for any number of surprise units, η. This view is similar in spirit to the notion of a margin of error in polling or a confidence interval in traditional statistics.[2] But remember that we are concerned with the distribution of the estimate of our single prediction $\hat{y}_t$, and the likelihood that the true estimate falls in some

---

[2] We will not go into detail about the so-called frequentist interpretation of confidence intervals or the related semantics and assumptions that accompany this interpretation. We would refer the reader to texts on classical statistics to explore these issues.

noise-polluted range. We are not making a statement about the likeli-hood that the actual outcome will fall within a given range.

To make these ideas clearer, we may translate the variance of $\hat{y}_t$ into a measure of precision for our estimate. Ideally, it would be nice to com-pare precision across prediction exercises that use different outcomes, y. We normalize the variance of the prediction by the variance of the outcomes overall, leading to:

$$\frac{\text{Var}(\hat{y}_t)}{\text{Var}(y)} = \frac{\sigma_{r,f}^2}{n-1} (n \times outlier\ influence_t - agreement_t) \qquad (178)$$

We should think of precision as the inverse of expected variance, or one divided by Equation (178):

$$Precision_t = \frac{\text{Var}(y)}{\text{Var}(\hat{y}_t)} = \frac{n-1}{\sigma_{r,f}^2(n \times outlier\ influence_t - agreement_t)} \qquad (179)$$

To gain further intuition for this measure of precision, recall that when $n = N$ and every observation is included in the prediction, we have $\sigma_{r,f}^2 = info(x_t)$. We may now write:

$$Precision_t = \frac{n-1}{info(x_t)(n \times outlier\ influence_t - agreement_t)} \qquad (180)$$

This expression reveals that precision is inversely related to $info(x_t)$. Owing to linearity, when we attempt to predict more unusual circum-stances, we amplify the noise along with the signal. By contrast, we saw earlier that fit is invariant to any scaling of the circumstances vector. There are other important differences between precision and fit. Preci-sion increases with the number of observations used in the predictive sum, while fit does not. And precision reinforces the importance of disaggregating fit into its two components, because it depends on the difference between them. The influence of outliers degrades precision. This term is more important to precision than to fit, because it is mul-tiplied by the number of observations. Intuitively, a prediction is more sensitive to noise if it hinges on just a few observations for which rele-vance and outcomes are aligned. Higher agreement, on the other hand, improves precision. Agreement indicates robustness because it means that patterns exist across many observation pairs.

Fit Applied

In Chapter 3, we explored a "pairs of pairs" approach to measuring co-occurrence. In essence, we evaluated whether the alignment of a pair of observations for some attribute *A* mirrored the alignment of that same pair of observations for attribute *B*. Now, rather than comparing two attributes, we are interested in the degree of alignment between pairs of observed relevance and pairs of observed outcomes. For a given pair of observations, such as the dark-shaded duo shown in Exhibit 5.2, this comparison is conceptually akin to co-occurrence; it gives us one piece of input toward the calculation of fit. If we repeat this comparison for every pair of observations, we obtain the fit for a single prediction.

Exhibit 5.2 plots two series of observations. On the top, each circle represents the z-score of an observation's relevance, based on the full-sample prediction we computed in Chapter 4. And below, each circle represents the z-score of an observation's outcome. For a given pair of observations, such as the shaded dots, we multiply their relevance values together to arrive at a product of z-scores—or put differently, the relevance between two relevance values (Equation (157)). We do the same for outcomes, multiplying the two observations' z-scores, which is equivalent to the relevance of the two outcomes to each other (Equation (158)).

Exhibit 5.3 reports these values for every pair. As before, we display only the first and last four values and their overlapping pairs, but one can imagine a large grid containing every pairwise value. The

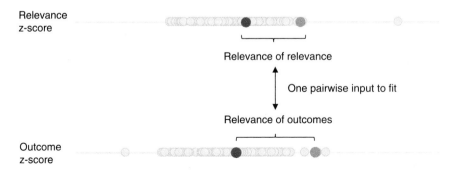

Exhibit 5.2 Pairwise Relevance and Fit

Exhibit 5.3 Pairwise Relevance and Outcomes

Product of Relevance z–scores

		1	2	3	4	• • •	291	292	293	294
1	Q1 1947	5.7	−1.5	1.0	0.6		0.6	0.8	1.2	−15.3
2	Q2 1947	−1.5	0.4	−0.3	−0.2		−0.2	−0.2	−0.3	4.0
3	Q3 1947	1.0	−0.3	0.2	0.1		0.1	0.2	0.2	−2.8
4	Q4 1947	0.6	−0.2	0.1	0.1		0.1	0.1	0.1	−1.6
	•									
	•									
	•									
291	Q3 2019	0.6	−0.2	0.1	0.1		0.1	0.1	0.1	−1.7
292	Q4 2019	0.8	−0.2	0.2	0.1		0.1	0.1	0.2	−2.2
293	Q1 2020	1.2	−0.3	0.2	0.1		0.1	0.2	0.3	−3.2
294	Q2 2020	−15.3	4.0	−2.8	−1.6		−1.7	−2.2	−3.2	41.3

Product of Outcome z–scores

		1	2	3	4	• • •	291	292	293	294
1	Q1 1947	0.7	1.0	1.2	0.4		−1.8	−1.6	−0.8	2.3
2	Q2 1947	1.0	1.5	1.9	0.5		−2.7	−2.5	−1.3	3.5
3	Q3 1947	1.2	1.9	2.3	0.7		−3.3	−3.0	−1.6	4.3
4	Q4 1947	0.4	0.5	0.7	0.2		−1.0	−0.9	−0.4	1.2
	•									
	•									
	•									
291	Q3 2019	−1.8	−2.7	−3.3	−1.0		4.8	4.4	2.3	−6.2
292	Q4 2019	−1.6	−2.5	−3.0	−0.9		4.4	4.0	2.1	−5.7
293	Q1 2020	−0.8	−1.3	−1.6	−0.4		2.3	2.1	1.0	−2.9
294	Q2 2020	2.3	3.5	4.3	1.2		−6.2	−5.7	−2.9	8.1

top panel shows z-score products for relevance. The diagonal entries are all positive. They represent the shaded dots that fall directly on top of each other, so that two positives are multiplied together to yield a positive, and two negatives are multiplied together to yield a positive. The observation for Q4 1947 falls close to average, so its squared z-score is near zero. The observation for Q2 2020 is extreme, so its squared value reaches double digits. The off-diagonal values are negative when the z-scores straddle a value of zero, and positive when both appear on the same side of center. The bottom panel of Exhibit 5.3 works the same way, but for outcomes.

The direction and degree of alignment for a given pair equals the product of the cells in these two panels. Exhibit 5.4 shows these cell-by-cell products. The value for Q2 2020 exceeds the others by a

Exhibit 5.4 Prediction Fit

Product of Relevance and Outcome z-scores

		1	2	3	4	• • •	291	292	293	294
1	Q1 1947	3.7	−1.5	1.3	0.2		−1.1	−1.3	−1.0	−35.1
2	Q2 1947	−1.5	0.6	−0.5	−0.1		0.4	0.5	0.4	13.9
3	Q3 1947	1.3	−0.5	0.4	0.1		−0.4	−0.5	−0.3	−12.1
4	Q4 1947	0.2	−0.1	0.1	0.0		−0.1	−0.1	−0.1	−2.0
	•									
	•									
	•									
291	Q3 2019	−1.1	0.4	−0.4	−0.1		0.3	0.4	0.3	10.4
292	Q4 2019	−1.3	0.5	−0.5	−0.1		0.4	0.5	0.4	12.8
293	Q1 2020	−1.0	0.4	−0.3	−0.1		0.3	0.4	0.3	9.4
294	Q2 2020	−35.1	13.9	−12.1	−2.0		10.4	12.8	9.4	332.7

Sum of nondiagonal pairs	412
Sum of diagonal pairs	752
Sum of all pairs	1164
Number of observations − 1, squared	85849
Agreement	0.005
Outlier influence	0.009
Fit	0.014

huge margin, because this observation has both large relevance and a large outcome. We saw in Chapter 4 that this observation's relevance and outcome are both strongly positive. But what if that were not the case? The diagonal value of 332.7 would remain unchanged even if the outcome was negative while the relevance stayed positive. Therefore, the average of diagonal terms is not only anchored to a biased (always positive) value, but it also does not reveal the direction of alignment. It reflects the influence of outliers, such as Q2 2020, and it is a large value in this case. The sum of nondiagonal pairs, which we call agreement, is not subject to the positive bias, and it does indeed capture the directionality of observations. We apply Equation (163) and Equation (165) to compute agreement and outlier influence, respectively. Fit equals the sum of these two subcomponents. It is important to remember that fit is defined in the context of one prediction task, and it will differ for others.

Next, we compute the variance of our prediction for economic growth, using Equation (176). Exhibit 5.5 reports the components that inform this variance, including the outlier influence and agreement from earlier. We also need the variance of outcomes (from Chapter 2) and the variance of relevance (Equation 63), together with the number of observations. Next, we use Equation (177) to convert the variance into the

Exhibit 5.5 Prediction Variance and Bounds

Variance of Prediction	
Variance of Outcomes	0.1%
Variance of Relevance	18.7
Number of Observations	294
Outlier Influence	0.009
Agreement	0.005
Variance of Prediction	0.02%
Standard Deviation of Prediction	1.5%

Prediction Bounds	
Prediction	8.2%
Standard Deviation of Prediction	1.5%
Prediction—Upper Bound	9.7%
Prediction—Lower Bound	6.7%

same units as the outcomes. This allows us to articulate a range of uncertainty around the prediction itself. The standard deviation of the prediction is 1.5%, which means that if history had turned out differently—by one standard dosage of randomness—our GDP growth prediction may fall to as low as 6.7% or rise as high as 9.7%. Recall from Chapter 2 that the standard deviation of annual GDP growth outcomes is 3.7%. Our prediction is more stable than the outcomes themselves, in part, because it draws from many observations; hence, noise will cancel out in the prediction process. On the other hand, outlier influence renders our prediction less stable; agreement counteracts this effect, but only partly. The variance of relevance—which as we have noted previously is equal to the informativeness of current circumstances—is high here, as we are predicting in the midst of unusual times. This fact also expands our cloud of uncertainty.

Exhibit 5.6 shows the components of precision, which we calculate according to Equation (180). Precision is nearly an exact inverse (reciprocal) of variance, but it is normalized so as not to depend on the variance of the underlying outcomes. A higher number is better. Precision reflects the stability that is present in our forecast, while fit reflects the amount of information it contains. We seek high values for both, although they are often in conflict.

The preceding illustrations of fit, variance, and precision all pertain to a full-sample prediction. We now explore the same calculations

Exhibit 5.6 Precision

Precision of Prediction	
Variance of Relevance	18.7
Number of Observations	294
Outlier Influence	0.009
Agreement	0.005
Precision	6.1

Exhibit 5.7 Calculating Prediction Fit for Partial Sample Prediction

Product of Relevance and Outcome z-scores										
		1	2	3	4	• • •	291	292	293	294
1	Q1 1947	n/a	n/a	n/a	n/a		n/a	n/a	n/a	n/a
2	Q2 1947	n/a	0.6	n/a	n/a		n/a	n/a	n/a	13.9
3	Q3 1947	n/a	n/a	n/a	n/a		n/a	n/a	n/a	n/a
4	Q4 1947	n/a	n/a	n/a	n/a		n/a	n/a	n/a	n/a
	•									
	•									
	•									
291	Q3 2019	n/a	n/a	n/a	n/a		n/a	n/a	n/a	n/a
292	Q4 2019	n/a	n/a	n/a	n/a		n/a	n/a	n/a	n/a
293	Q1 2020	n/a	n/a	n/a	n/a		n/a	n/a	n/a	n/a
294	Q2 2020	n/a	13.9	n/a	n/a		n/a	n/a	n/a	332.7

Sum of nondiagonal pairs	1,636
Sum of diagonal pairs	640
Sum of all pairs	2,276
Number of observations − 1, squared	5,329
Lambda, squared	0.20
Agreement	0.063
Outlier influence	0.025
Fit	0.087

as they apply to the partial sample prediction from Chapter 4. We use the same formulas as before to calculate agreement (Equation (163)) and outlier influence (Equation (165)). The main difference is that our constellation of pairs has become sparse: using the 25% most relevant observations, we have one quarter the observations and one-sixteenth as many pairs. We must also account for lambda, a scaling factor that was equal to 1 for the full sample but is lower for the partial sample.

Lambda counteracts the bias that would otherwise occur when we focus on a subset of high-relevance observations, rather than letting relevance occur throughout its full natural range.

Exhibit 5.7 reveals some differences for our partial sample prediction versus the prior full-sample prediction. Agreement and outlier influence are both much higher, resulting in a total fit more than six times as great.

In Exhibit 5.8, we present the variance, prediction bounds, and precision for the partial sample. The cloud of uncertainty around the prediction extends 2.5%—meaningfully more than its radius for the full-sample prediction. More prediction noise lingers when we blend fewer observations together, and outlier influences have increased too. Precision neatly summarizes this loss, dipping to 2.2 from 6.1 in the full sample. And while these costs of the partial sample may seem punitive, we must weigh them against the vastly improved fit we achieve.

Exhibit 5.8 Prediction Variance, Bounds, and Precision for Partial Sample Prediction

Variance of Prediction	
Variance of Outcomes	0.1%
Variance of Relevance	18.7
Number of Observations	74
Outlier Influence	0.02
Agreement	0.06
Variance of Prediction	0.1%
Standard Deviation of Prediction	2.5%
Prediction Bounds	
Prediction	11.0%
Standard Deviation of Prediction	2.5%
Prediction—Upper Bound	13.5%
Prediction—Lower Bound	8.6%
Precision of Prediction	
Variance of Relevance	18.7
Number of Observations	74
Outlier Influence	0.02
Agreement	0.06
Precision	2.2

6

Reliability

I n Chapter 5, we characterized prediction as a voting process in
which each observation casts a ballot. We argued that our confidence in a prediction depends on how closely the individual votes
tend to agree. And we showed that some predictions warrant more confidence than others by virtue of their fit. We would now like to broaden
our perspective to consider how reliable a particular voting procedure is
overall, based on the underlying data.

Reliability Conceptually

Let us continue with the voting analogy from earlier. The votes we
are talking about are not discrete choices like votes for candidates in
an election. Rather, each prediction vote is the product of a previously
observed outcome and its relevance. The average of all votes gives the
final prediction. For this discussion, it is important to distinguish between
information that is available at the time of a prediction, which is used
for voting, and the actual outcome of the event we are trying to predict,
which is unknown. The measure of fit we introduced in the previous
chapter comes from the observed information. It captures the information inside a single prediction, and it does not consider, in any way, the
unknown outcome to be revealed later.

As a brief review, the fit of a prediction tells us whether the most relevant voters tend to agree. In other words, do pairs of relevant observations have similar outcomes?[1] If the answer is usually yes, the fit is tight. Now, we must keep in mind that the answer may change dramatically as we vary the prediction task. To take a medical example, we might find that the results of a clinical trial are consistent for young men but not for older women. Thus, our predictions for young men are more likely to be accurate. Measuring fit for every combination of goals could lead to a sea of mixed results with both good fits and bad. We summarize this range of fits by its average, which we call reliability. It is not a simple average, however. As is often the case, extreme circumstances are more informative and should be weighed more heavily. Therefore, we take an information-weighted average of fit, in which the information weights reflect the informativeness of each prediction task.

The idea of reliability is straightforward: it is the fit you should expect, on average, if you are assigned a vector of prediction inputs at random. The average can only be high when strong fits are common. In our medical example, the outcomes for relevant events must be aligned consistently, whether the object of our prediction pertains to young men, young women, old men, or old women. Whereas fit pertains to one predictive instance, reliability pertains to an entire predictive routine, inclusive of the available data that it consumes. Reliable models have the capacity to locate sets of relevant examples that all point to similar conclusions. Success depends on having enough examples to make this a reality; our imagined clinical trial must include a broad swath of the population. Of course, success also depends on choosing predictive attributes for which there is a genuine relationship with outcomes.

The classical equivalent to our measure of reliability is the R-squared statistic, also called the coefficient of determination. Reliability, however, is not the R-word that prior researchers had in mind. The letter connection is to the Pearson correlation coefficient, as described in Chapter 3, which Pearson denoted as r and which, in this case, refers to the correlation between a model's many predictions and its actual outcomes. R-squared is equal to the squared correlation, and both are equal to reliability. This also means, of course, that our measure of reliability is not

---

[1] The calculation also reflects whether two observations with negative relevance had similar outcomes, and whether observations with opposite relevance had opposite outcomes. These scenarios are important for full-sample regressions, but less so for partial sample regressions in which large negatively relevant observations are removed.

new. What *is* new, to the best of our knowledge, is how the concept of reliability can be dissected to apply to individual—or, we might say, atomic—predictions for a linear regression. Moreover, the two notions diverge for partial sample regression and for other nonlinear models. Viewing reliability through the lens of observations offers considerable insight.

Reliability's equivalence to R-squared is not obvious. In fact, its equivalence is striking given the different paths used to arrive at the two measures. This equivalence holds in the special case of full-sample regression; therefore, it is instructive to consider that case more deeply.

First, we should review the definition of R-squared for a linear regression. It is equal to the variance of the predictions divided by the variance of the quantity to be predicted.[2] Although it is unclear exactly how the term *R-squared* fell into common usage, it clearly comes from Ronald Fisher's 1930s concept of analysis of variance, ANOVA for short, which provides more context around the notion of variance. In a fitted linear regression, the prediction variance is independent of variance in prediction errors, so the predictions' share of variance reveals its explanatory power across all the prediction trials posed by the data sample itself. We stress that R-squared (and likewise, the correlation *r*) is defined and computed from the actual outcomes of each prediction trial.

By contrast, our measure of reliability does not look at the outcomes of prediction trials. As noted earlier, it is defined exclusively in terms of the votes cast for each individual prediction. The central insight that links reliability to R-squared is that when we compute reliability across the trials found in the data sample, two special identities arise for full-sample regression. First, the closeness in outcomes for pairs of observations inside of each prediction fit merge together across the trials. As a result, we need not consider closeness in outcomes for each prediction trial, but just similarity in outcomes for every pair of observations in the sample. Second, the same effect holds for relevance. The relevance of observation pairs within prediction trials merge so that we need not consider them separately, either. We may simply consider the relevance of every observation to every other observation, in pairs. The punchline is that we can compute reliability, and therefore R-squared, without ever computing an actual prediction. We need only measure the

---

[2] We could refer to the sum of squared prediction deviations from average, and the sum of squared outcomes from average, which is equivalent to a ratio of variances in the absence of adjustments to degrees of freedom, which we address later.

alignment of relevance for every pair of observations with the closeness of outcomes for every pair of observations. In the presence of data where relevant observations coincide with close outcomes, a linear regression has high reliability and a high R-squared. Thinking back to the clinical trial, a model is reliable if patients who are relevant to each other in terms of their attributes (age, gender, and so forth) react in like fashion to the treatment.

Let us recap in one sentence what we have just outlined. A full-sample linear regression's reliability, and hence its R-squared, is equal to the relevance-weighted closeness in pairwise outcomes, averaged across all the observations in a sample.[3]

This perspective on pairwise alignment leads to additional insights. First, we notice an obvious bias in the measure of a model's explanatory power because the evaluation is performed on the same sample that gives the predictions. In other words, we are forced to assess the efficacy of a prediction that makes use of all the observations, in part, on the outcome of one of those same observations. The overlap is not optimal. This fact is well known for R-squared, of course. But it becomes abundantly clear from the observation-centric view that this bias arises from counting an observation's ability to explain itself. For a full-sample regression, even if there is no relationship whatsoever between inputs and outcomes, we will end up with a reliability equal to approximately K/N. But any suggestion of predictive reliability is a mirage in this scenario. All else equal, the larger the number of attributes (K), the more impressive the meaningless relevance of each data point to itself will appear. The greater the number of observations (N), the fewer self-relevance entries we have relative to genuine comparisons to other observations. The conventional view of this problem is to say that the model overfits the observations. That may be so, but the problem is not the model itself so much as the mistakenly inflated perception that the apparent reliability comes from genuine relationships in the data.

The remedy for this issue is to omit the offending terms from the sum. We should instead focus on the agreement portion of the fit—and, by extension, the reliability—as this component reflects real patterns of

---

[3] To be precise, the closeness in outcomes for the dependent variable is measured as the relevance between them. We avoid referring to relevance between dependent variables, so that we do not confuse the main notion of relevance, which is determined by the independent variables. But it is mathematically legitimate, and we make these definitions precise in the math section.

alignment across observations. This approach is conceptually related to the so-called adjusted R-squared, although it is not identical. In fact, many different adjustments have been proposed to render the R-squared an unbiased estimate. Most of these are approximations, as it is very difficult to systematically adjust a measure whose degree of bias depends on the underlying relationship itself. Recall that R-squared is a ratio of variances. The bias in the numerator and denominator are both known, but mathematically, the bias of the ratio does not equal the ratio of the biases. Summing alignment across observation pairs offers a more direct view of the relationship.

The interpretation of reliability diverges from that of R-squared when the predictive model is not a full-sample regression. For instance, consider partial sample regression from Chapter 4. Reliability speaks to the agreement in votes within various prediction trials in which we surgically remove each trial's own information from its predictions to eliminate bias. The average fit that gives reliability in this case reflects an expectation based on the observed data. By contrast, the correlation between simulated predictions and out-of-sample outcomes tells us something different: how effective these predictions are on unseen data. This effectiveness depends on fit, but it also depends on the randomness of the resulting outcomes. The effect of the randomness of outcomes for partial sample regression may not equal the effect of randomness on the prediction outcomes for a full-sample regression. Thus, out-of-sample efficacy differs from reliability in a general setting, but both are useful.

Key Takeaways

- Reliability is a measure of the fit to be expected from a random circumstance, which is to say, a random set of values for the prediction attributes. It is equal to the informativeness-weighted average fit across prediction tasks.

- Reliability pertains to an entire predictive approach, whereas fit pertains to a specific prediction.

- Reliability is equivalent to R-squared. Hence, reliability is equal to the squared Pearson correlation between predictions and outcomes.

- We can compute reliability, as well as R-squared, without forming any explicit predictions; we need only measure the alignment of relevance for every pair of observations with the closeness of outcomes for every pair of observations.

- A full-sample linear regression's reliability, and hence its R-squared, is equal to the relevance-weighted closeness in pairwise outcomes, averaged across all the observations in a sample.

- By focusing on pairwise alignment, it becomes clear that R-squared is biased upward because it includes an observation's ability to explain itself. It may therefore be prudent to focus on the agreement component of reliability to capture genuine patterns of alignment across observations.

- The reliability of a partial sample regression differs from the reliability of a full-sample regression, because the randomness of outcomes used to form predictions will differ between partial sample regression and full-sample regression.

Reliability Mathematically

In Chapter 5, we introduced measures of fit and confidence that pertain to a prediction for $\hat{y}_t$. As such, these measures took the prediction task as a given, and evaluated everything through that lens. In other words, the fit and confidence in Chapter 5 were specific to the circumstances of the prediction, x_t. Next, we want to evaluate a predictive process across multiple tasks. To do so, we will use the same approach we used in Chapter 4 to summarize asymmetry across many observations.

The most obvious set of tasks to evaluate are those of actual circumstances that occurred in history. Therefore, we may treat each x_i as an x_t, the input about which a prediction is formed. We define reliability as the average fit across prediction tasks, weighted by the informativeness of each task.

$$Reliability = \frac{1}{N-1} \sum_{t=1}^{N} info_t obj_t \qquad (181)$$

Where:

$$obj_t = fit_t \qquad (182)$$

$$info_t = info(x_t) \qquad (183)$$

Therefore:

$$Reliability = \frac{1}{N-1} \sum_{t=1}^{N} info(x_t) fit_t \qquad (184)$$

Note that we take the sum across all N observations, even for partial sample regression, because we want to evaluate every task. For reliability to be large, a model must exhibit a strong fit consistently, particularly for tasks where x_t is most different from average conditions; that is, when its informativeness is largest.

In the case of a full–sample linear regression, our measure of reliability equals the traditional R–squared statistic. To illustrate this equivalence, we begin by estimating the correlation between predictions and realizations for the dependent variable in the classical tradition as a sum over t. We use capital N to stress the use of the full-sample for both prediction and evaluation. We continue to use the index t to denote predictions, although soon we will recast the summation index variables for clarity.

$$\rho(\hat{y}, y) = \frac{1}{N-1} \sum_t \left(\frac{y_t - \bar{y}}{\sigma_y} \right) \left(\frac{\hat{y}_t - \bar{y}}{\sigma_{\hat{y}}} \right) \tag{185}$$

Substituting the prediction of each $\hat{y}_t$ as a sum over i gives:

$$\rho(\hat{y}, y) = \frac{1}{(N-1)\sigma_y\sigma_{\hat{y}}} \sum_t (y_t - \bar{y}) \left(\frac{1}{N-1} \sum_i r_{it}(y_i - \bar{y}) \right) \tag{186}$$

$$\rho(\hat{y}, y) = \frac{1}{(N-1)^2\sigma_y\sigma_{\hat{y}}} \sum_t \sum_i r_{it}(y_t - \bar{y})(y_i - \bar{y}) \tag{187}$$

For reasons that will soon become clear, we recast the double summation from t and i to be instead over i and j. The labeling of the summation indexes is of no consequence to the calculation itself. Thus:

$$\rho(\hat{y}, y) = \frac{1}{(N-1)^2\sigma_y\sigma_{\hat{y}}} \sum_i \sum_j r_{ij}(y_i - \bar{y})(y_j - \bar{y}) \tag{188}$$

To simplify this expression further, we need to dig deeper into $\sigma_{\hat{y}}$, which is estimated as:

$$\sigma_{\hat{y}}^2 = \frac{1}{N-1} \sum_t (\hat{y}_t - \bar{y})^2 \tag{189}$$

Inserting the summed definition of $\hat{y}_t$, we have:

$$\sigma_{\hat{y}}^2 = \frac{1}{N-1} \sum_t \left(\frac{1}{N-1} \sum_i r_{it}(y_i - \bar{y}) \right)^2 \tag{190}$$

$$\sigma_{\hat{y}}^2 = \frac{1}{(N-1)^3} \sum_t \sum_i \sum_j r_{it}r_{jt}(y_i - \bar{y})(y_j - \bar{y}) \tag{191}$$

$$\sigma_{\hat{y}}^2 = \frac{1}{(N-1)^3} \sum_i \sum_j (y_i - \bar{y})(y_j - \bar{y}) \sum_t r_{it}r_{jt} \tag{192}$$

When we sum across every observation t, which spans the same values as i and j for a full-sample regression, we simplify to:

$$\frac{1}{N-1} \sum_t r_{it}r_{jt} = r_{ij} \tag{193}$$

To see why, we write out:

$$\frac{1}{N-1} \sum_t r_{it} r_{jt} = \frac{1}{N-1} \sum_t (x_i - \bar{x})\Omega^{-1}(x_t - \bar{x})'(x_t - \bar{x})\Omega^{-1}(x_j - \bar{x})' \tag{194}$$

$$\frac{1}{N-1} \sum_t r_{it} r_{jt} = (x_i - \bar{x})\Omega^{-1} \left(\frac{1}{N-1} \sum_t (x_t - \bar{x})'(x_t - \bar{x}) \right) \Omega^{-1}(x_j - \bar{x})' \tag{195}$$

$$\frac{1}{N-1} \sum_t r_{it} r_{jt} = (x_i - \bar{x})\Omega^{-1}\Omega\Omega^{-1}(x_j - \bar{x})' = (x_i - \bar{x})\Omega^{-1}(x_j - \bar{x})' \tag{196}$$

This important result holds that the joint relevance of any two observations to a given prediction stems directly from the two observations' relevance to each other. Thus, for a full-sample regression, we express the general predictive capacity of a dataset in terms of the pairwise relevance of the observations within it. So:

$$\sigma_{\hat{y}}^2 = \frac{1}{(N-1)^2} \sum_i \sum_j r_{ij}(y_i - \bar{y})(y_j - \bar{y}) \tag{197}$$

This result bears a striking similarity to the equation for the correlation between predictions and realizations. We now return to Equation 188 from earlier, and square both sides:

$$R^2 = \rho(\hat{y}, y)^2 = \frac{1}{(N-1)^4 \sigma_y^2 \sigma_{\hat{y}}^2} \left(\sum_i \sum_j r_{ij}(y_i - \bar{y})(y_j - \bar{y}) \right)^2 \tag{198}$$

Substituting Equation 197 into 198, we obtain:

$$R^2 = \frac{1}{(N-1)^2} \sum_i \sum_j r_{ij} \left(\frac{y_i - \bar{y}}{\sigma_y} \right) \left(\frac{y_j - \bar{y}}{\sigma_y} \right) \tag{199}$$

Or equivalently:

$$R^2 = \frac{1}{N-1} \sum_t \frac{1}{(N-1)^2} \sum_t \sum_i r_{it} r_{jt} \left(\frac{y_i - \bar{y}}{\sigma_y} \right) \left(\frac{y_j - \bar{y}}{\sigma_y} \right) \tag{200}$$

We now return to our definition of fit and, in the case of full-sample regression, show why it is equivalent to this expression for R-squared. Recall that fit for a full-sample regression prediction of $\hat{y}_t$ is given by:

$$fit_{t,full} = \frac{1}{(N-1)^2} \sum_i \sum_j z_{r_{it}} z_{r_{jt}} z_{y_i} z_{y_j} \qquad (201)$$

Next, we expand the z-scores and apply Equation 63, which shows that $\sigma_{r,f}^2 = info(x_t)$ to obtain:

$$fit_{t,full} = \frac{1}{info(x_t)} \frac{1}{(N-1)^2} \sum_i \sum_j r_{it} r_{jt} \left(\frac{y_i - \bar{y}}{\sigma_{y,f}}\right)\left(\frac{y_j - \bar{y}}{\sigma_{y,f}}\right) \qquad (202)$$

We now take the informativeness weighted sum over t, following Equation 183. Note that this procedure matches the approach we used in Chapter 4 to summarize asymmetry across many observations. For a full-sample prediction, we find that:

$$Reliability_{full} = \frac{info(x_t)}{N-1} \sum_t \frac{1}{info(x_t)} \frac{1}{(N-1)^2} \sum_i \sum_j r_{it} r_{jt} \left(\frac{y_i - \bar{y}}{\sigma_{y,f}}\right)\left(\frac{y_j - \bar{y}}{\sigma_{y,f}}\right)$$
$$(203)$$

$$Reliability_{full} = \frac{1}{N-1} \sum_t \frac{1}{(N-1)^2} \sum_i \sum_j r_{it} r_{jt} \left(\frac{y_i - \bar{y}}{\sigma_{y,f}}\right)\left(\frac{y_j - \bar{y}}{\sigma_{y,f}}\right)$$
$$(204)$$

This expression is identical to the R-squared in Equation 200. And based on this equivalence for the full sample, we may repurpose Equation 199 to express the reliability of a full-sample linear regression in terms of pairwise relevance of circumstances and outcomes, without any explicit reference to formulating point predictions. In other words, we may view full-sample regression reliability as a property of the dataset—a high-level measure of alignment.

$$Reliability_{full} = \frac{1}{(N-1)^2} \sum_i \sum_j r_{ij} z_{y_i} z_{y_j} \qquad (205)$$

$$Reliability_{full} = \frac{1}{(N-1)^2} \sum_i \sum_j r(x_i, x_j) r(y_i, y_j) \qquad (206)$$

In Chapter 5 we showed that fit does not drop to zero even if there is truly no relationship. This is because fit includes comparisons of observations with themselves that are all nonzero and positive. As noted earlier, we interpret these self-comparisons as outlier influence and the remaining terms as agreement. In the event that there is no true relationship, we should expect agreement to equal zero, but outlier influence will not. Thus, the expected value for reliability when the data represents pure noise is the expected value of the outlier influence component, where $i = j$:

$$\text{Expected Reliability} = E\left[\frac{1}{(N-1)^2}\sum_i r_{ii}\left(\frac{y_i - \bar{y}}{\sigma_y}\right)^2\right] \tag{207}$$

Under the assumption that there is no relationship between X and Y, the terms involving y_i are independent from those involving r_{ii}, and the expected value of their product equals the product of their expected values.

$$\text{Expected Reliability} = \frac{1}{(N-1)^2}\sum_i E[info(x_i)]E[info(y_i)] \tag{208}$$

From the identities in Chapter 4, we know that the sum of informativeness equals $(N-1)K$, where K equals the number of chosen attributes for X, and 1 for Y, so:

$$\text{Expected Reliability} = \frac{1}{(N-1)^2}\sum_i \frac{(N-1)K}{N}\frac{(N-1)1}{N} \tag{209}$$

Therefore:

$$\text{Expected Reliability} = \frac{K}{N} \tag{210}$$

The ratio of predictive attributes to observations aligns with the traditional concept of overfitting. The risk increases with the number of attributes, and it decreases when there are more observations. We can subtract this quantity from our estimate of reliability to remove the bias for a full-sample regression. Then, the expected reliability will be zero, and we can interpret any positive value as evidence of a relationship in the data.

The derivation of this adjustment relies on the fact that the average of $r_{it}r_{jt}$ across all t in a full sample equals r_{ij}. We cannot use the same adjustment for a partial sample regression, but we can evaluate the agreement component of fit on its own to determine whether there is a nontrivial relationship. The observation-centric perspective, together with the pairwise calculation procedure, makes this possible.

How does this approach to measuring full-sample reliability compare to the conventional adjusted R-squared statistic? The answer to this question is rather complex. The R-squared statistic is typically interpreted as the ratio of explained variance of a regression's predictions to total variance of Y. To adjust it, the numerator and denominator are both scaled by different amounts to render them individually unbiased. The revised ratio is a less-biased estimate of the true population R-squared, but it is still biased. This remaining bias occurs because the degree of bias depends on the level of the true R-squared itself. To prove this point with an extreme example, a random process with a true R-squared of 1 (perfect explanatory power) will not incur any bias when it is estimated, because the statistic will never stray from 1 and it is impossible to overestimate the truth. However, a true R-squared of 0 will experience significant bias due to noise and overestimation.

The most common formulation of the adjusted R-squared is from Ezekiel (1929):

$$Adjusted\ R^2 = 1 - \frac{N-1}{N-K-1}(1-R^2) \qquad (211)$$

Many variations of this general formula have been proposed, each of which replaces the fractional coefficient with a slightly different value. Olkin and Pratt (1958) augmented this coefficient with another term involving an infinite sum, which they proved is the most efficient unbiased estimator of the population R-squared. Unfortunately, it is so complicated to compute that it is almost never used. For practical purposes, especially when N is large and K is small, these differences are of little consequence.

Our proposition is philosophically distinct from these efforts. We do not seek the best estimate of the R-squared statistic; rather, we suggest that it could be more enlightening to break apart the definition into the two components described earlier: outlier influence and agreement. The outlier influence component is always positive, and it is consistent. The agreement component may be positive or negative, and for data that consists of pure noise, it averages to zero. Exhibit 6.1 shows the result of predicting each of 500 random noise outcomes using three attributes drawn from random noise of their own. The values for agreement are sorted from highest to lowest and shown along with their corresponding outlier influence values. Each vertical slice represents one prediction out of 500 for this noise sample.

Exhibit 6.2 illustrates how the positive bias of the outlier influence grows, as does the scale of variation in agreement, if we adjust the ratio

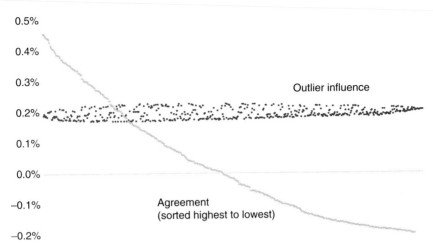

Exhibit 6.1 Components of Fit for Simulated Random Noise

Note: $K = 3$ attributes, $N = 500$ observations.

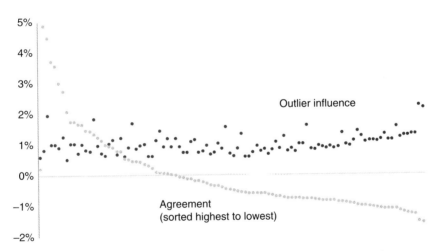

Exhibit 6.2 Components of Fit for Simulated Random Noise

Note: $K = 20$ attributes, $N = 100$ observations.

of predictive attributes for the number of observations feeding the prediction. Here, we include 20 predictive attributes rather than just 3, and we decrease the number of observations fivefold to 100. Take care to note that the vertical axis is now scaled to plot values 10 times larger than in the previous exhibit.

Before closing this topic, we should note that the number of attributes has another implication for fit. As we stated earlier, informativeness sums to $(N - 1)K$ across any sample, so the average informativeness of an observation is equal to K. We saw in Equation 184 that reliability is an average across $info(x_t)$ times fit_t. This means that if we augment a set of predictors with an attribute that reflects only noise, and yet reliability remains the same, it must be the case that the average fit degrades by $-1/(K+1)$ percent to offset the $1/K$ percent growth in total informativeness. For example, if $K = 4$ and we add a fifth attribute that is not useful at all, average fit will register 20% lower. Thus, fit depends on how many attributes we use. This is intuitive and helpful. Suppose we have two competing prediction routines with equal reliability (R-squared), but one uses three attributes while the other uses 20. And suppose that, unlike in Exhibits 6.1 and 6.2, both have predictive capacity, and we hold the number of observations constant. We will discover that average informativeness is $20 \div 3 \approx 6.67$ times larger when we use 20 attributes, and its average fit is 6.67 times smaller. The fit should indeed be smaller, because less of the information in X is aligned with outcomes. Or, to put it differently, we should be more skeptical of the attribute-hungry routine because, all else being equal, it is more likely to uncover a spurious fit.

Still, you might object to this method of accounting. Imagine that our two prediction routines are perfect at predicting outcomes; they both have reliability equal to 1. The 20-attribute version will still have a much lower average fit. In fact, even for three attributes, the fit will never reach as high as 1. If desired, we could reallocate the multiples to compute a modified $Kfit_t$. In parallel, we must deflate the informativeness terms to $info(x_t)/K$. The modified informativeness averages to 1, and $Kfit_t$ will be distributed above and below reliability, which in our present perfect-predictor example equals 1. This slightly altered view has merit as a weighted average of terms that are centered on the ultimate reliability number. The drawback is that the objects of interest, $Kfit_t$, are no longer guaranteed to lie between 0 and 1.

In line with this discussion, we may express reliability in terms of explicit nonnegative weights $w_t > 0$ that sum to 1, $\sum_{t=1}^{N} w_t = 1$, by distributing the number of predictive attributes K as follows:

$$Reliability = \sum_{t=1}^{N} w_t(Kfit_t) \qquad (212)$$

Where:

$$w_t = \frac{info(x_t)}{K(N-1)} \qquad (213)$$

Reliability Applied

In Chapter 5, we computed fit for a single prediction task; namely, predicting growth for the year following Q4 2020. We now repeat that process (using Equation 159) 294 times over, treating each historical observation as the circumstances of prediction, x_t. The column labeled "Fit" in Exhibit 6.3 shows these results. Next, following Equation 212 we multiply fit by the number of attributes, $K = 4$, and formulate weights that sum to 1 using Equation 213. The resulting weighted average of 0.04 is the reliability. Reliability may range from 0 to 1, and higher is better, so 0.04 may not seem very impressive by the standards in some fields. In finance and economics, though, such a low number is common. As we stated earlier in our numerical application, our focus in this section is on illustration, not on predictive quality. Fortunately, we will see higher numbers for the partial sample approach.

We next show that, for our full-sample prediction, reliability may be calculated as the alignment between the pairwise relevance of X and the pairwise relevance of Y. Exhibits 6.4 and 6.5 show how a pairwise calculation (Equation 206) leads to precisely the same answer. By now, measuring across pairs of observations should feel familiar. In Exhibit 2.9, we computed pairwise information spreads for a single attribute. In Exhibit 3.7, we computed pairwise co-occurrence for

Exhibit 6.3 Calculating Reliability

		Weight	Fit	Fit × K
1	Q1 1947	21.5/1,172	0.00	0.01
2	Q2 1947	20.5/1,172	0.00	0.00
3	Q3 1947	1.4/1,172	0.01	0.05
4	Q4 1947	1.1/1,172	0.01	0.05
	•	•	•	•
	•	•	•	•
	•	•	•	•
291	Q3 2019	1.2/1,172	0.00	0.01
292	Q4 2019	4.6/1,172	0.00	0.02
293	Q1 2020	2.2/1,172	0.01	0.05
294	Q2 2020	43.5/1,172	0.01	0.03
		Reliability = Weighted average:		0.04

Exhibit 6.4 Pairwise Relevance and Pairwise Outcomes

Pairwise Relevance of Attributes

		1	2	3	4	• • •	291	292	293	294
1	Q1 1947	21.5	16.1	4.5	3.5		−2.2	−5.9	−0.6	−18.7
2	Q2 1947	16.1	20.5	4.0	3.5		−3.1	−8.7	−1.8	1.2
3	Q3 1947	4.5	4.0	1.4	1.2		−0.7	−2.1	−0.2	−3.1
4	Q4 1947	3.5	3.5	1.2	1.1		−0.6	−2.0	−0.1	−1.6
	•									
	•									
	•									
291	Q3 2019	−2.2	−3.1	−0.7	−0.6		1.2	1.3	1.5	−0.5
292	Q4 2019	−5.9	−8.7	−2.1	−2.0		1.3	4.6	0.5	−2.1
293	Q1 2020	−0.6	−1.8	−0.2	−0.1		1.5	0.5	2.2	−1.6
294	Q2 2020	−18.7	1.2	−3.1	−1.6		−0.5	−2.1	−1.6	43.5

Pairwise Relevance of Outcomes

		1	2	3	4	• • •	291	292	293	294
1	Q1 1947	0.7	1.0	1.2	0.4		−1.8	−1.6	−0.8	2.3
2	Q2 1947	1.0	1.5	1.9	0.5		−2.7	−2.5	−1.3	3.5
3	Q3 1947	1.2	1.9	2.3	0.7		−3.3	−3.0	−1.6	4.3
4	Q4 1947	0.4	0.5	0.7	0.2		−1.0	−0.9	−0.4	1.2
	•									
	•									
	•									
291	Q3 2019	−1.8	−2.7	−3.3	−1.0		4.8	4.4	2.3	−6.2
292	Q4 2019	−1.6	−2.5	−3.0	−0.9		4.4	4.0	2.1	−5.7
293	Q1 2020	−0.8	−1.3	−1.6	−0.4		2.3	2.1	1.0	−2.9
294	Q2 2020	2.3	3.5	4.3	1.2		−6.2	−5.7	−2.9	8.1

two attributes. And in Exhibit 5.3, we computed pairwise products of relevance for the specific prediction of x_t, including every attribute. Now, we compute the pairwise relevance of the observations themselves, including every attribute. These values are shown in the top panel. Below that, we compute the pairwise relevance of outcomes—which, in fact, is identical to the bottom panel of Exhibit 5.3.

The diagonal elements are equal to the informativeness of an observation. The others are equal to the average of each constituent's informativeness, plus their similarity (which is negative). Large positive values occur for pairs of notable observations that are similar. Large negative values occur for pairs of notable observations that are highly dissimilar (more dissimilar from each other than they are dissimilar from average).

Exhibit 6.5 Pairwise Calculation of Full-Sample Reliability

Pairwise Product of Relevance of Attributes and Relevance of Outcomes

		1	2	3	4	• • •	291	292	293	294
1	Q1 1947	14.0	15.9	5.5	1.2		3.9	9.5	0.5	−42.8
2	Q2 1947	15.9	30.8	7.4	1.9		8.5	21.3	2.2	4.0
3	Q3 1947	5.5	7.4	3.1	0.8		2.2	6.4	0.3	−13.2
4	Q4 1947	1.2	1.9	0.8	0.2		0.5	1.8	0.1	−2.0
	•									
	•									
	•									
291	Q3 2019	3.9	8.5	2.2	0.5		5.8	5.7	3.3	3.2
292	Q4 2019	9.5	21.3	6.4	1.8		5.7	18.7	0.9	12.1
293	Q1 2020	0.5	2.2	0.3	0.1		3.3	0.9	2.4	4.7
294	Q2 2020	−42.8	4.0	−13.2	−2.0		3.2	12.1	4.7	350.5

Sum of all pairs	3,188
Number of observations − 1, squared	85,849
Reliability	0.04

Exhibit 6.5 shows the pairwise calculation of reliability. Each cell equals the product of the corresponding cells in Exhibit 6.4. We arrive at the predictions' reliability without ever explicitly forming a single prediction.

We now show how the conventional R-squared statistic produces an identical value. Any prediction model, no matter its approach, may be judged by the correlation of actual outcomes to the predictions it renders. As shown in Equation 41 from Chapter 3, correlation is an average over products of z-scores. As demonstrated by Exhibit 6.6, the correlation between outcomes and predictions for our full-sample method is 0.19. When we square it, we get the same 0.04 from earlier.

We use the first of these three methods—the weighted average fit—to compute reliability for partial sample regression. Exhibit 6.7 presents these values.

Exhibit 6.8 shows the fit (times K) graphically for every prediction task. The weighted average settles on a value of 0.12.

There are a few points worth emphasizing. First, Exhibit 6.8 makes clear that individual fits tend to vary dramatically from one prediction to another. The reliability (or R-squared) is a useful summary, but it belies the fact that the available evidence is more useful in some cases than others. Second, reliability is not the same as R-squared for partial

Exhibit 6.6 Traditional Approach to Calculating R-squared

		Outcome	Full-Sample Prediction	Outcome z-score	Prediction z-score	Product of z-score
1	Q1 1947	9.3%	5.5%	0.8	−1.2	−1.0
2	Q2 1947	10.8%	6.3%	1.2	0.0	0.0
3	Q3 1947	11.9%	5.9%	1.5	−0.7	−1.0
4	Q4 1947	7.9%	5.9%	0.4	−0.6	−0.3
	•	•	•	•	•	•
	•	•	•	•	•	•
	•	•	•	•	•	•
291	Q3 2019	−1.7%	6.1%	−2.2	−0.3	0.7
292	Q4 2019	−1.0%	6.8%	−2.0	0.7	−1.4
293	Q1 2020	2.6%	5.7%	−1.0	−0.8	0.9
294	Q2 2020	16.7%	8.4%	2.8	2.9	8.3

Sum of product of z-scores	56.5
Number of predictions − 1	293
Correlation	0.19
R^2	0.04

Exhibit 6.7 Calculating Reliability for Partial Sample Regression

		$info(x_i)$ Weight	Fit	Fit $* K$
1	Q1 1947	21.5/1,172	0.07	0.27
2	Q2 1947	20.5/1,172	0.02	0.07
3	Q3 1947	1.4/1,172	0.02	0.08
4	Q4 1947	1.1/1,172	0.01	0.02
	•	•	•	•
	•	•	•	•
	•	•	•	•
291	Q3 2019	1.2/1,172	0.01	0.05
292	Q4 2019	4.6/1,172	0.04	0.15
293	Q1 2020	2.2/1,172	0.00	0.00
294	Q2 2020	43.5/1,172	0.08	0.30

Reliability = Weighted average:	0.12

sample regressions. Reliability gauges confidence at the time of prediction, whereas R-squared is usually defined after the fact on realized outcomes. Third, from Equation 210, we should expect even a truly useless model to deliver a reliability equal to the ratio of attributes to

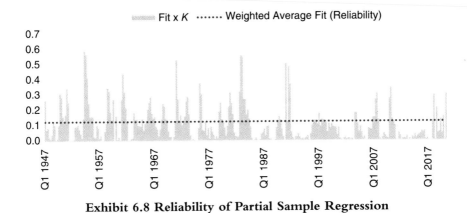

Exhibit 6.8 Reliability of Partial Sample Regression

Exhibit 6.9 Removing the Impact of Biased Terms

		$info(x_t)$ Weight	Full-Sample Agreement	Full-Sample Agreement × K	Partial Sample Agreement	Partial Sample Agreement × K
1	Q1 1947	21.5/1,172	0.00	−0.01	0.06	0.23
2	Q2 1947	20.5/1,172	0.00	−0.02	0.01	0.03
3	Q3 1947	1.4/1,172	0.01	0.03	0.01	0.05
4	Q4 1947	1.1/1,172	0.01	0.04	0.00	0.00
	•	•	•	•	•	•
	•	•	•	•	•	•
	•	•	•	•	•	•
291	Q3 2019	1.2/1,172	0.00	−0.01	0.00	0.01
292	Q4 2019	4.6/1,172	0.00	0.00	0.03	0.12
293	Q1 2020	2.2/1,172	0.01	0.03	−0.01	−0.03
294	Q2 2020	43.5/1,172	0.00	−0.01	0.05	0.21
		Weighted average:		0.02		0.09

observations. In our full-sample regression this benchmark reliability is around 0.01, and for partial sample regression with one quarter the observations, it is four times as large, rounding up to 0.05. Thankfully, the actual fits exceed these baseline values.

To address this point directly, we compute reliability in the same fashion as before, but instead of total fit we use agreement, which, for a useless noninformative prediction process, will average to zero. In Exhibit 6.9, the agreements of 0.02 and 0.09 for the full and partial sample, respectively, tell us that our dataset contains a pattern worth noticing.

Exhibit 6.10 Addressing the Bias of R-Squared

Adjusted R^2 versus Alternatives	
R^2	0.04
Number of observations, N	294
Number of attributes, K	4
$(N-1)/(N-K-1)$	1.01
Adjusted R^2	0.0238
K/N	0.01
Reliability minus K/N	0.0235
Agreement component of reliability	0.0175

Finally, let us consider how agreement, as a solution to avoiding bias, compares to other approaches in the case of a full-sample prediction method. Exhibit 6.10 repeats the weighted average agreement from Exhibit 6.9, although we add two more digits of precision: 0.0175. We now compute the adjusted R-squared using Equation 211. Interestingly, it is nearly equal to another simple alternative we have proposed, which is to subtract from reliability the ratio of the number of predictive attributes to the number of observations, K/N—this is the value we should expect in the presence of no relationship. Agreement is convenient because in the absence of a relationship, we should expect a value of 0.

References

Ezekiel, M. 1929. "The Application of the Theory of Error to Multiple and Curvilinear Correlation." *Journal of the American Statistical Association* 24 (165).

Olkin, I., and J. W. Pratt. 1958. "Unbiased Estimation of Certain Correlation Coefficients." *Annals of Mathematical Statistics* 29 (1).

7

Toward Complexity

Our relevance-based approach to prediction is intended to overcome the failure of linear regression analysis to address asymmetric relationships between inputs and predictions. But you may question the need for yet another apparatus to deal with complexities such as asymmetry, given the rapidly expanding suite of machine learning algorithms. In this chapter we describe how partial sample regression is related to machine learning and why we should view these approaches as complementary rather than mutually exclusive. We also explain why partial sample regression might often be the preferred approach.

Toward Complexity Conceptually

The idea that machines could match, or exceed, the power of human decision making has captivated people for centuries. Often the test of a machine's ability to match human decision making has focused on popular games like chess. One notorious and amusing example dates to 1770. A Hungarian inventor known as Wolfgang von Kempelen unveiled an elaborate cabinet full of gears topped by a life-sized replica of a man dressed in traditional Ottoman clothing with a turban and a smoking pipe. His invention, known as the Turk, was able to grasp and move chess pieces and play effectively enough to win most matches. The spectacle mystified crowds across the world. The contraption publicly defeated

Napoleon Bonaparte and Benjamin Franklin, among others. But the machine's talent was a clever illusion. A skilled chess player would sit inside a cramped compartment and maneuver the Turk's arm and hand with levers.

About 180 years later, in 1949, Claude Shannon wrote a scientific paper on how to program a computer to play chess. As we noted in Chapter 2, Shannon's early work proved that electrical circuits could execute the core components of logic, raising the prospect of artificial intelligence. These ideas were not put into practice, though, until a decade later. In 1959, an IBM engineer named Arthur Samuel unveiled a software program that could play a competent game of checkers. IBM's stock jumped 15% in one day. Samuel's program ran on a computer with 72 memory tubes for a capacity of 9 kilobytes, enough to remember about four pages of this book. Ironically, Samuel approached the checkers project with confidence because he mistakenly assumed that Shannon had built a functioning machine to play chess. But Shannon had only written a paper. In any event, Samuel coined the term *machine learning* and paved the way for more sophisticated data analysis. He empowered his checkers program with rote learning to recall known board positions from memory. Later, he programmed it to learn from playing against itself and to optimize the reward function it assigned to various positions.

Progress was uneven in the decades that followed. The artificial intelligence advocates were at times euphoric and at times despondent. But amazing breakthroughs eventually emerged. In 1988 IBM's Deep Blue defeated Gary Kasparov, the world's reigning chess champion. And DeepMind's Alpha Go beat the best human player at the game of Go, a much more complex game than chess. Triumphs like these owed much of their success to raw computing power. But they also relied on innovative approaches to data processing and prediction.

Learning by Example

Early attempts at artificial intelligence failed because they tried to specify knowledge as rigid decision rules. Imagine, for example, trying to teach a classroom of children how to navigate their way through life. Would they not learn the rules of life more effectively through experience?

Based on this principle, artificial neural networks, inspired by the human brain, sift through examples to learn prediction rules. Then, they correctly determine whether an image depicts a fish or a cat, for instance, based on pixels. Put simply, machine learning algorithms extrapolate from examples to predict the unknown. This is the same philosophy we used for relevance-weighted predictions in Chapter 4. But powerful machine learning models extrapolate from historical observations in a more complex way.

Why is complexity helpful? Consider the fact that people often learn faster than machines. A toddler can distinguish a fish from a cat after just a few encounters, but it takes thousands of sample images for a computer to do the same. One interpretation of this fact, in line with this book's central thesis, is that the human mind is surprisingly adept at finding relevance in disparate observations. In fact, studies have shown people are so eager to draw connections that we see them where they don't exist, which causes its own problems. As we write this book, science knows very little about how the human mind and its 86 billion (or so) neurons work. But we can speculate that even the first time a toddler sees a cat, he might remember other animals with four legs or animals that live indoors. He might relate fish to other things that are underwater. And he might instinctively predict that the cat moves very differently from the fish, having never seen a cat before. Complicated machine learning algorithms can learn patterns like these eventually. Linear regressions never will.

This thought experiment leads to some further insights about relevance. First, a broad range of experience is valuable. Second, with broad experience, only a tiny fraction of observations is relevant to the task at hand. And third, relevance could be applied in nested layers or different domains to determine what a leg is and what it means to have four of them.

Expanding on Relevance

Let us return to the relevance-weighted predictions from Chapter 4 as a starting point. We showed that by including every observation, our predictions match those of linear regression. We also argued that censoring irrelevant observations may lead to better predictions, and then our results no longer match linear regression. By selectively focusing on subsets of observations, partial sample regression uses the attributes in new ways. Each attribute helps determine the relevant subset, and the predictive effect of each attribute shifts according to the subset. Changing the value of one attribute creates a ripple effect that changes what we conclude from the other attributes. The relationship of an input value to the final prediction is not linear.

In fact, partial sample regression is a special case of a more general idea. We can augment the definition of relevance to include logic beyond the raw values of informativeness and similarity. With partial sample regression, we add a layer of processing that sets the relevance of certain points to 0, based on the sign or rank of their relevance, and rescales the rest. In principle, we could adjust relevance in more complicated ways. For example, we could amplify the weights of relevant observations even more, focusing on a handful of the most relevant ones, and compress the weights of others.

Going further, we could add a layer of processing that is informed dynamically by fit and confidence. For example, the recipe for relevance in a given circumstance could evaluate the fit (from Chapter 5) for that prediction across many different thresholds, select the best method, and use the final result as the weights for each observation. In this way, a model can dynamically recalibrate its thresholds for relevance based on how well the data performs for each prediction task. Some predictions enjoy lots of historical precedence. Others stretch the limits of our experience. The key point is that this entire process can itself be viewed as a broader recipe for evaluating relevance.

We do not need to stop there. We have gone to great lengths in this book to motivate the precise definition of relevance as a sum of similarity and informativeness, using the Mahalanobis distance. This specification is simple, elegant, intuitive, and effective. It shares the virtues of unbiasedness and efficiency with linear regression. Still, there may be applications for which other definitions of relevance work better.

Many popular machine learning models are based on decision trees. A tree is a set of simple rules that directs you to some endpoint. Once you have defined a tree, your decision proceeds as if it were a squirrel running from the tree trunk to the tip of a branch where the ultimate prediction is formed. Each path leads to a different prediction, as shown in the left panel of Exhibit 7.1. Decision trees operate on the principle of similarity, which we have already discussed at length. To see why, it may be more helpful to leave the tree image behind and consider the same logic in terms of postal codes for attribute values, shown in the right panel.

In this illustration, we characterize days in terms of temperature (in degrees Fahrenheit) and chance of rain. There are many reasons why this might be useful; for example, we may want to predict how crowded it will be at our favorite beach. Thresholds define regions (shown as rectangles in Exhibit 7.1), akin to postal codes, where input values are

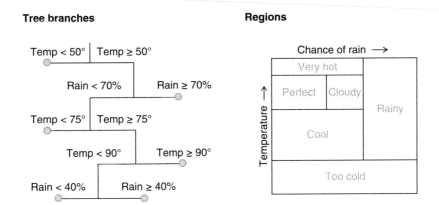

Tree branches

Regions

Exhibit 7.1 Decision Tree

similar. They predict the same outcome for any inputs that land in that zone—usually with a simple average of all the past outcomes that landed there too. For more than two inputs, we can visualize postal codes that carve up three-dimensional space as if for planets or galaxies. Although we cannot visualize dimensions beyond three inputs, defining them is straightforward.

It is worth noting that the tree-based version of similarity, unlike partial sample regression, does not assign distance values to each observation. Therefore, it cannot discriminate between the relevance of two observations in the same group. It does not include a measure of informativeness, either. It may, however, find nuanced boundaries that distinguish some experiences from others, which could be helpful in gauging relevance. Perhaps we can combine these considerations, which once again conform to a weighted average prediction, with other aspects of relevance.

Two tree-based learning models that receive a great deal of interest are gradient-boosting machines, introduced by Friedman (2001), and random forests, introduced by Ho (1995) and Breiman (2001). Boosting is an iterative process that carves up postal codes intelligently, focusing on parts of the map that demand the most understanding and nuance. For example, there are many more important distinctions to make among neighborhoods in a big city than in a rural town with just a handful of residents. Drawing an equally spaced grid across an entire country is too coarse. The boundaries we want from a model should help us gain an understanding of the neighborhoods where observations reside.

Random forests, by contrast, pull out vastly simplified descriptions of observations and dispatch miniature models to predict from each description. By restricting each individual analyst's view to just a few of the available attributes, this method avoids a false sense of confidence in predictions, or what is often called overfitting. Averaging hundreds of such miniature predictions cancels errors and, in many cases, allows robust relationships to shine through. The same insight could be applied to relevance as measured by the Mahalanobis distance. We could determine relevance many times over, using different sets of attributes to describe observations. Each alternate process—or miniature model—could vote on relevance, either through a democratic process or one that favors models with tighter fits. Though far more complicated than basic regression, this approach still maintains the intuitive appeal of relevance-based prediction.

A broader range of experience is likely to improve prediction, especially for difficult tasks. One solution is to expand the sample of informative observations. Another is to include a wider set of attributes. Doing so is challenging. If we include more attributes than we have observations, we will struggle to estimate covariance matrices that are internally consistent, which will make it more difficult to compute relevance. And even if we are able to compute a valid covariance matrix, we run the risk of false confidence, because as we track more and more attributes, we increase the odds of uncovering an illusory pattern that is driven by noise.

A possible way forward is to define alternative models based on the goal of the prediction or based on the nature of the relevant sample. Our relevance engine could bring in additional attributes or additional observations on demand. These processes would better inform the higher-level attributes that feed into the final predictions. Intuitively, this process of reaching for supplemental information is related to how an artificial neural network model works. Different goals require different inputs. Each, in turn, reaches for the inputs it needs for its own role in the process. Whereas random forests enlist armies of prediction models to stand side by side and work on variations of the same problem, neural networks engage a team of nested models that are each tuned for their specific purpose.

In our discussion so far, we have portrayed relevance-based prediction as an approximation to more advanced machine learning algorithms with the potential to incorporate more complexity. Yet there are two important features of relevance-based prediction that set it apart favorably from most machine learning algorithms.

First, we can assess relevance without any knowledge whatsoever of Y. It is easy to overlook this point, especially if linear regression is viewed as measuring a causal link between X and Y. The story of a causal model is that we learn something about Y by studying its past behavior, namely its covariation with the attributes in X. But, as we showed in Chapter 4, we can tell an equivalent story in terms of observations. With this alternative perspective, all the information we need to judge the relevance of past experiences is contained in X. In our observation-based approach, X does all the hard work, directing our attention to some occurrences over others. We reach for Y only after we have determined relevance. This sounds impossible. How can X predict Y if it has never seen Y and knows nothing about it? This is possible because the relevance weights will predict Y if there is a relationship. Predictions will be good if similar circumstances tend to have similar outcomes. If not, then the predictions will tend toward zero plus a dose of noise.

By contrast, machine learning algorithms gravitate toward a solution by searching for relationships iteratively based on the success of their predictions. These algorithms depend jointly on X and Y, so they must guard against overfitting to spurious patterns in Y. As a result, they require a lot of new scaffolding to test, select, and configure a prediction process effectively.

Second, as we let go of simplicity, machine learning algorithms become more difficult to interpret. For practitioners, understanding a prediction is often as important as producing it. Relevance demystifies the prediction process. It casts decisions in terms of the information that comes from experience—an intuitive perspective that fits most people's natural way of thinking. It says something about cause and effect that is easy to understand. It simplifies the full reality, while staying faithful to the information that truly matters.

Key Takeaways

- In partial sample regression, the relationship of an input value to the prediction is not linear. By changing the value of one attribute, we change the relevance of the observations and the effect they have on our prediction. In this sense, partial sample regression is a simple, yet efficient, machine learning algorithm.

- We could expand the definition of relevance to include logic beyond informativeness and similarity or incorporate processes to calibrate these quantities dynamically in response to feedback about fit and precision. We can, therefore, think of machine learning algorithms and relevance-based prediction as potential complements to one another rather than mutually exclusive techniques.

- Relevance-based prediction is not simply a convenient approximation to more complex machine learning algorithms. It compares favorably in two ways. It enables us to assess relevance without any knowledge of prior outcomes. And it opens a window into the cause and effect of predictors and outcomes, thereby enabling us to assess the sensibility of our model.

Toward Complexity Mathematically

It may be helpful to take a step back and characterize the prediction process in general terms. For example, the relevance-weighted prediction formula from Chapter 4 is a special case of a general predictive function f that transforms observed inputs into an output:

$$\hat{y}_t = f(x_t, X, Y) \tag{214}$$

As before, x_t can represent any circumstance we wish to consider, while X comprises the full set of observations available for those attributes, and Y the corresponding outcomes. There are many ways we can process these inputs. A full-sample linear regression is linear with respect to changes in x_t. The linear weights that govern this relationship are commonly interpreted as regression coefficients collected in a row vector, β. In this expression, which hopefully feels familiar at this point in our discussion, Ω, $\bar{x}$, and $\bar{y}$ are themselves functions of X and Y:

$$f_{full}(x_t, X, Y) = \bar{y} + (x_t - \bar{x}) \frac{1}{N-1} \sum_{i=1}^{N} \Omega^{-1}(x_i - \bar{x})'(y_i - \bar{y}) \tag{215}$$

$$f_{full}(x_t, X, Y) = (\bar{y} - \bar{x}\beta') + x_t\beta' \tag{216}$$

The linear rate of change in the prediction is given by the derivative with respect to x_t, which is a constant vector:

$$\frac{\partial f_{full}(x_t, X, Y)}{\partial x_t} = \beta \tag{217}$$

A full-sample regression is also linear with respect to changes in Y, the column vector of all N outcomes for y_i. The linear weights in this case represent relevance.

$$f_{full}(x_t, X, Y) = \bar{y} + \frac{1}{N-1} \sum_{i=1}^{N} r_{it}(y_i - \bar{y}) \tag{218}$$

$$\frac{\partial f_{full}(x_t, X, Y)}{\partial y_i} = \frac{r_{it}}{N-1} \tag{219}$$

In other words, if it turned out that one of our historical observations for y_i was missing and we wanted to consider how different values for this input would affect our ultimate prediction, the range of hypothetical possibilities would trace out a straight line.

To turn this approach into partial sample regression, we introduce a nonlinear function g that modifies r_{it} by censoring and scaling the values:

$$f_{partial}(x_t, X, Y) = \sum_{i=1}^{N} g_{partial}(r_{it}) y_i \qquad (220)$$

Where:

$$g_{partial}(r_{it}) = \frac{\delta(r_{it})}{n} \left(1 + \frac{n}{(n-1)} \lambda^2 r_{it} \right) \qquad (221)$$

Here, $\delta(r_{it})$ is a censoring function that returns 1 if $r > r^*$ and 0 if $r \leq r^*$, with r^* serving as a threshold for relevance. We use $n = \sum_i^N \delta(r_{it})$ to denote the number of observations that are included in the relevant subset. The first element in the parentheses generates the simple average of Y. In the second term, $\frac{n}{n-1}$ will be close to 1 for all practical purposes. The term $\lambda^2 r_{it}$ incorporates the specific information from observation y_i according to the abnormal relevance of that observation within the subset. This formulation of partial sample regression is equivalent to a recipe we presented in Chapter 4. We express it this way so that the simple average $\bar{y}$ can be subsumed into the logic of censoring observations. To be explicit about the information that flows into the determination of relevance, we can write that g is a function of x_i, x_t, and X, but, importantly, not Y:

$$g_{partial}(x_i, x_t, X) = \frac{\delta(r_{it})}{n} \left(1 + \frac{n}{(n-1)} \lambda^2 r_{it} \right) \qquad (222)$$

For a given x_t, partial sample prediction is linear with respect to y_i. In contrast to a full-sample linear regression, the linear weights are now defined by $g(r)$ instead of r:

$$\frac{\partial f_{partial}(x_t, X, Y)}{\partial y_i} = g_{partial}(r_{it}) \qquad (223)$$

However, partial sample regression is not linear with respect to the input conditions, x_t. Each component that involves $\delta(r_{it})$ changes abruptly when x_t changes enough to include a new observation in the relevant subset or exclude an old one. More generally, we can imagine two disparate choices such as x_t and $-x_t$, which may comprise entirely distinct subsets of observations. The nature of the relationship between X and Y could be completely different in these subsets. Thus, if we vary x_t from very low to very high, it is not likely to change the predictions according to a straight line.

Let us now compare these methods to other common approaches in machine learning. The nearest neighbor algorithm is a good place to start. It instructs us to measure the distance of x_t from x_i and retain any points that fall within a given circumference, averaging their outcomes to get a prediction. In other words, we define g as:

$$g_{neighbor}(x_i, x_t) = \frac{\delta(\|x_i - x_t\|)}{n} \tag{224}$$

Note that g for partial sample regression was defined in terms of relevance, which means that it was implicitly based on x_i, x_t, and indeed the entire covariance matrix Ω of X. By contrast, g for the nearest neighbor prediction is based on x_i and x_t only. It uses this information in a much simpler way, comparing the Euclidean distance $\|x_i - x_t\|$ to a threshold to determine which observations to censor and which to include. In this sense, we may think of the nearest neighbor algorithm as defining its own notion of relevance: equal relevance for each point that is nearby. There is an aspect of similarity here, but it does not consider variances or correlations as does the Mahalanobis distance. And informativeness does not play a role.

Prediction trees offer another way to gauge similarity. Through sequential branches of logic, trees apply thresholds to each of the attribute values in an observation. These thresholds partition the space where x_i and x_t might land into nonoverlapping regions $\mathcal{R}_1, \mathcal{R}_2, \ldots, \mathcal{R}_p$. In this case, we set our censoring function $\delta(x_i, x_t, \mathcal{R}_1, \mathcal{R}_2, \ldots, \mathcal{R}_p)$ to return 1 if x_i and x_t belong to the same group, and 0 otherwise. We then take the average of y_i in the appropriate subset as our prediction.

$$g_{tree}(x_t, x_i) = \frac{\delta(x_i, x_t, \mathcal{R}_1, \mathcal{R}_2, \ldots, \mathcal{R}_p)}{n} \tag{225}$$

There are many ways these P regions could be defined. Usually, they are calibrated so that they produce the best possible predictions, on average, for a set of training observations. Thus, each $\mathcal{R}_p$ may be influenced by the observations for X and Y. This fitting process must be solved by an iterative search that tries predicting with a set of thresholds and revises them to yield even better predictions repeatedly. Though we cannot write an explicit formula for how the final regions incorporate the information from X and Y, they clearly do, so it is accurate to say that $\{\mathcal{R}_1, \mathcal{R}_2, \ldots, \mathcal{R}_p\} = h(X, Y)$. Here, the function h describes a fitting procedure. Recall that for our relevance-weighted predictions from earlier, and for the nearest neighbor predictions, the weights applied to y_i were based entirely on X and did not depend on Y. The fitting procedure we have just outlined for a tree represents a meaningful departure. We should emphasize this dependency as follows:

$$g_{fitted\ tree}(x_t, x_i, X, Y) = \frac{\delta(x_i, x_t, h(X, Y))}{n} \tag{226}$$

This fitted tree prediction is nonlinear with respect to y_i because it makes use of the information in Y in two ways that interact and compound: first, by setting the thresholds that define the regions and, second, by including the outcome in an average. Still, despite the increased complexity that comes from using Y to determine relevance, the fitted tree prediction is anchored to the same principle of similarity that we have discussed at length.

Our original conception of relevance—using the Mahalanobis distance to measure similarity and informativeness—did not depend on Y because if a relationship exists between X and Y, it will be captured, and if no relationship exists, the predictions will fall close to average. But there is no reason we cannot extend our original notion of relevance to incorporate a procedure, h, that makes decisions about relevance based on observed outcomes for Y.

For example, we could allow our prediction logic to apply a different threshold r^* for partial sample regression depending on the prediction circumstances, x_t. We could set the threshold using a calibration function $r_t^* = h(X, Y)$. For a given prediction task, our procedure could evaluate the fit or agreement (from Chapter 5) for a range of thresholds and return the maximizing choice. Because the fit depends on Y, our definition of relevance depends on Y. We have thereby introduced an aspect of calibration and nonlinearity to the prediction routine.

The notion that $g(x_i, x_t, X, Y)$ determines the relevance of observations, which then inform a weighted average of y_i outcomes, is quite general. There is no limit to the sophistication or complexity of this procedure and the way it learns from data. This formulation preserves the intuition that predictions are ultimately averages of what has occurred in y_i. Even when the circumstances of our prediction are novel, they still extrapolate from previous events. Determining relevance is where the magic happens.

Let us consider some forms of g that relate to popular machine learning procedures. It may be useful to define relevance as an average across a range of submodels, as follows:

$$g(x_i, x_t, X, Y) = \frac{1}{Q} \sum_{q=1}^{Q} g_q(x_i, x_t, X, Y) \qquad (227)$$

So-called random forest models, originally introduced by Ho (1995) and Breiman (2001), follow this logic. We can think of each g_q as a prediction tree that limits its focus to a randomly selected subset of the attributes (columns) and observations (rows) in X and Y. The prediction from a random forest is typically described as the average of the final predictions from each tree. But we may also interpret it as a weighted average across y_i, where we observe the relevance of each observation as judged by the ensemble of trees. In similar fashion, we could extend our Mahalanobis-based relevance prediction to average across submodels that consider different attributes.

We could also employ nested logic, where the output of some entire prediction processes informs the inputs of others, such as determining which attributes and observations to include in the next step. This type of procedure resembles the architecture of artificial neural networks. Although this nested structure is too complex to be viewed as one relevance-weighted average across observations, we may be able to view interim steps in this way. In other words, nested algorithms can combine separate domains of relevance. A function g_{q+1}, which determines relevance across attributes X and Y in each step $q + 1$ of a procedure, might be informed by the predictions that come from a prior step, q, based on entirely different data, X^* and Y^*. The notion of relevance may help us interpret the building blocks of such a complex approach. Of course, there will be models that do not fit this mold. We merely wish to emphasize the intuition that comes from the observation-based view, anchored to the notions of similarity, informativeness, and relevance.

Let us turn now to a simpler extension of the framework we have presented, but one that may prove useful. We generalize the censoring function, δ, to allow a smooth transition from 0 to 1, rather than an abrupt, discontinuous jump. Suppose we use the S-shaped logistic function from Chapter 4's discussion of binary outcomes. As an aside, this function also goes by the name sigmoid, and it is used, along with other similarly shaped curves, as a nonlinear threshold for artificial neural net-work models. We could calibrate this transition to be as gentle or abrupt as we like. Applied to partial sample regression, it reweights relevance to accord with a subset, but offers a smoother transition from inclusion to exclusion for observations near the boundary of relevance. Specifically, we define:

$$\delta(r_{it}) = \frac{1}{1 + e^{-(a+br_{it})}} \tag{228}$$

The parameters a and b are set to control the location and speed, respectively, of the transition between censorship weights of 0 and 1. Unlike the step function from earlier, this variant allows us to compute its derivative, which makes it easier to study how predictions will change along with their inputs.

Complexity Applied

The empirical examples in Chapters 2 through 6 are intended to illustrate the essence of our observation-centric view as plainly as possible. The purpose of this chapter is to show how relevance and complex machine learning algorithms are related and how they could be adapted to complement one another. We resist extending our empirical analysis to illustrate these ideas because doing so might overly complicate our central message rather than reinforce it. We, therefore, leave the application of these ideas to you—our intrepid reader—and to others.

References

Breiman, L. 2001. "Random Forests." *Machine Learning* 45 (1): 5–32.

Friedman, J. H. 2001. "Greedy Function Approximation: A Gradient Boosting Machine." *Annals of Statistics* 29 (5): 1189–1232.

Ho, T. K. 1995. "Random Decision Forests." *Proceedings of the 3rd International Conference on Document Analysis and Recognition, Montreal, QC, 14–16 August 1995*, 278–282.

8

Foundations of Relevance

O ur proposal for using relevance to refine how we observe data is predicated on a long list of scientific discoveries. Although it is beyond the scope of this book to document all the discoveries that underpin our research, we have chosen to highlight the following eight scientists whose contributions stand out for their importance to the development of relevance.[1]

Abraham de Moivre (1617–1754) discovered the normal distribution by solving for a curve to fit the ratio of the coefficients of the terms in a binomial expansion to the sum of the coefficients.

Pierre-Simon Laplace (1749–1827) used his expertise in deriving approximations to integrals to prove the Central Limit Theorem, which holds that the sum of independent random variables will tend toward normality as the number of random variables increases, even if the random variables themselves are not normally distributed.

Carl Friedrich Gauss (1777–1835) invented the method of least squares, although this method was first published by Adrien-Marie Legendre. The normal distribution is sometimes called the Gaussian distribution, because Gauss's proof that the line of least squares best fits a set of observations rests on the assumption that the errors around the line of least squares are normally distributed.

---

[1] The facts contained in these brief biographies come from several excellent sources, which are listed as references at the end of this chapter. We enthusiastically recommend these sources for readers who wish to learn more about these legendary scientists.

Francis Galton (1822–1911) introduced the notion of regression to the mean, and he developed a first approximation of the correlation coefficient. He came to these insights by observing nature rather than by developing these concepts from a mathematical perspective. Galton also invented an ingenious device called the quincunx, which gives a physical demonstration of the Central Limit Theorem.

Karl Pearson (1857–1936) established a probabilistic foundation to Galton's conception of the correlation coefficient. He also introduced the chi-square statistic.

Ronald Fisher (1890–1962) is widely considered to be the father of modern statistics and experimental design. He originated the concept of analysis of variance (ANOVA) and helped to develop and popularize maximum likelihood estimation. Fisher is perhaps best known for his contributions to hypothesis testing, including the F-test, the z-distribution, and the p-value.

Prasanta Chandra Mahalanobis (1893–1972) introduced the Mahalanobis distance to measure the statistical distance of one group from another, taking into account their average values and covariation. He originally developed his measure of distance to analyze human skulls. The Mahalanobis distance has since been applied in engineering, finance, and medicine, to name but a few fields that have benefited from Mahalanobis's invention.

Claude Shannon (1916–2001) created the field of information theory. He first showed that all information can be expressed as 1s and 0s, which is to say he invented digitization. He then went on to develop a stochastic theory of redundancy to optimally balance the accuracy and speed of communication. His theory of communication rests on the principle that information is inversely related to probability.

Observations and Relevance: A Brief Review of the Main Insights

Before we proceed to the foundations of relevance, it might be useful to pause and revisit the main insights that emerged from our observation-centric view of prediction and to connect these insights to the discoveries of the eight scientists we profile.

Spread

Variance is conventionally computed as the average of the squared differences of observations from their mean. However, we can compute variance equivalently as half the average squared distance across every pair of observations. Measuring variance as a function of pairwise distance reveals why we must divide by $N - 1$ rather than N to obtain an unbiased estimate of a sample's variance; it is because the zero distance of an observation from itself (the diagonal in a matrix of pairs) conveys no information.

Because distances between pairs depend on two observations jointly, large distances are rare. A distance twice as large as another conveys four times as much information. We square distances to reflect the heightened importance of large spreads, which arises from their rarity and thus their informativeness. We will soon explore pivotal discoveries by de Moivre, Laplace, and Gauss, each of which reveals the normal distribution as a fundamental expression of these principles of rarity.

When we compute variance from the distances across pairs, we multiply squared distances by one half to match the common definition of variance. But this scaling is arbitrary. Because information equates to surprise, it is a ratio of one observation (or pair) to the average of many observations (or pairs). In other words, information does not depend on the units of measurement, and scaling the squared distance has no effect. Without Shannon's information theory, these central intuitions would not be possible.

Co-occurrence

We measure co-occurrence for a pair of attributes as the product of their z-scores divided by the average of their squared z-scores. Importantly, co-occurrence pertains to just a single observation. This concept allows us to atomize the relationship between attributes so that it can be studied from an observation-centric perspective. The information-weighted average co-occurrence for a pair of attributes across all observations equals the well-known Pearson correlation. We will soon explore the circumstances in which Galton and Pearson first formalized the measurement of correlation.

Relevance

Not all observations are equally relevant to a prediction. Observations that are unusual are more informative and therefore more relevant. Also, observations that are more similar to current circumstances are more relevant.

Informativeness is measured as the Mahalanobis distance of a circumstance from average, a fact that underscores the profound importance of Mahalanobis's metric. Likewise, similarity is measured as the negative of half the Mahalanobis distance of a historical circumstance from the current circumstance.

Relevance is not an arbitrary notion. It rests on Shannon's information theory, which holds that information is inversely related to probability. It also rests on a mathematical equivalence: that the prediction from a linear regression equation is equivalent to a weighted average of the past outcomes in which the weights are the relevance of the attributes used to predict the outcomes.

This equivalence reveals that linear regression analysis places as much importance on nonrelevant observations as it does on relevant observations; it just flips the sign of the effect of the nonrelevant observations on the prediction.

These insights invite the question of whether one could form a more reliable prediction by focusing on a subset of relevant observations. Partial sample regression offers an alternative to full-sample linear regression. It is a two-step process. It first identifies a subset of relevant observations, and then it forms the prediction as a relevance-weighted average of the past values of the outcomes.

Asymmetry

Partial sample regression focuses on a subset of relevant observations. This focus introduces conditionality to the subset of relevant observations because the relevant subset changes with new circumstances. Partial sample regression will produce a more reliable prediction than full-sample linear regression if outcomes have an asymmetric relationship with the attributes used to predict the outcomes. Full-sample linear regression always assumes a symmetric relationship, whereas partial sample regression recognizes that the relationship between outcomes and attributes could change depending on the circumstances.

If the benefit gained from responding to asymmetry outweighs the additional noise that arises from shrinking the sample of observations, partial sample regression will produce a more reliable prediction than full-sample linear regression.

Fit and Reliability

Fit measures the relationship between relevance and outcomes for a single prediction. In doing so, it summarizes the relationships among many observations that inform the prediction. To the extent the product of the z-scores of relevance and outcomes is positive, indicating that relevance is aligned with outcomes, we should have more confidence in the prediction. If relevance and outcomes are not aligned, we should view our prediction with more caution. Fit is specific to a given prediction. It addresses questions of confidence about prediction similar to those addressed by Fisher, although from a different angle.

The average fit across all predictions gives a general measure of a model's reliability and is equal to a linear regression's R-squared. Thus, the fit of a prediction is an elemental component of reliability in the same way that co-occurrence is an elemental component of correlation. An analog exists also for precision, a measure that complements fit.

Among the most interesting insights from our pairwise perspective about prediction is that we can compute reliability without ever explicitly forming a prediction; we need only measure the alignment of relevance for every pair of observations with the closeness of outcomes for every pair of observations.

Moreover, a pairwise perspective lends intuition to the upward bias of R-squared (it is inflated by an observation's association with itself), thereby suggesting a new adjustment to address this bias.

Partial Sample Regression and Machine Learning Algorithms

Partial sample regression can be thought of as an efficient and transparent machine learning algorithm, because the relationship between inputs and predictions is not linear. When we change an attribute, we redefine the relevant subset and the effect of the observations on our predictions.

Abraham de Moivre (1667–1754)

Abraham de Moivre was born in the Champagne region of France on May 26, 1617. His father was a surgeon who encouraged de Moivre's educational pursuits by first arranging for a series of tutors and then sending him to Paris to study physics at the College de Harcourt. When he returned from Paris, he carried on with his studies, focusing on mathematics, soon surpassing what his tutors could teach him.

De Moivre belonged to a group of French Protestants known as Huguenots. Henri IV had issued the Edict of Nantes in 1598, which protected the rights of Protestants, although France was a Catholic country. Henri was sympathetic to Protestants because he was originally Protestant but converted to Catholicism to become king. However, in 1685, Louis XIV issued the Edict of Fontainebleau, which prohibited Protestant worship and closed all Protestant schools. As a consequence of this religious persecution, de Moivre moved to England around 1686.

Not long after de Moivre arrived in England he had a near chance encounter with Isaac Newton. While de Moivre was about to visit the Earl of Devonshire, who was a patron of mathematicians, he noticed a man who was leaving just as he arrived. While de Moivre was waiting in the Earl's antechamber, he spotted a book, which he began to read but had trouble understanding. It was Newton's *Principia*, and it was Newton whom he saw leaving the Earl's residence. He soon thereafter obtained a copy of *Principia* and studied it assiduously. De Moivre subsequently developed a close relationship with Newton, as well as with the famous astronomer Edmond Halley, who is well-known for the comet that bears his name.

Despite these powerful connections, de Moivre was unable to secure a university professorship, and supported himself by tutoring students of mathematics and consulting to gamblers and insurance brokers. Nonetheless, with Newton and Halley's support, de Moivre published important papers that advanced Newton's work on the binomial formula. This enabled de Moivre to become a member of the prestigious Royal Society.

De Moivre is most famous for deriving the formula for the normal distribution, which he published in Latin in a paper in 1733 and then again in English in the second edition of his popular book, *The Doctrine of Chances*, in 1738. Exhibit 8.1 illustrates the challenge de Moivre addressed that resulted in his discovery of the formula for the normal distribution.

Exhibit 8.1 Binomial Distribution

Number of Coin Tosses	1			2			3			
Possible Outcomes	H			HH			HHH	TTH		
	T			HT			HHT	THH		
				TH			HTT	THT		
				TT			TTT	HTH		
Number of Heads	1H	0H	2H	1H	0H	3H	2H	1H	0H	
Probability of Heads	.5	.5	.25	.5	.25	.125	.375	.375	.125	
Expansion	$H+T$			$H^2+2HT+T^2$			$H^3+3H^2T+3HT^2+T^3$			
Coefficients	1 1			1 2 1			1 3 3 1			
Sum of Coefficients	2			4			8			
Coefficients/Sum	.5 .5			.25 .5 .25			.125 .375 .375 .125			

The top panel shows the potential outcomes for tossing a coin once, twice, and three times. De Moivre wanted to estimate the probability of getting a certain number of heads. For a small number of trials, it is easy to write down all the potential outcomes and compute the fraction of times a certain number of heads results. For example, if we toss a coin three times, we see that three heads occur in only one of the potential eight outcomes, two heads in three of the eight outcomes, one head in three of the eight outcomes, and zero heads in only one of the eight outcomes.

The bottom panel presents an alternative approach for computing the probable frequency of heads for a given number of tosses. It was this approach that intrigued de Moivre. For a single toss, which is called a Bernoulli trial, the distribution of outcomes is the probability of a head and the probability of a tail. For two tosses, the distribution is the product of the probability of a head and a tail. It is the binomial distribution for a sample of two tosses. To get the binomial distribution for a sample of three tosses, we raise the probability of a head and a tail to the third power. Newton had previously derived the binomial distribution. It was well known at the time that the probability of getting a certain number of heads was equal to the coefficient of the term in the binomial expansion associated with that number of heads divided by the sum of the coefficients. However, this approach becomes unwieldy as we increase the number of tosses. For example, if we were to toss a coin 20 times and we wanted to know the likelihood of getting 10 heads, we would need to consider 184,756 potential combinations of 10 heads.

De Moivre's approach was to fit a curve that would approximate the ratio of the coefficients to their sums. He had already found a formula for the ratio of the middle term of a binomial expansion, which gives the height of the curve at its middle point, based on earlier work by Newton for finding the area under a curve. Then, based on work by James Bernoulli, de Moivre found that he could simplify his formula by substituting e^{-1} for a more cumbersome term. And another mathematician, James Stirling, showed de Moivre that another awkward term could be expressed as a function of π. The only remaining task was to write standard deviation as σ rather than as terms of a binomial distribution. By solving for the ratio of the middle term of the binomial distribution as n approached infinity, de Moivre was able to extend his formula to estimate the ratios before and after the middle term, thereby deriving a formula that gives all the values of what later came to be known as the normal distribution.

What stands out about de Moivre's triumph is how his solution built upon earlier work by Newton, and then progressed to a solution based on insights by Bernoulli and Stirling, although their contribution was merely to help de Moivre simplify the notation. Perhaps Louis XIV did a service for society by compelling de Moivre to decamp to England, where he had the good fortune to mingle with the most brilliant mathematicians of the day. De Moivre never returned to France and understandably maintained a hostile attitude toward the country throughout his life; nevertheless, near the end of his life he was elated to learn that he had been admitted to the Royal Academy of Sciences in Paris.

Pierre-Simon Laplace (1749–1827)

Pierre-Simon Laplace was born in Beaumont-en-Auge, France, to humble beginnings. His parents were peasants, but not much else is known about Laplace's early years because he was embarrassed to reveal his humble beginnings. At the age of 18 he moved to Paris and quickly established himself as a brilliant mathematician, which led to his appointment as professor of mathematics at the Military School of Paris.

Laplace is more than deserving of acclaim for his prodigious contributions to physics and mathematics. For example, he proved the stability of the solar system showing, within bounds, that the planets' distances from the sun were fixed. And he is considered by many as the founder of the theory of probability. Yet, unfortunately, he also had a less flattering reputation; for example, he was known to seek the spotlight and pursue titles. And, putting it generously, he did not always give credit in his work to deserving predecessors and contemporaries.

Laplace's greatest scientific contribution was to prove the Central Limit Theorem. De Moivre before him had shown that the number of successes in a series of trials approaches a normal distribution as the number of trials increases. Laplace, relying upon his well-known expertise in deriving approximations to integrals, generalized this result to show that it applied to any sum or mean.

Laplace presented his result to the Royal Academy of Sciences in Paris on April 9, 1810, thereby establishing his reputation as one of the greatest mathematicians of all time. His self-confidence matched his greatness. Upon presenting Napoleon with a copy of his famous book, *Mécanique Céleste*, Napoleon teased Laplace by saying, "You have this huge book on the system of the world without once mentioning the author of the world." To which Laplace retorted, "Sire, I had no need of that hypothesis." When Napoleon recounted this conversation to Joseph-Louis Lagrange, another brilliant mathematician of the day, Lagrange replied, "That's a fine conclusion indeed—it explains many things."

Carl Friedrich Gauss (1777–1853)

Friedrich Gauss, as he preferred to be called, was born in Brunswick, Germany, in 1777. His grandfather was a peasant, and his father did little to advance their family's station in life. Moreover, his father, for whom Gauss had no affection, discouraged Gauss from pursuing his intellectual interests. Fortunately, however, his mother's brother, Friedrich, recognized Gauss's potential and did his best to help Gauss develop his prodigious talents, which included a photographic memory. It was Gauss's appreciation for his uncle's support that led him to go by his middle name, Friedrich.

Gauss gave evidence of his extraordinary talent for mathematics at an early age, solving math problems even before he learned to speak, and he continued to display his precocious talent for math at elementary school. Gauss was assigned to the class of Herr Büttner, a teacher with a no-nonsense reputation, and not known for his kindness and compassion. Instead, he would assign laborious progression problems to his class. One such problem, according to legend, was to sum the numbers from 1 to 100. Gauss began by summing $1 + 2 + 3$ ... but become bored.

So, he started backwards by summing $100 + 99 + 98$ ... He quickly noticed that the sum of the forward and backward sequences was 101 ($1 + 100$, $2 + 99$, $3 + 98$, and so on). He immediately saw the solution as $(101 \times 100)/2$ to offset the double counting. When Büttner recognized Gauss's genius he made an exception to his usual harsh treatment of his students and purchased a math book for Gauss. By the time Gauss was 19, it was already anticipated that he would become the greatest mathematician in all of Europe. His growing reputation persuaded the Duke of Brunswick to become Gauss's benefactor and to fund his education.

The normal distribution is often referred to as the Gaussian distribution, even though it was discovered originally by Abraham de Moivre. Gauss's connection to the normal distribution was by way of his invention of the method of least squares. Gauss showed that by minimizing the sum of the squared distances of the observations around lines passing through a scatter plot of data, one could obtain the line that best fit the data. That minimizing the sum of the squares yielded the best fit rested on the assumption that the deviations from the best fit line would be normally distributed. This assumption is known as the Gaussian Law of Normal Distribution of Errors.

Gauss's discovery of the method of least squares led to a lifelong feud with Adrien-Marie Legendre, who claimed precedence for the method of least squares, which he published in 1806. Legendre accused Gauss of dishonesty when he referred to his own earlier discovery of the method of least squares in a subsequent publication. Gauss, in a letter to a friend, countered that he shared his discovery of least squares with then–astronomer Heinrich Wilhelm Olbers in 1802. Olbers had the manuscript, but Legendre never consulted him about it.

The posthumous publication of Gauss's papers revealed many cases in which Gauss had preceded others in their presumed discoveries, but he made no claim of priority. Gauss had too many discoveries to publish, especially given his preference to publish work only when it reached a certain level of completeness and unassailability. His focus was to advance science. Some claim, however, that Gauss's reluctance to publish his discoveries delayed the progress of science by many decades.

Nonetheless, the work that Gauss did publish made him a legend in his own time, as evidenced by the many honors that were bestowed upon him. He spent the later years of his life content to continue his research at the University of Gottingen.

Francis Galton (1822–1911)

Francis Galton was a multi-disciplined scientist who contributed to several fields, including criminology (he invented fingerprint identification), geography, meteorology, and psychology. But he is best known for discovering the notion of regression to the mean, which led to the development of the correlation coefficient. Although he was not an especially accomplished mathematician, he had great intuition and a knack for clever experimentation.

Galton had the good fortune to be able to support himself from an inheritance and studied medicine at Cambridge University. He developed an interest in the statistical properties of heredity owing, in part, to the influence of his older first cousin, Charles Darwin.

Galton approached the concept of regression to the mean, which he first referred to as reversion to mediocrity, not from a mathematical perspective, but rather based his observations of nature. He first concerned himself with the size of peas. He co-opted a group of friends to grow peas. Each friend was given a different size pea from which to produce the next generation. Galton then analyzed the size of the next generation of peas. He observed that peas that originated from peas of above average size were larger than the average pea size of its generation but smaller than the pea from which it was produced. Likewise, he observed that peas originating from below-average parent peas were smaller than average but not as small as their pea parents. He measured the size of the offspring peas to be one-third the size of the parent peas and two-thirds the size of the average.

Galton then conducted a similar experiment regarding the height of children from parents of varying heights. He used the average of the mother's and father's heights to analyze its influence on the height of their offspring. He observed the same phenomenon regarding the height of children as he did with peas.

Galton's work with heredity led him to an abiding conviction in the supremacy of nature over nurture. In fact, he coined the term *nature and nurture*. He came to believe that just as animals could be bred to excel at certain tasks, so could people be bred to improve the quality of the human race, which led to his ignominious advocacy of eugenics, yet another term that he invented.

The upside of Galton's dark side was his discovery of correlation, which he initially called co-relation. Galton hypothesized that a common natural factor that caused a person to have a longer than average arm would also cause him to have a longer than average leg. He reasoned that natural traits were normally distributed, and he measured their co-relation by comparing their standardized differences from their medians. His first pass at the correlation coefficient used a fraction of one standard deviation to measure dispersion, or to use his term, error, and he used the median rather than the mean to measure central tendency. Also, he only considered positive correlations. His good friend and protégé, Karl Pearson, who was a much more adept mathematician than Galton, refined Galton's approximation to its current form.

Galton strongly believed that the distribution of natural phenomena conformed to a normal curve, and he invented an ingenious device to demonstrate the force of normality. He called this device a quincunx. At its top is a funnel filled with pellets. These pellets are released into a lattice of pins arranged such that the pins of each successive row are placed halfway between the pins of the preceding row. The word quincunx derives from the pattern of dots as they appear on the five side of a die. At the bottom of the quincunx is a row of adjacent, equally sized narrow bins to collect the cascading pins. When the pellets are released from the funnel, they bounce off the pins on their way to the bins. Most of the pellets land in the middle bins with fewer and fewer landing in the bins further to the left and right side of the quincunx. The shape of the histogram formed by the pellets conforms to a normal curve.

Galton's quincunx is a physical demonstration of the Central Limit Theorem, which holds that the sum of independent random variables, which themselves may not be normally distributed, will tend toward normality as the number of random variables increases. Each pellet bouncing from pin to pin is a random variable because its destination is determined randomly, just as the toss of a die or the flip of a coin is. As more and more pellets are released from the funnel, they accumulate into a summation of random variables that forms a normal curve; hence, verification of the Central Limit Theorem.

Exhibit 8.2 is a somewhat impressionistic depiction of Galton's quincunx. Obviously, the pellets are not suspended in air within the funnel but rather piled upon one another. When they are released from the funnel, they accumulate in the bins and form a normal distribution. The larger the number of pellets, the better the resulting histogram will approximate a normal distribution.

Galton was an extraordinarily prolific writer, having published 340 articles and books. Among his more whimsical missives was a letter published in the journal *Nature*, in which he described how to cut a cake in a way that would allow the remaining parts of the cake to fit together and prevent them from drying out.

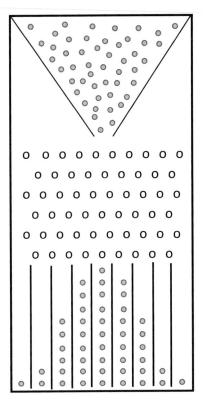

Exhibit 8.2 Galton's Quincunx

Galton was knighted in 1906, most likely not for his contribution to cake cutting, but instead for launching the study of modern statistical analysis with his profound insights about regression to the mean and correlation.

Karl Pearson (1857–1936)

Karl Pearson was an English mathematician and biostatistician who is widely regarded as the founder of mathematical statistics. He was born to Quaker parents but raised in the Church of England. In 1875 Pearson was awarded a scholarship to Kings College, Cambridge, and graduated with honors in 1879. As a student of Edward Routh, a renowned mathematician, Pearson demonstrated his mathematical prowess by achieving Third Wrangler in the prestigious Tripos Exam.

During his college years he abandoned his religious faith, became an agnostic, and studied German philosophy and literature. These interests led him to a year of study in Germany before returning to England in 1884 to accept a position as professor of applied mathematics and engineering at University College in London.

Along with contributions from Edgeworth and George Yule, Pearson refined Galton's conception of correlation by providing a probabilistic foundation. The formula for correlation that is in common use today is referred to as Pearson's *r* as acknowledgment of Pearson's contribution to its derivation.

Although he is best known for his work on the correlation coefficient, his contributions extend well beyond that achievement. For example, he developed the chi-square statistic to determine whether an observation belongs within a particular grouping, and he worked with W. S. Gosset to develop the t-test. Pearson is also credited with developing principal components analysis.

In preparation for a lecture, Pearson studied Galton's influential book *Natural Inheritance*, and wrote a manuscript about it. Like Galton, Pearson became interested in applying quantitative methods to the social sciences, especially the theory of evolution. Pearson became a fierce advocate of eugenics, which led to many disputes with leading scientists regarding environmental versus hereditary causation.

Although Pearson was undisputedly a brilliant statistician, his caustic style of engagement and his advocacy of eugenics left him with a mixed legacy. For example, he famously rejected a manuscript submitted by the famous statistician Prasanta Mahalanobis to the journal *Biometrika*, which Pearson founded. And he did so even though this article was a precursor to Mahalanobis's landmark papers about his famous distance measure, which improved upon Pearson's CRL statistic (coefficient of racial likeness), and even though Mahalanobis had worked in Pearson's lab converting CRL measurements into Mahalanobis distances.

Pearson also battled with Ronald Fisher, a younger yet equally brilliant statistician who is considered the creator of modern statistics. Pearson apparently struggled to accept Fisher's ascendance as his own reputation receded.

Pearson was unquestionably a devoted disciple of Galton, as evidenced by his three-volume biography of Galton published in 1914, 1924, and 1930. He was happy to devote such a large portion of his later years to this endeavor because he so admired and loved Galton and because he felt he was the only person who could adequately describe Galton's prolific contributions.

Ronald Fisher (1890–1962)

Ronald Fisher is widely regarded as the father of modern statistics and experimental design and the greatest statistician of the twentieth century. According to evolutionary biologist Richard Dawkins, Fisher was the greatest biologist since Charles Darwin. But he had a dark side, which we will come to later.

Fisher grew up in a middle-class family in London. As a pre-college student at Harrow, Fisher gave an early indication of his mathematical talent by winning the Neeld Medal in mathematics. He continued his study of mathematics at Cambridge University and enjoyed continued success there, gaining a First in Mathematics.

Following his graduation from Cambridge in 1912, Fisher embarked upon a career in education and took a series of positions at several public schools and colleges. Following these teaching appointments, he switched to a research position in 1919 at the Rothansted Experimental Station, where he remained for 14 years and studied, among other topics, crop data.

In 1921 he published a paper called "Studies in Crop Variation," in which he introduced the statistical method analysis of variance (ANOVA). He followed his publication about ANOVA with an article in 1924, in which he introduced the F-distribution, which is the null distribution for evaluating statistical models that have been fitted to data. Then in 1925 Fisher published a book called *Statistical Methods for Research Workers*, in which he popularized the p-value, which gives the two standard deviation threshold for determining significance. Fisher is also credited with developing maximum likelihood estimation, which is used to estimate the parameters of a probability distribution such that the data we observe are the most probable data.

Clearly, Fisher's contributions to statistical analysis were a profound force for good, not just in a purely intellectual sense, but in their practical impact as well. His methods for statistical inference advanced the practice of medicine from a science based mainly on biological analysis to one in which diagnoses and treatments are also guided by statistical probability. And as the founder of experimental agricultural research, he is responsible for saving millions of people from starvation. Fisher was also a force for good on a personal level. For example, in 1937 he visited the Indian Statistical Institute in Calcutta to give a boost to the fledgling organization and its founder, Prasanta Mahalanobis. Moreover, he coined the term *Mahalanobis distance* for the statistical measure invented by Mahalanobis to assess multivariate similarity, thereby contributing to the growing stature of Mahalanobis.

But, sadly, as we alluded to earlier, there was a dark side to Fisher. He was a fierce advocate of eugenics and the notion that race differences are genetically based. He was the head of the department of eugenics at University College London, and between 1950 and 1951, he lent his considerable reputation to refute a statement by UNESCO that put forth the position that within different populations, psychological attributes are due to historical and social factors rather than differences of temperament and intelligence. Fisher argued instead that gene differences influence the congenital inclinations and capacities of the mind. He also revealed a tendency toward bias in his scientific work. He spoke out against a study showing a correlation between tobacco usage and cancer while he was a consultant to tobacco firms.

Fisher retired to Adelaide, Australia, in 1957 and died a few years later of complications from surgery for colon cancer.

Prasanta Chandra Mahalanobis (1893–1972)

Prasanta Chandra Mahalanobis was born in Calcutta, India, in 1893. He went on to become an acclaimed statistician who founded the Indian Statistical Institute, the Central Statistical Organization, and the National Sample Survey. But he is most acclaimed for creating the Mahalanobis distance.

Mahalanobis was not at first a standout student in mathematics—he excelled more in physics. His early struggles in mathematics were not because the subject was too challenging for him, but rather because it was not challenging enough. In a letter to his future wife, Rani, dated October 30, 1916, he wrote:

"Things that can be easily done never attracted me; that is the reason why I almost failed in the mathematics paper in B.Sc. even though I always had a taste for mathematics. That is because my interest was up to the point of knowing the theory. What comes next, e.g., working out steps which can be done easily if only one labours, always appeared boring to me." Nonetheless, he performed well enough academically to graduate from Presidents College in 1912 with Honours in Physics and to be accepted to study at Cambridge University.

In 1913, Mahalanobis sailed off to England to begin his studies at Cambridge. He performed admirably there, completing the course for

Tripos Part II, which normally takes four years, in just one year. Moreover, he was the only student to receive first class that year.

During his years in England, Mahalanobis pursued a variety of interests, including anthropology, demography, psychology, and education. While at Cambridge, he became an amateur astronomer and spent hours making star maps. He also developed close friendships with two luminaries while at Cambridge, the famous Bengali poet and philosopher Rabindraneth Tagore, who won the Nobel prize in literature in 1913, the year Mahalanobis arrived at Cambridge, and Srinivasa Ramanujan, the mathematical genius discovered by G. H. Hardy.

Ramanujan and Mahalanobis both studied at Kings College. Mahalanobis tells the story of a puzzle, whose solution he had figured out by trial and error, that he put to Ramanujan. Not only did Ramanujan solve the puzzle quickly and analytically; his solution solved a class of problems of which Mahalanobis's puzzle was a special case. When Mahalanobis pressed him about how he solved the puzzle, Ramanujan said, "the answer came to my mind." Even though he was a brilliant mathematician himself, Mahalanobis was in awe of Ramanujan's genius.

Unlike Ramanujan, who focused on pure mathematics, Mahalanobis was very much interested in applying mathematics to solve real-world problems. He made important contributions in meteorological research, operations research, educational testing, field experimentation, and anthropometric measurement. It is this latter work that started him on the path to creating the Mahalanobis distance.

At a chance encounter, Nelson Annadale, a Scottish zoologist and the director of the Zoological Survey of India, asked Mahalanobis to analyze anthropometric measurements of people with mixed British and Indian parentage. Mahalanobis first considered scatter plots of two characteristics of skulls. He looked for clusters and used the nearness of their means to draw inferences about interrelationships between different populations. It is not possible to graph more than two characteristics; however, Mahalanobis recognized that he could study interrelationships based on more than two variables by using a matrix of the variances and covariances of the measurements, which led him to his famous discovery.

Around the time of his discovery, Mahalanobis was influenced by two prominent statisticians, Karl Pearson and Ronald Fisher. Pearson is credited with establishing the discipline of mathematical statistics, and Fisher is considered the creator of modern statistics. Unfortunately, these scholars were rivals and could not tolerate one another. This tension created some awkwardness for Mahalanobis, who regarded both men very highly. Whereas Fisher supported Mahalanobis in at least two important ways, Pearson's connection to Mahalanobis was less helpful.

Fisher used his reputation to encourage the government of India to support Mahalanobis's initiative to undertake random sampling in the form of the National Sample Survey. He also promoted Mahalanobis's discovery of D^2, and he coined the term *Mahalanobis distance*, thereby establishing the legend of Mahalanobis.

Pearson is best remembered as having introduced the Pearson correlation, which measures the association between two variables. He is also known for introducing the chi-square statistic, which is used to determine whether there is a statistically significant difference between the observed frequency and expected frequency of observations within a category for a given distribution.

Pearson was not especially kind to Mahalanobis. For example, Mahalanobis submitted an early version of his paper on his new distance measure to a journal called *Biometrika*, which was founded by Pearson. Pearson refused to publish it, even though Mahalanobis had worked for months in the Pearson laboratory converting Pearson's CRL (coefficient of racial likeness) measures into D^2 measures.

As Mahalanobis's stature grew, he was able to attract a steady stream of scholars to the India Statistical Institute, including Harold Hotelling, Norbert Weiner, Andrey Kolmogorov, Simon Kuznets, and John Kenneth Galbraith, to name but a few. And his fame extended beyond mathematics and science, as he developed close ties with political leaders as well as Indian movie stars. He enjoyed celebrity status up until his death in 1972.

Throughout his life, Mahalanobis harbored self-doubt about his success as a scientist, despite his global acclaim and unquestioned record of accomplishment. Perhaps if he were alive today to see the ubiquitous application of his invention, he would be less self-critical; at least, one would hope.[2]

Claude Shannon (1916–2001)

Claude Shannon was born in 1916 in Gaylord, Michigan, a small town in the center of the state. His father, also named Claude, had moved there, having been a traveling salesman, and set up a small furniture business. He went on to become the town's probate judge. His mother was at first

---

[2] For an excellent and exceptionally thorough biography of Mahalanobis, see Rudra (1996).

a schoolteacher, but she lost that job when it was deemed that such positions should not be taken up by women whose husbands had successful employment. She subsequently pursued various volunteer positions in town and participated in various musical performances as a vocalist.

As a child, Shannon already showed an interest in mechanics and engineering, figuring out how to use a wire fence to transmit coded messages. He was also the go-to person in town for repairing radios. From Gaylord, Shannon went on to the University of Michigan at Ann Arbor, where he studied mathematics and engineering, earning dual degrees. Shannon's first publication occurred when he was only 17. His solution to a codebreaking problem appeared in the *American Mathematical Monthly* and foreshadowed his later intelligence work during World War II.

At age 19, having completed high school in three years and earning two undergraduate degrees, Shannon continued his education at MIT in Cambridge, Massachusetts, where he studied Boolean logic and circuit design. And as a graduate student, he served one summer as an intern at Bell Labs, the acclaimed research center of AT&T. Following this internship in 1937, Shannon published his master's thesis, called "A Symbolic Analysis of Relay and Switching Circuits," by which he transformed circuit design into a mathematical science resting on Boolean logic. He showed that all knowledge could be expressed as 0s and 1s.

He continued at MIT to pursue his PhD and spent part of his studies at the renowned genetics lab at Cold Springs Harbor in Long Island, New York. Without any prior training in genetics, nor an enduring interest in the field, Shannon was able to produce a PhD thesis by applying the same mathematical abstraction and symbolism he used to transform circuit design to genetics. More importantly, while at Cold Springs Harbor, Shannon began work on the transmission of intelligence.

Upon graduation from MIT and following a brief stint at the Institute for Advanced Study at Princeton, Shannon returned to Bell Labs as a research mathematician. Bell Labs was arguably the world's preeminent research facility and the perfect landing spot for Shannon. He had free rein to pursue his research interests, and to do so without any teaching obligations. This was a very good outcome for Shannon, for Bell Labs, and for the rest of us, for it was at Bell Labs that Shannon produced his masterpiece that forever changed the world.

As we mentioned earlier, Shannon first showed in his master's thesis that all information can be represented by binary choices with equal odds, which he expressed as 0s and 1s, which is to say he invented digitization. He then took up where his Bell Labs predecessors, Harry

Nyquist and Ralph Hartley, had left off. They had discovered that information is inversely related to the number of ways something can happen. In other words, they showed that unusual occurrences contain more information than common occurrences. More specifically, they showed that informativeness is an inverse logarithmic function of the number of ways something can happen. But they proved this relationship under the restrictive assumption that each binary outcome was equally probable. Shannon extended their insight to cover the probabilistic spectrum from impossible to fully determined, and he derived a precise measure of information intensity, which he called a bit. He was therefore able to show precisely how much information was contained in each outcome based on its likelihood of occurrence. This enabled Shannon to introduce the notion of redundancy—a notion of profound importance to the science of communication.

Keep in mind that Shannon worked for the phone company—granted, an ultra-elite branch of the phone company, but nonetheless an organization whose primary purpose was to enable fast and accurate communication. The phone company's chief challenge was to transmit signals of information quickly and accurately across great distances in the presence of static or noise, which explains the term signal-to-noise ratio. Shannon's first great insight was that the speed of transmission is a direct inverse function of redundancy. That is to say, we can speed up the transmission of information by reducing the redundant symbols used to convey the information. For example, in the English language, the letter *q* is almost always followed by the letter *u*. Therefore, *u* is almost always redundant when preceded by *q*. By removing *u* whenever it is preceded by *q*, we can convey the same information with fewer symbols, thereby enabling quicker transmission of the message. Perhaps a starker example of redundancy is the fact that we can remove the word *the* throughout this entire book without giving up any information contained herein. It would not read as well, and it might take the reader a little longer to grasp the meaning of our text, but the information contained in it could be transmitted more quickly. This example suggests another feature of Shannon's theory of communication. He was not concerned with conveying meaning, but rather information or messages that might mean different things to different people.

This notion of redundancy enabled Shannon to estimate the maximum achievable information intensity of a message based on the probabilistic occurrence of the symbols used to convey the message. High-probability symbols were more likely to be redundant than low-probability symbols. The more likely the symbol, the safer it would be to remove it without compromising the information of the message, which follows from the notion that information is related to probability. Shannon then proceeded to sort out the maximum speed that a message can be transmitted based on the channel of transmission. To this day the Shannon limit remains the goal of communication engineers.

The second great insight of Shannon is that redundancy also determines the accuracy with which a message can be conveyed. Recall that Shannon showed that all information can be coded as 0s and 1s. The risk to transmitting a message accurately is that static might cause a 0 to be received as a 1, thereby distorting the message. By inserting redundant sequences of 0s and 1s, the risk that static would distort two or more redundant components of a message diminishes exponentially, thereby protecting the accuracy of the message. This feature of communication presents a redundancy tradeoff. We reduce redundancy to increase the speed of transmission, but we increase redundancy to improve accuracy. Based on probability, Shannon showed how to achieve near-perfect accuracy within the speed limit of a given communication channel. Put plainly, he conquered noise by his stochastic theory of communication.

After publishing his revolutionary theory of communication and having spent nearly two decades at Bell Labs, Shannon returned to MIT with appointments in both engineering and mathematics. He settled into a large nineteenth-century house, built by a descendant of Thomas Jefferson and styled after Monticello, in the leafy community of Winchester, just a few miles from the MIT campus. Aside from the times he taught or gave lectures, he spent most of his time at his home in Winchester, which he referred to as Entropy House. He left it to others to apply and extend his theories about information and turned his attention to artificial intelligence and more whimsical pursuits such as a mathematical description of juggling, a skill at which he achieved considerable proficiency. Shannon became a celebrity among the cognoscenti and was given numerous prestigious awards from organizations throughout the world. Sadly, he succumbed to Alzheimer's disease and died in 2001 at the age of 85.

To understand the profundity of Shannon's information theory is to imagine a world without email, without the Internet, without cell phones, or without the ability to send a photograph across the world or to download music and videos nearly instantaneously. Consider that all these capabilities are enabled by 0s and 1s configured probabilistically bouncing off satellites orbiting Earth. And to appreciate further the brilliance of Shannon, consider that the logical and mathematical structure of information theory explains the transmission of information by the genes in our bodies as well as how we communicate with one another. The mark of a great theory is the magnitude and generality of its influence. By that standard, Shannon's information theory ranks as one of the greatest technological achievements ever.

References

Abraham de Moivre

Bellhouse, D., and C. Genest. 2004. "Maty's Biography of Abraham De Moivre. Translated, Annotated and Augmented." *Statistical Science* 22 (1): 109–136.

Bernstein, P. 1996. *Against the Gods: The Remarkable Story of Risk.* New York: John Wiley & Sons, 125–129.

Rosenfeld, R. 2019a. "Origin of the Normal Curve—Abraham De Moivre (1667–1754)." Vermont Mathematics Initiative.

Stigler, S. M. 1986a. *The History of Statistics.* Cambridge, MA and London: The Belknap Press of Harvard University Press, 62–98.

Pierre-Simon Laplace

Bell, E. T. 1986a. *Men of Mathematics.* New York: Simon & Schuster, 182.

Stigler, S. M. 1986b. *The History of Statistics.* Cambridge, MA and London: The Belknap Press of Harvard University Press, 99–158.

Carl Friedrich Gauss

Bell, E. T. 1986b. *Men of Mathematics.* New York: Simon & Schuster, 218–269.

Stigler, S. M. 1986c. *The History of Statistics.* Cambridge, MA and London: The Belknap Press of Harvard University Press, 139–158.

Francis Galton

Galton, F. 1889a. "Co-relations and Their Measurements, Chiefly from Anthropometric Data." *Proceedings of the Royal Society of London* 45: 273–279.

Galton, F. 1889b. *Natural Inheritance.* London: Macmillan.

Galton, F. 1890. "Kinship and Correlation." *North American Review* 150: 419–431.

Rosenfeld, R. 2019b. "The Invention of Correlation. Francis Galton (1822–1911), Karl Pearson (1857–1936)." Vermont Mathematics Initiative.

Stigler, S. M. 1986d. *The History of Statistics.* Cambridge, MA and London: The Belknap Press of Harvard University Press, 265–299.

Karl Pearson

Pearson, K. 1920. "Notes on the History of Correlation." *Biometrika* 1 (October): 25–45.

Rosenfeld, R. 2019c. "The Invention of Correlation. Francis Galton (1822–1911), Karl Pearson (1857–1936)." Vermont Mathematics Initiative.

Stigler, S. M. 1986e. *The History of Statistics*. Cambridge, MA and London: The Belknap Press of Harvard University Press, 326–361.

Stigler, S. M. 1989. "Francis Galton's Account of the Invention of Correlation." *Statistical Science* 4 (2): 73–86.

Ronald Fisher

Bodmer, W., R. A. Bailey, B. Charlesworth, A. Eyre-Walker, V. Farewell, A. Mead, and S. Senn. 2021. "The Outstanding Scientist, R.A. Fisher: His Views on Eugenics and Race." *Heredity* 126: 565–576. https://doi.org/10.1038/s41437-020-00394-6.

Rudra, A. 1996a. *Prasanta Chandra Mahalanobis: A Biography*. Oxford University Press, 269–270, 296–300.

Prasanta Chandra Mahalanobis

Rudra, A. 1996b. *Prasanta Chandra Mahalanobis: A Biography*. Oxford University Press.

Ghosh, J. K., and Majumder, P. 1994. "Letter to the Editor." *Annals of Human Biology* 21 (3): 287–289. DOI: 10.1080/03014469400003292.

Claude Shannon

Poundstone, W. 2006. *Fortune's Formula: The Untold Story of the Scientific Betting System That Beat the Casinos and Wall Street*. New York: Hill and Wang, a division of Farrar, Straus and Giroux.

Soni, J., and R. Goodman. 2017. *A Mind at Play: How Claude Shannon Invented the Information Age*. New York: Simon & Schuster.

Concluding Thoughts

We recognize that this book is packed with numerous conceptual subtleties and mathematical details, which in total may be challenging to assimilate with just one pass through these pages. Therefore, we conclude by summarizing the main elements of our new approach to prediction, with the hope that interested readers will revisit certain sections of this book to explore these topics more thoroughly.

Perspective

We introduce a new perspective for forming predictions from data that differs from conventional practice in two important ways.

First, we shift the focus from the selection of predictive variables to how we should observe those variables.

- This shift to an observation-centric view leads to the notion that some observations are more relevant to a prediction than others.
- Moreover, we show how to measure relevance precisely as the sum of informativeness and similarity.

Second, we summarize data, not as a distribution of observations around their mean, but as a collection of pairs of observations. This pairwise view illuminates several statistical notions that are commonly accepted but less commonly understood.

- We square distances between observations to gauge their informativeness because a distance depends on the joint probability of two outcomes.
- We divide by $N - 1$ to calculate a sample's variance because the diagonal of a matrix of pairs is made up of the distances of observations to

209

themselves, which convey no information and thus should not influence the calculation.

- We adjust R-squared because it is biased upward by including an observation's ability to explain itself.

- We divide the Mahalanobis distance used to measure *similarity* in half because it measures the distance between a pair of observations, where pairs are prone to double counting, but we do not divide the Mahalanobis distance used to measure *informativeness* in half because it measures the distance of observations from their average.

Insights

Our new perspective on prediction leads to several intriguing insights.

- Variance equivalence: We can compute variance as an average across pairs, in which we average half the squared distance between observations.

- Regression equivalence: We can compute a linear regression prediction as a weighted average of observed outcomes for Y, in which the weights are the relevance of the observations as determined by X.

- Regression symmetry: Linear regression relies as much on nonrelevant observations as it does on relevant ones; it just flips the sign of the observations' effect on the prediction.

- Prediction-specific fit: Each prediction task generated by a prediction model has its own unique fit that is separate from the overall reliability of the prediction model.

Prescriptions

These insights suggest two important modifications to prediction.

- Partial sample regression: We should consider a two-step approach to prediction:
  1. Identify a subset of relevant observations.
  2. Form a prediction as a relevance-weighted average of past outcomes.

- Scale bets: We should consider scaling our response to individual prediction tasks based on our confidence in each specific prediction task rather than on our confidence in an overall model.

Index

212

INDEX